The *Sams Teach Yourself* in 24 Hours Series

Sams Teach Yourself in 24 Hours books provide quick and easy answers in a proven step-by-step approach that works for you. In just 24 sessions of one hour or less, you will tackle every task you need to get the results you want. Let our experienced authors present the most accurate information to get you reliable answers—fast!

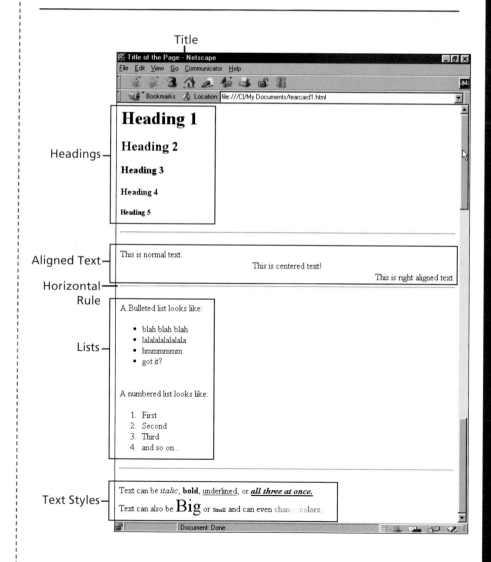

Title

Headings —

Aligned Text —

Horizontal Rule —

Lists —

Text Styles —

Table
with
Borders

Banner

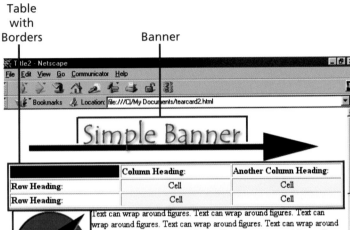

Image
Aligned
Left

Image
Aligned
Right

Table
Without
Borders

Footer

SAMS

Ned Snell

SAMS
Teach Yourself
to Create Web Pages
in 24 Hours

SAMS

A Division of Macmillan Computer Publishing
201 West 103rd St., Indianapolis, Indiana, 46290 USA

Sams Teach Yourself to Create Web Pages in 24 Hours

Copyright © 1999 by Sams Publishing

International Standard Book Number: 0-672-31346-4

Library of Congress Catalog Card Number: 98-85218

Printed in the United States of America

First Printing: September 1998

00   99   98   4   3   2

Trademarks

Warning and Disclaimer

EXECUTIVE EDITOR
Mark Taber

DEVELOPMENT EDITOR
Scott D. Meyers

MANAGING EDITOR
Patrick Kanouse

COPY EDITORS
Christina L. Smith
Sara Bosin
Patricia Kinyon

INDEXER
Heather Goens

SOFTWARE DEVELOPMENT SPECIALIST
Adam Swetnam

INTERIOR DESIGN
Gary Adair

COVER DESIGN
Aren Howell

PRODUCTION
Marcia Deboy
Susan Geiselman

PROOFREADER
Michael Henry

Overview

Contents

Dedication

For my family.

About the Author

Ned Snell has been making technology make sense since 1986, when he began writing beginner's documentation for one of the world's largest software companies. After writing manuals and training materials for several major companies, he switched sides and became a computer journalist, serving as writer and eventually as an editor for two national magazines, *Edge* and *Art & Design News*.

A freelance writer since 1991, Snell has written 12 computer books and hundreds of articles and is the courseware critic for *Inside Technology Training* magazine. Between books, Snell works as a professional actor in regional theater, commercials, and industrial films. He lives with his wife and two sons in Florida.

Acknowledgments

Thanks to the folks at Macmillan Computer Publishing—especially Scott Meyers, Mark Taber, and Patrick Kanouse. And to Laura Lemay, whose book, *Sams Teach Yourself Web Publishing with HTML in a Week,* provided the inspiration for this book in its original form.

Tell Us What You Think!

As the reader of this book, *you* are our most important critic and commentator. We value your opinion and want to know what we're doing right, what we could do better, what areas you'd like to see us publish in, and any other words of wisdom you're willing to pass our way.

As the Executive Editor for the Web Publishing team at Macmillan Computer Publishing, I welcome your comments. You can fax, email, or write me directly to let me know what you did or didn't like about this book—as well as what we can do to make our books stronger.

Please note that I cannot help you with technical problems related to the topic of this book, and that due to the high volume of mail I receive, I might not be able to reply to every message.

When you write, please be sure to include this book's title and author as well as your name and phone or fax number. I will carefully review your comments and share them with the author and editors who worked on the book.

Fax: 317-817-7070

Email: webdev@mcp.com

Mail: Mark Taber
          Executive Editor, Web Publishing
          Macmillan Computer Publishing
          201 West 103rd Street
          Indianapolis, IN 46290 USA

Introduction

Books that aim to teach beginners how to create a Web page almost always start out the same way: They tell you what a Web page is and why you might want one of your own.

I figure that if you picked up this book, you've already been online (at least a little), you've seen a Web page, and you know why you want one. So I won't waste even one of our 24 hours together on that stuff. Instead, I'll get you creating your own Web pages as quickly and simply as possible.

In fact, before your first three hours are up, you'll already know your way around in the easy-but-powerful Web page creation program (Netscape Composer) included on the CD that comes with this book, and you will already have created your first Web page. How's that for cutting to the chase?

Who I Wrote This Thing For

To understand this book without even breaking a mental sweat, you do not need to be any kind of Internet expert or computer guru.

If you can operate basic programs (such as a word processor) in Windows 95, 98, or NT, and if you can surf from page to page on the Internet, then you already know everything you need to know to get started with this book.

By the end of this book, you'll know not only how to create cool-looking Web pages for yourself or your business, but also how to publish them on the Web for all to see.

Why Do I Need the Programs on the CD?

Well, you don't need them, exactly. Technically, you can create a Web page using a simple text-editing program—and here you'll learn a thing or two about how to do it that way.

But for nearly everybody, Web page creation is quickest and easiest when you use a top-notch Web page editor. That's why this book includes a complete copy of Netscape Communicator.

Netscape Communicator is an all-in-one Internet package (see Figure I.1) that includes a terrific Web page editor (Netscape Composer), plus a Web browser (the popular Netscape Navigator), email program, and more—everything you need to create Web pages *and* enjoy the Internet. (Although the Net surfing stuff in Communicator is terrific, you don't have to use it. You can do your Web page authoring in Composer and still use your own Web browser and email program if you like.)

FIGURE I.1.

Included with this book, Netscape Communicator has a Web page editor, a Web browser, and other Internet tools.

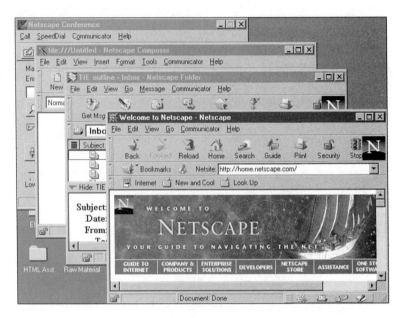

Because I know you have Netscape Composer, I demonstrate many Web page creation techniques in Composer to help you get started. By the end of this book, you'll know how to do just about anything in Composer.

But this book is not limited to Composer, and neither are you. Along the way, you'll explore important Web authoring concepts that will enable you to quickly learn and use just about any other Web authoring program. You'll also discover a number of powerful techniques that don't involve Composer at all. And in the final hour of this tutorial, I'll introduce you to a variety of other popular Web page creation tools, so you can decide where to go if you outgrow Composer.

In addition to Communicator, the CD also includes a variety of utility programs, free graphics, and other stuff that will help you create professional-looking pages in a flash. You'll learn about these programs as you go along, but you can also find out exactly what's on the CD by checking out Appendix D, "What's on the CD-ROM?."

How to Use This Book

This book is divided into six parts, each four hours long:

Part I, "First Steps, First Web Page," kicks off with an easy primer on the technology behind a Web page and a Web page's basic anatomy. After that, you'll learn your way around in Composer, and even create your very first Web page, using the interactive Page Wizard.

Part II, "Titles, Text, and Tables," moves ahead to the nitty-gritty of Web authoring, getting your text into the page and making it look exactly the way you want it to look. You'll also pick up handy techniques like spell checking, creating tables, and saving typing time by copying text from other documents.

Part III, "Linking to Stuff," lays out for you the wonderful world of links. You'll find out not only how to add links to your Web pages, but also how to link to stuff other than Web pages, such as newsgroup messages or email addresses.

Part IV, "Adding Pizzazz with Multimedia," shows how to add audiovisual content to your page, including pictures, backgrounds, sound, video, and animation.

Part V, "Fine-Tuning Your Page," takes you beyond Composer, into editing the raw code of a Web page to create frames, pictures with multiple links, and other advanced (but not too tough) Web page features.

Part VI, "Getting It Online," takes you step-by-step through publishing your pages on the Internet and shows you how to test, update, and publicize your pages. It also shows you how to expand your skills to new tools and techniques.

As you can see, the parts move logically from easy stuff to not-so-easy stuff—so it's generally best to read the hours in order. But here and there, I'll tip you to stuff you can skip if you're not immediately interested in a particular activity or technique.

After Hour 24, you'll discover four useful appendixes:

Appendix A, "Installing Netscape Communicator," shows how to install, set up, and update Netscape Communicator after copying it from the CD at the back of this book.

Appendix B, "HTML Reference," supplies a guide to the Web authoring commands you may optionally apply when editing raw Web page code (as you learn to do in Part V).

Appendix C, "Online Resources for Web Authors," contains a directory of Web pages you can visit to learn more about Web authoring, pick up great new Web authoring programs, or gather picture files, animations, and other fun stuff to spice up your own creations.

Appendix D, "What's on the CD-ROM?" describes all of the programs and files included on the bonus CD-ROM.

Finally, there's a Glossary, although I must point out that I use very, very little technical terminology, and I explain it very well when I do. So you'll probably never need the Glossary. But just in case you want a glossary, you've got one. I aim to please.

Things You'd Probably Figure Out By Yourself

As you go along, you'll run into a variety of different tip boxes and other special elements. When you do, you'll immediately recognize what each element offers—they really require no explanation. But just for the record, you'll see the following:

"To Do," Tips, and Terms

Here and there, I use step-by-step instructions, called "To Dos," to show you exactly how to do something. I generally explain how to do that thing in the text that precedes the steps, so feel free to skip 'em when you want to. However, anytime you feel like you don't completely understand something, do the steps, and you'll probably get the picture before you're done. Sometimes we learn only by doing.

NEW TERM   I call attention to important new terms by tagging them with a New Term icon. It won't happen often, but when it does, it'll help you remember the terms that will help you learn the Internet.

You'll also see three different kinds of tips set off in boxes:

A Tip box points out a faster, easier way to do something, or another way to save time and effort. These boxes are completely optional.

A Note box pops out an important consideration, or interesting tidbit related to the topic at hand. They're optional, too, but always worth reading (otherwise, I wouldn't interrupt).

A Caution box alerts you to actions and situations where something bad could happen, like accidentally deleting an important file. Since there's very little you can do in Web authoring that's in any way dangerous, you'll see very few Cautions. But when you do see one, take it seriously.

Workshops

At the end of every hour, there's an easy, fun Workshop designed to reinforce the most important skills and concepts covered in the hour. Each workshop contains

Q&A: A few quick questions and answers explaining interesting stuff that wasn't included in the Hour because it doesn't directly contribute to teaching yourself how to create a Web page (even though it's interesting).

Quiz: Three or four multiple-choice questions that help you recall important points, and also provide me with a good place for jokes I couldn't work into the book elsewhere.

Activity: Something you can do to practice what you learned in the hour, or to prepare for the hour that follows.

One More Thing

Actually, no more things. Start the clock and hit Hour 1. Twenty-four working hours from now, you'll know Web page authoring inside out.

Thanks for spending a day with me.

PART I

First Steps, First Web Page

Hour

HOUR 1

Understanding Web Authoring

When Francis Ford Coppola makes a movie, he tosses the script out the window and improvises. When Steven Spielberg makes a movie, he makes a rigid plan before shooting begins and sticks to it. Both directors have made good and bad movies, so I suppose either approach can work.

But starting out with Web authoring, it pays to work more like Spielberg than like Coppola. Before building that first page, you need to acquire that rudimentary understanding of how Web pages are born and to do some planning about what you want your page to be like. Could you improvise? Sure—but improvising at this stage might produce a less effective page, take much longer, put you millions of dollars over budget and weeks behind schedule, antagonize the critics, and so on.

In this hour, you'll get a quick tour of what Web pages are made of and a rundown on the important issues to consider when conceiving your own Web documents. At the end of the hour, you will be able to answer the following questions:

- What are Web pages are made of, and how do they work?
- What's HTML, and why should I care?
- How does multimedia—pictures, sound, video, and animation—become part of a page?
- What are *extensions* and the pros and cons of using extensions in your Web page?
- How should I approach organizing multiple pages into a complete Web site?

Anatomy of a Web Page

There are other optional parts, but most Web pages contain many of the elements described in this section. It's important to know what these parts are because the principle task in Web authoring is deciding what content to use for each standard part, and a principle challenge is dealing with the different ways each browser treats the different parts. (More on that later.)

Parts You See

The following are the elements of a Web page typically visible to visitors through a browser (see Figure 1.1):

FIGURE 1.1.

Some of the common parts of a Web page.

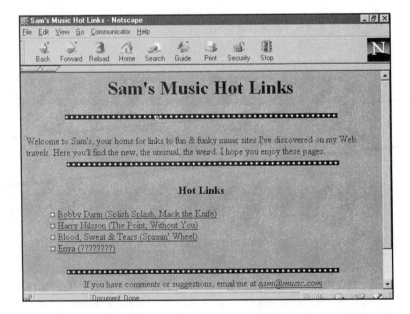

- A *title*, which graphical browsers (most Windows, Macintosh, and X Window browsers) typically display in the title bar of the window in which the page appears.

> The real title of a Web page does not appear within the page itself, but as the title of the browser window in which the page is displayed. However, most pages have another *title* of sorts, or rather, text or a graphic on the screen doing the job we typically associate with a title in books or magazine—sitting boldly and proudly near the top of the page to give it a name.

- *Headings*, which browsers typically display in large, bold, or otherwise emphasized type. A Web page can have many headings, and headings can be *nested* up to six levels deep; that is, there can be subheadings, and sub-subheadings, and so on.

- *Normal text*, which makes up the basic, general-purpose text of the page. Traditionally, Web authors refer to lines or blocks of normal text as *paragraphs*. But in the parlance of the Netscape Editor, *any* discrete block of words on the page is called a paragraph—whether it's a heading, normal text, or something else that is determined by *properties* assigned to that paragraph.

- A *signature*, typically displayed at the bottom of the page. A signature usually identifies the page's author and often includes the author's (or Webmaster's) email address so that visitors can send comments or questions about the page. The email address is sometimes formatted as a mailto link, so visitors can click it to open their email program with a message preaddressed to the author.

- *Horizontal lines*, which dress up the page and separate it into logical sections.

- *Inline images*, which are pictures that are incorporated into the layout of the page to jazz it up or make it more informative.

- *Background pattern*, which is an inline image that, unlike regular images, covers the entire background of the page so that text and other images can be seen on top of it.

- *Animations*, text or pictures that appear within the layout of the Web page but move in some way. Pictures can flash on and off or cycle though simple animations, and text can flash or scroll across the screen.

- *Hyperlinks* (or simply *links*) to many different things: other Web pages, multimedia files (external images, animation, sound, video), document files, email addresses, and files or programs on other types of servers (such as Telnet, FTP, and Gopher). Links may also lead to specific spots within the current page.

- *Imagemaps*, inline images in which different areas of the image have different links beneath them.

- *Lists*, which can be bulleted (like this one), numbered, and otherwise.

- *Forms*, areas in which visitors can fill in the blanks to respond to an online questionnaire, order goods and services, and more.

Parts You *Don't* See

In addition to the stuff you see in a Web page, the page—or rather, the set of files making up the page—has a number of other elements that can be included. These elements aren't usually visible to the visitor, but here are their effects:

- *Identification*—Web page files can include a variety of identification information, including the name (and/or email address) of the author and special coding that helps search engines determine the topic and content of the page.

- *Comments*—Comments are text the author wants to be seen when the HTML code of the page is read directly, not when the page is displayed in a browser. Comments generally include notes about the structure or organization of the HTML file.

NEW TERM   **HTML.** Short for *Hypertext Markup Language*, HTML is the computer file format in which Web pages are stored. An HTML file is really just a text file with special codes in it that tell a browser how to display the file—the size to use for each block of text, where to put the pictures, and so on.

- *JavaScript code*—Within an HTML file, lines of JavaScript program code can add special dynamic capabilities to the page.

- *Java applets*—In separate files, Java program modules can enhance interaction between the visitor, the browser, and the server.

- *Imagemap and forms processing code*—Program code (written in JavaScript or another language called CGI) used to process imagemaps and interactive forms.

To Do: Identify parts of a Web page

▼ To Do

1. Open your Web browser, connect to the Internet and go to any Web page you like. (You can use the copy of Netscape Navigator included with this book or use any other browser you may have.)

2. Look at the title bar of the window in which the browser appears (the bar along the very top, where you usually see the name of a program you're using). You'll probably see there the name of the browser program you're using, followed by the title of the Web page you're viewing.

3. Explore the page (and others), and see if you can identify all of the following in the pages you visit:

▼

▼ Headings (usually large, bold text, and only a few words)

Normal text

Lists (both bulleted and numbered)

Links (attached to underlined text or pictures)

Pictures

Signature (a link that opens your email program when you click it)

In most browsers, at the very bottom of the window a status bar appears. Whenever you point to a link (without clicking), you may see in the status bar the address to which that link leads.

Besides exploring where links lead, you can learn about the picture files you see in a Web page. Point to a picture, right-click, and then choose Properties from the menu that appears. A dialog box appears to tell you the filename, file size, and file type of the picture to which you pointed.

Using these techniques, you can develop your Web authoring skills by learning more about the design of the Web pages you visit.

▲

How a Web Page Works

When you author a Web page, no matter how you go about it—running a page generator (as you'll do in Hour 3, "Wizarding Up an Instant Web Page"), by using an editor such as Netscape Composer or Microsoft's FrontPage, or just typing it into a text file—what you end up with is an HTML file that can be published on a Web server.

An HTML file (see Figure 1.2) contains all of the text that appears on the page, plus codes, called *tags*, that label each chunk of text as a particular element of the page. For example, HTML tags identify one line of text as the page's title, blocks of text as paragraphs, certain lines or words as links, and so on. Other HTML tags designate the file names of inline images to be incorporated into the page by the browser when the page is displayed.

Another type of HTML code, called an *attribute*, controls the effects of tags with which they are associated. For example, a tag can determine that the page will have a colored background. An attribute within that tag specifies which color to use.

In addition to identifying the elements of the page, HTML tags and their attributes control, to a varying extent, the formatting of the page—but more about this a little later.

The point of most Web page editors, including Netscape Composer, is to insulate you from having to work directly with HTML code. Instead, you work in a *WYSIWYG* (what you see is what you get) environment, arranging and formatting text and graphics onscreen as they would appear when seen through a browser. As you do this, Composer creates the HTML document for you, behind the scenes.

Nevertheless, there are reasons to become familiar with HTML. In Part V, "Fine-Tuning Your Page," you'll discover powerful features you can deploy in your Web page for which the editor supplied with this book (and most other editors, as well) has no tools. To exploit those features, you'll pull the curtain and work with HTML—which isn't difficult, as you'll discover.

FIGURE 1.2.

The HTML source file of the page shown in Figure 1.1.

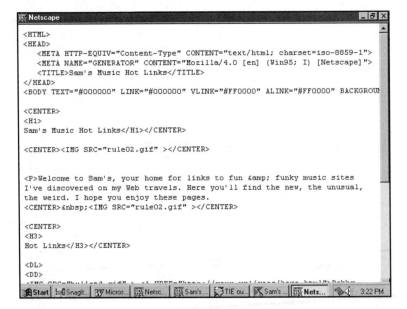

A Web browser is a program that knows how to do at least two things:

- Retrieve HTML documents from remote Web servers (by using a communications protocol called HTTP, about which you need know nothing right now).
- Interpret the HTML tags in the document to display a heading as a heading, treat a link like a link, and so on.

What's important to remember is that the HTML tags do not offer you the kind of control over the precise formatting of a page that you would have in a word processor.

Except when extensions are used, HTML mostly just identifies what's what. Each browser decides differently how to format those elements onscreen.

NEW TERM **Extension.** Extensions are special additions to the standard HTML language, usually created by a browser-maker to enable that browser to do stuff that's not included in HTML. See "Extensions: Love 'Em!, Hate 'Em!," later in this hour.

At this writing, the two most popular browsers—various versions of Netscape Navigator and Internet Explorer—comprise the overwhelming majority of the browser market. While there are subtle differences in the HTML tags each supports, the perpetual competition between these two has resulted in two browsers that display most Web pages identically. This means that, to most potential visitors on the Web, your Web page will look roughly the same as it does to you in Communicator.

To folks using browsers other than the two bigshots, your page will always show the same text content and general organization, but its graphical content and other aesthetics might vary dramatically browser-to-browser. In fact, in some cases, pictures and any other graphical niceties might not show up at all.

> You can download the browsers shown in Figures 1.3 and 1.4 and display your pages in them to see how your work appears in various browsers. Web addresses for getting these browsers appear in Hour 23, "Testing and Maintaining Your Page Online."

To illustrate this browser-to-browser variation, Figures 1.3 and 1.4 show the exact same Web page as shown earlier in Figure 1.1. Figure 1.1, however, displays the page through Netscape Navigator, while Figures 1.3 and 1.4 show it through two other browsers: Cello and DOSLynx. Compare Figures 1.3 and 1.4 to Figure 1.1 and observe how the presentation differs in each.

DOSLynx, the browser shown in Figure 1.4, is a *text-only* browser for DOS. (You still remember DOS, don't you?) Disappearing rapidly from the Web (but still out there), these browsers cannot display inline graphics and display all text in the same size typeface, though important elements such as headings can be made to stand out with bold type or underlining. Some people use text-only browsers out of choice, although most do so because they lack the proper type of Internet account or the proper hardware for a graphical browser.

FIGURE 1.3.

The same page as Figure 1.1, but shown in Cello.

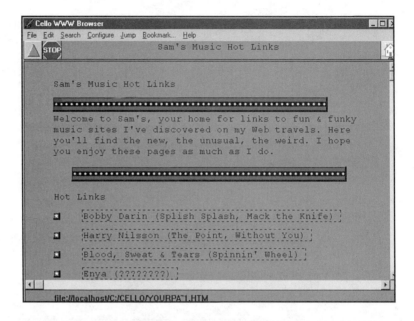

FIGURE 1.4.

The same page as Figure 1.1 and 1.3, but shown in DOSLynx.

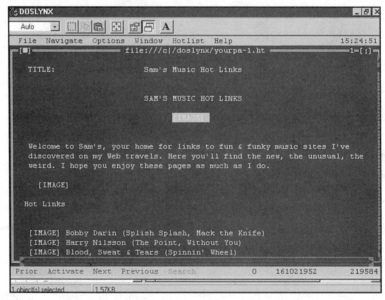

Because of the lingering presence of text-only browsers (and because some surfers switch off the display of inline graphics when browsing to speed up their Web sessions), it's important to duplicate in text any important information that's also communicated in a graphic. In particular, links buried in an imagemap should be duplicated with text else-where on the page. You'll learn more about this in Hour 9, "Understanding Links."

▼ To Do

To Do: Examine the HTML source code of a Web page

1. Open your Web browser, connect to the Internet, and go to any Web page you like.

2. Change the view of your browser so that it shows the raw HTML source code of the page:

   In Netscape Navigator (included with this book), choose View, Page Source.

   In Internet Explorer 4, choose View, Source.

   In another browser, look for a menu option that mentions "Source" or "HTML."

3. Explore the HTML code. Don't worry if a lot of it looks like gibberish—you don't really need to be able to "decode" an HTML file on sight. But if you look closely, you'll see within the various codes:

   The actual text that appears on the page

   File names of pictures in the page

   Web addresses to which the links point

4. When finished examining the HTML source code, close the window in which the code appears to return to normal browser view.

> To get started off right in Web authoring, you need the basic introduction to HTML you're picking up in this hour. However, after this hour, you can pretty much forget about the HTML, at least until Part V.
>
> For beginning Web authors, HTML is kind of like a septic tank. You need to know what it is and where it is, but once you know, you can pretty much ignore it unless a problem bubbles up.

▲

Pictures, Sound, and Other Media

Because an HTML file contains only text, the graphics that you see in Web pages, and the multimedia you can access from them, are not exactly a part of the HTML source file, itself. Rather, they're linked to the page in either of two ways:

- *Inline images* are graphics files whose filenames and locations are noted in the HTML file itself and identified as images by tags. Inline images are images incor-porated into the layout of the page—all of the images you see through a browser when you access the page.

- *External media* are image, sound, or video files whose names and locations appear as links in the HTML file. These files do not appear or play automatically as part of the page. Instead, the page shows links that, when activated, download the file to play or display it.

Whether inline or external, the media files you use in your Web pages challenge the browsers that will be used to view your page. The browser must be capable of displaying graphics to display inline graphics. External media files can be played by the browser, itself, or, more commonly, played by helper applications (or plug-ins) opened by the browser.

When choosing to incorporate media into your page, you'll have to consider carefully the file types you use. The text-only rule of HTML files is what allows users of many different types of computers to access Web pages. Graphics files are less likely to be readable by a wide range of systems, and sound and video files even less so. Even within the confines of PCs and Macintoshes, you'll need to consider whether your media will be supported by a broad spectrum of browsers and/or helper applications. You'll learn more about this in Hour 13, "Getting (or Making) Pictures for Your Page."

Extensions: Love 'Em!, Hate 'Em!

HTML is standardized so that any Web browser can read any Web documents—sort of.

Here's the deal: All modern browsers support HTML 2, the latest set of tags that has been sanctioned as a *bona fide* standard by the committees that oversee Internet standards. Standardization is good, because it provides Web authors with a way to ensure that most browsers will be able to read what they publish. Because any browser can understand and interpret all of the HTML 2 tags, authors need only stick within the confines of those tags to ensure that their pages are accessible to the biggest possible online audience.

The problem with standards, though, is that they evolve slowly. On the Web, only downloads are permitted to be slow; *evolution* is required to be *fast*. Think about it: The first graphical browser emerged four years ago, and now we're talking real-time video. The entire birth and maturation of the Web as a graphical, interactive environment has taken place within a single presidential administration. Yikes!

HTML 2 includes support for all of the basics—headings, normal text, horizontal lines, lists, links, inline pictures, and so on. But now there's HTML 3, which includes all of the HTML 2 tags but also adds tags for stuff like the following:

- Centered and right-aligned text
- Tables
- Math functions
- Ways to position text alongside inline images (instead of just above or below images)

> When creating pages for an intranet, where all users have the same browser, you don't need to consider the extensions issue—you can apply all tags supported by the browser.

Leading browsers, including both Navigator and Internet Explorer, support all of HTML 3, and even some parts of a newer, emerging standard, HTML 4. Still, the pace of Web page enhancement is so great that both Netscape and Microsoft continue to incorporate in their browsers new tags and other capabilities that are not part of any approved HTML standard.

When used in a Web document, the effects of these *extensions* to HTML, as they're called, can be seen only through a browser that specifically supports them. Of course, Navigator supports all of Netscape's extensions, and Internet Explorer supports all of Microsoft's. However, not all browsers support all extensions. That's why you need to be careful with 'em.

In general, when an incompatible browser accesses a page that uses these tags, nothing dire happens. The fancy extension-based formatting doesn't show up, but the meat of the page—its text and graphics—remain readable.

> Authors who want to take advantage of extensions are concerned that some visitors are not seeing the page in its full glory. That's why, more and more, you'll see messages like Best when viewed through Netscape Navigator or Enhanced for Internet Explorer on Web pages. That's the author telling you that he or she has used extensions—and if you want to enjoy all the features of the page, you'd best pick up a compatible browser.

Ways to Organize a Document

Finally, before you dive into creating a Web document, you must give some thought to the following issues:

- How can my message be broken down into an organized series of topics?
- How long a page, or how many pages, will be required to say what I have to say?

> After you've developed and refined the topic breakdown and outline of your message, you might find that you've already composed the headings for your document.

Jot down a list of the topics or subtopics your document will cover. How many do you have, and how much material will be required for each topic? After this simple exercise, you'll begin to get a good sense of the size and scope of your document.

Now look at the topics. Do they proceed in a logical order from beginning to end, with each new part depending on knowledge of the parts that came before? Or does the material seem to branch naturally to subtopics (and sub-subtopics)? How might you reorder the topics to make the flow more logical or group related topics together?

As you work on your breakdown (not *that* kind of breakdown—your topic breakdown), a simple outline begins to emerge. The more you refine the outline before you begin composing your document, the more focused and efficient your authoring will be. More importantly, the resulting Web document will present your message in a way that's clear and easy to follow.

> To plan a document with three or more pages, *storyboard* it by roughing out each page on a piece of paper to decide which information belongs on each page. Tape the papers to a wall and draw lines or tape strings to plan links among the pages.

While you're building your outline, consider the logical organization of your presentation and how its material might fit into any of the common organizational structures seen on the Web:

Billboard—A single, simple page, usually describing a person, small business, or simple product. Most personal home pages are this type. They'll often contain links to related (or favorite) resources on the Web, but not to any further pages of the same document. (The Netscape Page Wizard builds this type of page.)

One-page linear—One Web page, short or long, designed to be read more or less from top to bottom. Rules are often used to divide up such a page into virtual "pages."

Readers can scroll through the entire page, but a table of contents and targets can be used to help readers jump down quickly to any section. This type is best used for fairly short documents (less than 10 screenfuls) wherein all the information flows naturally from a beginning to an end.

Multipage linear—Same general idea as one-page linear, but broken up into multiple pages that flow logically, one after the other, from beginning to end, like the pages of a story. You can lead the reader through the series by placing a link at the bottom of each page, leading to the next page.

Hierarchical—The classic Web structure. A top page (sometimes confusingly called a *home page*) contains links to other pages, each covering a major subject area. Each of those pages can have multiple links to still more pages, breaking the subject down further and getting into even more specific information. The result is a tree structure, like the one shown in Figure 1.5.

FIGURE 1.5.

A hierarchical structure.

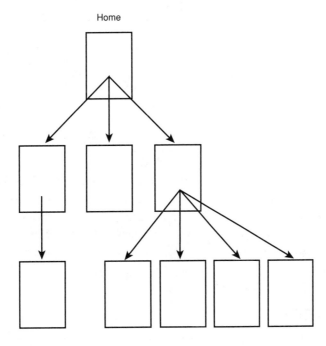

Home

Web—A Web structure (see Figure 1.6) is a hierarchical structure without the hierarchy. It's a multipage document in which any page can have a link leading to any other page. There may be a "top" page, but from there, readers can wander around the Web in no particular path. Web structures are loose and free-flowing and are, therefore, best suited to fun, recreational subjects, or to subjects that defy any kind of sequential or hierarchical breakdown. (Hint: Before you resort to a Web structure, make sure your message really calls for one—you might just be having trouble focusing.)

FIGURE 1.6.

A Web structure.

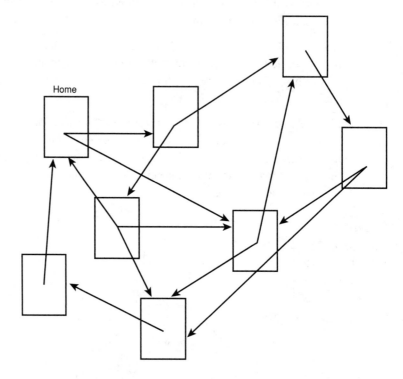

There are other ways to organize information; variations on each of the structures presented here. But one of these structures should resemble the general shape of your message, and thus your document. To put it another way, if you can't yet decide which of these structures is best for the Web page you want to create, you need to play with your message some more and break it down in different ways until a structure reveals itself to you.

Summary

You could, if you so choose, create your Web page by getting some good coffee, sitting down and fiddling for awhile with a Wizard (Hour 3) or any Web page editor. In the end, you'll have an HTML file suitable for publishing (if not for reading).

But will it be a file that achieves your goals for wanting a Web page in the first place? If you're looking for cyber-friends, will your page appeal to them? If you're looking for clients or customers, will your page make you look better than your competitors do? If you're offering useful information, are you doing so in a way that visitors to your page will find intuitive and easy to navigate?

Clearly, Web authoring is more than mechanics; it's also aesthetics, ergonomics, social science, and much more. To create a page that hits its mark, you must first ground yourself in the basics of how a Web document works, and what it can and cannot do. That's what you've picked up in this hour. I didn't attempt to dictate how your document should look, feel, or operate—that has to be your inspiration. But I've tried to feed your thoughts so that you can make informed choices during whatever tasks you choose to take on next.

Workshop

Q&A

Q So basically you're telling me I can do all these cool things to my page, but I should stick with the boring stuff since the cool stuff is based on extensions and also some people can't see graphics. Isn't that, well, ever so slightly a bummer?

A Bummer—not. In practice, it's really not such a big deal. First of all, remember that the overwhelming majority of the folks browsing the Web can view graphics, and most use a browser that can cope with most extensions. So even if you go completely nuts with pictures and extension-based formatting, your page will look great to most people. By using techniques I'll show you in later hours, you can accommodate the graphics-impaired or extension-impaired so that your page is as useful to them as to everyone else.

But still, it's important to remember that just because you're writing a page *in* Netscape's page editor doesn't mean you're writing it solely *for* users of Netscape. A smart author makes his or her document informative *and* cool to look at *as well as* accessible to all.

Quiz

Take the following quiz to see how much you have learned.

Questions

1. The real "title" of a Web page always appears:
    a. In bold type, within the body of the page.
    b. In the title bar of the browser window.

    c. Both a and b.

    d. None of the above.

2. True or False: The pictures you see in a Web page are not really part of the Web page file but are stored separately in picture files and inserted in the display by the browser.

3. Web pages are stored in a file format called:

    a. Hyper Speed Mockup Literature (HSML)

    b. Hypertext Markup Language (HTML)

    c. Stephen (S)

    d. Hyper Auto Retro Variant (HARV)

Answers

1. (b) Web authors often repeat the page title as a heading (choice a), but not always. The only place the real title always appears is b.

2. True. Each picture is in its own separate file, whose name and location are described in the HTML file so that the browser knows which picture to show where.

3. (b)

Activity

On your next surf of the Web, keep an eye on the area in your browser where the address and filename of the current page are shown (usually in the Address bar, just below the toolbar and above the page). Observe that most pages you view are files ending in the extension .htm or .html. Those are HTML files, just like those you're about to start creating.

HOUR 2

Getting Started with a Web Authoring Program

When you work in a WYSIWYG Web page editor (like Netscape Composer, included with this book), your page looks (with minor exceptions) just the way it will look to most visitors on the Web.

That's a powerful convenience; without it, Web authors have had to guess about the appearance of their page while fiddling with all the HTML code. To check their work, they had to open the file in a browser, and then go back to the HTML code to make adjustments. With a WYSIWYG editor, you can see and do it all in one window, live and in color.

This hour examines the general operation of Netscape Composer so you'll know your way around when you approach the specific authoring tasks coming up in later hours. At the end of the hour, you will be able to answer the following questions:

- In what ways can I open Composer for different kinds of tasks?
- How do I start, save, and re-open Web pages in Composer?

- How do I test the way my page will look online?
- Can I print my work?

> This hour assumes you have already installed Netscape Communicator, as described in Appendix A, "Installing Netscape Communicator."

Opening Composer

You can open Composer in a variety of ways, depending on where you begin and what you want to do with it.

To Open Composer from Windows 95, 98, or NT

When you want to work in Composer and Netscape Communicator is closed, open Composer directly from the Windows Start menu by choosing Programs, Netscape Communicator, Netscape Composer (see Figure 2.1). Composer opens to a new, blank Web page file. You can begin creating a Web page from this new file immediately, or open an existing file as described in the section "Open a File (and Sometimes Composer with It)," later in this hour.

> When using the Macintosh version of Communicator, you must open Navigator before you can open Composer.

> By default, opening the Netscape Communicator icon on the desktop opens Communicator's browser component (Navigator). But you can change that icon so that it opens Composer instead.

To Open Composer from Within Another Component

When you open Communicator, the Component bar opens automatically. Using the Component bar or Communicator menu, you can jump from any Communicator component to Composer.

FIGURE 2.1.

Opening Composer from the Windows Start menu to create a new Web page.

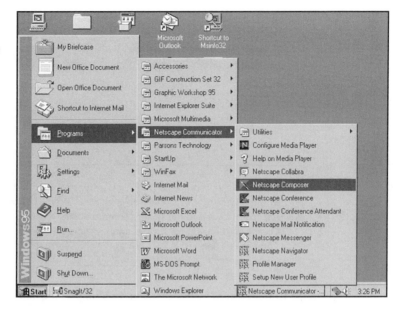

2

NEW TERM **Component bar.** A toolbar displayed by Communicator containing four icons, each of which opens a different Communicator component: Navigator (to browse the Web), Mailbox (email), Discussions (newsgroups) and Composer. The Component bar can appear in two forms: As a floating toolbar or "docked" in the lower-right corner of the window.

The first time you jump to Composer from another component within a Communicator session, Composer opens to a new, blank document, just as it does when you open it from the Start menu. When you open or create a file in Composer and then switch to another component, the file remains open in Composer. After you switch back to Composer from another component, you can resume working on the file.

To Do: Switch to Composer from other components

1. Open Navigator by opening the Start menu and choosing Programs, Netscape Communicator, Netscape Navigator. (If your Internet connection begins to open automatically, cancel it.)

2. Locate the Component bar. It will appear either as a floating toolbar with four icons (see Figure 2.2), or "docked" as a row of icons in the lower-right corner of the Navigator window.

FIGURE 2.2.

The Component bar appears as a floating toolbar, or docked as a row of icons in the lower-right corner of the window.

To switch the Component bar from a floating toolbar to its docked position in the lower-right of the window, choose Communicator, Dock Component Bar from the menu bar of any Communicator component. To undock the Component bar (make it float again), choose Communicator, Show Component Bar.

3. On the Component bar, click the icon for Composer. Composer opens.

4. On the Component bar, click the icon for Messenger to switch to Messenger.

5. From the menu bar, choose Communicator, Page Composer to switch back to Composer.

6. Use the Component bar and Communicator menu to switch among components a few more times to get the feel of it.

When you jump from another component to Composer, note that all open components remain open, as do their files and any online sessions. For example, if you're working online in Navigator and then jump to Composer using any of the methods just described, Navigator and the online session remain open behind the scenes.

Starting a New Web Page

From the File menu within any component, you have three ways to start a Web authoring session:

- **File, New, Blank Page**—Opens Composer with a new, blank Web page file ready for editing.

- **File, New, Page from Template**—Opens the New Page from the Template dialog box. In the dialog box, you enter the location of a Web page template to use as a head start on a new page. (See Hour 4, "Making a Fast, Fancy Page with a Template.")

- File, New, Page from Wizard—Opens Navigator (if you're not already there) and connects to Netscape's Page Wizard, which helps you quickly create a simple home page. (See Hour 3, "Wizarding Up an Instant Web Page.") After you complete the home page in Navigator, choose File, Edit Page to switch to Composer and save the page.

To Do: Open a file (and sometimes Composer with it)

The steps to open a file for editing in Composer are the same whether you begin in Navigator or Composer. Isn't that nice?

1. From within either Navigator or Composer, choose File, Open Page. The Open Page dialog box appears (see Figure 2.3).

FIGURE 2.3.

The Open Page dialog box, accessible from both Navigator and Composer.

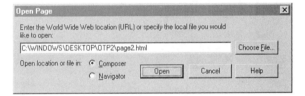

2. Enter the path and filename or click the Choose File button to open a standard Windows Open dialog box, which you can use to browse for the file. You can see from Figure 2.3 that you do not need to enter the path and filename in URL form.

3. When the correct path and filename appear in the Open Page dialog box, make sure that the radio button next to Composer is selected, and then click Open. The selected file opens in Composer, ready for editing.

> In Composer, instead of choosing File, Open Page, you can click the Open button on the Composition toolbar. This button does not open the Open Page dialog box; it opens a regular Windows Open dialog box that you can use to browse for and select a file.

Opening a File Using the New Button

Just in case you want to create a new page file or open an existing one, but you don't like any of the umpteen ways I've already offered for doing so, here's one more (it's the last one, I swear). As you'll see, using the New button is usually less convenient than the methods already described.

Click the New button on Composer's Composition toolbar to open the Create New Page dialog box (see Figure 2.4). From the dialog box, select the button you need:

- The first three buttons, Blank Page, From Template, and From Page Wizard, have the same effect as the three menu items of the same names under **File**, **New**.
- Open Local File has the same effect as clicking the Open button on Composer's toolbar (it opens a regular Windows Open dialog box, from which you select a file).

FIGURE 2.4.

Composer's Create New Page dialog box.

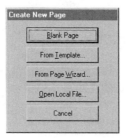

Saving and Naming Files

When you save a file in Composer, you give it a name—presumably the name by which it will be stored on a Web server when published. And when it comes time to publish a Web page, names can be tricky.

For example, Windows 95, 98, NT and even the Macintosh all allow you to use spaces and punctuation in filenames, but you should not do so when naming Web page files. Composer will permit you to do it, but when you attempt to publish the files (or even view them in Navigator), you'll find that a browser cannot open them.

In general, as long as you use an extension of .htm or .html and eliminate spaces and punctuation, you can give your page files any name you like. However, the filename must conform to the system the server uses. For example, if the Web server on which you will publish your document (see Hour 21, "Publishing Your Page") is a DOS server, your filenames must conform to DOS's 8.3 filename rule: A name must be no more than eight characters with an extension of no more than three (.htm, not .html).

Also, when a page is the "top" page of a multipage Web presentation, standard practice is to name it index.html. Some servers are configured to open the file index.html automatically when a visitor specifies a directory but not a specific file. However, this only works if you have your own directory on the server. Usually, you will. But if you share a directory with others, odds are you won't be the first to post a file called index.html, so the server won't accept your document.

The bottom line: Choose your server and find out about its naming guidelines before settling on final names for your HTML files.

Using AutoSave

Composer includes an AutoSave feature that saves any open file every time a set number of minutes pass (by default, 10 minutes).

The saving happens automatically and with no help from you, but only after the first time you have deliberately saved the file. Until the file has been saved the first time, AutoSave does not save automatically; instead, it prompts you, asking whether you want to save (see Figure 2.5). Click Yes in the dialog box to save the file, or No to close the dialog box without saving, which leaves AutoSave enabled to prompt you later. After you've saved the file, future autosaving happens automatically.

If you click Cancel in the AutoSave dialog box, two things happen (or rather, two things don't happen):

- The file is not saved.
- AutoSave is temporarily disabled for the current file, so it no longer attempts to save the file automatically. It will not prompt you again until after you have saved the file yourself. Once you do that, AutoSave is automatically re-enabled and resumes prompting you every 10 minutes thereafter.

You can enable or disable AutoSave and select the number of minutes AutoSave waits before prompting you to save. From Composer, choose Edit, Preferences to open the Preferences dialog box.

To change the number of minutes, enter a new number in the box next to "minutes" near the top of the dialog box. To disable AutoSave, clear the checkbox next to "Automatically save page every..."

FIGURE 2.5.

The AutoSave prompt.

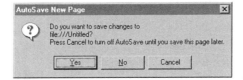

To Do: Save a file

1. Click the Save button on the Composition toolbar, or choose **F**ile, **S**ave. A standard Save dialog box opens.

> When you save a Web page file before giving it a title in Page Properties, a dialog box opens automatically, in which you can enter a title. For now, just enter any title you like—you'll learn all about titles and other page properties in Hour 5, "Choosing a Title, Colors, and Other Page Properties."

2. Select a folder if you wish and type a name for your file. You don't need to enter an extension; an extension of .htm is added automatically.

3. Click OK.

Testing Composer Files in Navigator

As you'll discover throughout this book, Composer is *mostly* WYSIWYG; in most cases, your page will look the same whether viewed through Composer or Navigator. However, a few page elements do not appear the same in Composer as they do in a browser.

So from time to time, it's smart to "preview" your creations in Navigator to see the way the page will appear to visitors (or to visitors using Navigator).

> Save your Composer file immediately before clicking the Preview button. If you don't, a prompt appears after you click Preview, forcing you to save before Navigator shows the file.

To preview a page you're editing in Composer, choose File, Browse Page from Composer's menu bar (or click the Preview button on Composer's toolbar). The file currently being edited in Composer opens in Navigator.

If, before you click Preview, Navigator is already open but displays a different file, a new Navigator window opens to display the file being edited. If Navigator already shows the file being edited (as it would if you had clicked Preview earlier in your editing session), that window opens and reloads the page automatically to show any changes you've made since you last browsed the file.

To return to your editing session after viewing the document in Navigator, choose Page Composer from the Component bar or Communicator menu.

After browsing a file you're editing, do not use **File**, **E**dit Page to jump back from Navigator to Composer. Doing so will not return you to your previous Composer editing session; instead, Edit Page opens a new Composer window and a new copy of the page for editing. You will then have two open Composer windows editing the same Web page file.

After viewing a file in Navigator, use the Windows taskbar, Ctrl+4, or the Component bar to switch back to Composer.

2

Working with Composer's Toolbars

All of Composer's functions are available from the menu bar, but for quicker access, many of the most frequently used functions are also available from one of Composer's two toolbars (see Figure 2.6).

Each button on the toolbars is discussed in the hour covering the action it performs. For example, the Insert Link button is covered in Hour 10, "Making Links."

- *Composition*—Contains buttons for opening and creating files, checking files in Navigator, editing text, printing, and adding page elements such as links and images.
- *Formatting*—Contains buttons and drop-down lists for creating lists and performing text formatting tasks such as applying paragraph styles, fonts, and text attributes.

When both toolbars are onscreen, they cut into the size of the edit window, so you can see less of the page you're working on. When you don't need one or both, you may hide a toolbar by choosing an option from the top of the View menu.

Observe in Figure 2.6 that there are two rows of buttons on top of the editing window. Each row is a separate toolbar, though the two bars create the impression of a single toolbar when positioned together.

Composition toolbar   Formatting toolbar

FIGURE 2.6.

Composer's toolbars.

Identifying Toolbar Buttons

The folks who invented the graphical user interface believed that self-explanatory onscreen buttons enabled *intuitive* operation, wherein the user instinctively clicked the required button by subconsciously comprehending the meaning of the button's picture icon.

Most of Composer's toolbar buttons are pretty intuitive after you get used to them. For example, the Print button has a picture of a printer; the Insert Link button has a picture of a chain (*link*—get it?). However, a few buttons might look pretty cryptic to you. Fortunately, all of Composer's toolbar buttons include tooltips. To learn the name of any toolbar button in Composer, rest the pointer on it for a moment, and the button's name appears.

NEW TERM **Tooltip.** Used in many Windows programs, tooltips are labels that pop up to identify toolbar buttons. You display a button's tooltip simply by resting the pointer on the button for a second or two.

> Here's a handy way to locate any button you need in a toolbar: Rest the pointer on the toolbar's far-left button. When the tooltip appears, move the pointer slowly to the right across the buttons—the tooltip of each button appears instantly as you go along.

Moving Toolbars

The order of the Composer toolbars—Composition and Formatting—is not fixed. Within the general toolbar area at the top of the window, you can put Formatting over Composition, or vice-versa.

To change the order, point to the vertical bar at the far left edge of a toolbar. Click and hold, and then drag the toolbar up or down within the toolbar area to its new home and release.

> Toolbar settings are file-specific. If you move a toolbar or change show/hide options and then save the page, those settings return whenever you open that page.

Printing from Composer

To print a page you're editing, click the Print button on the toolbar or choose File, Print. The document is printed exactly as it would be from Navigator—text formatting and pictures are included on the printout, but any background patterns you may have added are omitted to keep text legible. The page is broken up into appropriately sized chunks to fit on paper pages.

2

Although you might want to print your pages for reference, do not rely on printouts as accurate representations of your page's appearance online.

Summary

Composer does a lot—too much, in fact, for this hour to even scratch the surface. Still, in this hour you've wrapped your arms around the job and learned how to get into, out of, and around Composer. As mundane as those tasks are, they're the essential foundation to productive Web authoring. You're on your way.

But for all that it is, there's one thing Composer is not: smart. It can't tell you whether the content you've created is well organized, well presented, or well written. And although it applies HTML tags to your document dutifully, it cannot tell you whether you've selected the most effective tags for presenting the content at hand.

Thus, Composer is a replacement only for time and labor, not for judgment. To author an effective Web document, you must acquire a sense of Web aesthetics. You'll pick up much of this sense as you work through this book. But you must also study other pages you see online and mentally catalog the design aspects and content approaches that sing to you—and those that annoy, bore, or baffle you, as well.

Workshop

Q&A

Q Looking over the toolbar and menu items in Composer, I see the stuff described in this hour, plus other stuff I know you'll cover in later hours, such as images. But where are the menu items or toolbar buttons for other page elements I've seen on the Web, such as video?

A Composer is pretty full-featured, supplying tools for 90 percent of the things that 99 percent of Web authors do. But it is not a universal, all-encompassing Web authoring system. It does not do everything.

That's why this hour and others remind you at appropriate points that no matter what you do in Composer, you're building an HTML document underneath. When you move on to the page elements for which Composer supplies no tools, you'll need to switch off the cruise control and press the HTML pedals directly. You'll begin that experience in Hour 17, "Editing HTML," and I think you'll discover that it's not so challenging. Until then, explore and enjoy the things Composer *does* do, as covered in Hours 3 through 16.

Quiz

Take the following quiz to see how much you have learned.

Questions

1. When Communicator's component bar is "docked," you'll see it:

    a. On Pier 11.

    b. With a smaller paycheck.

    c. Floating on the screen.

    d. In the lower-right corner of the window.

2. You click the Preview button in Composer to test what your creation would look like if:

    a. You published it on the Web without making further changes.

    b. It were finished.

    c. Somebody else had created it.

    d. You started over.

3. True or False: You can use the filename "My New Web Page.htm" as a Web page filename.

Answers

1. (d) When it is undocked, (c) becomes true.

2. (a) The preview shows the current state of your page, as it would look online through a browser.

3. False. You can't use spaces in Web page filenames. (However, "MyNewWebPage.htm" would probably be okay.)

Activity

Begin exploring Composer as an editor. Open a new file and start typing text into it. See if you can figure out how to format that text. (Hint: Try the Formatting toolbar.)

HOUR 3

Wizarding Up an Instant Web Page

Netscape's Page Wizard is one of a growing field of fill-in-the-blanks "home page generators" that enable new Web authors to crank out personal home pages in a matter of minutes. Like anything built for speed and simplicity, the Page Wizard forces the author to compromise a lot of freedom when compared with other approaches. It's like a Polaroid camera: You can't do much with it and the results are small, fuzzy, and unprofessional looking, but the gratification is almost instantaneous.

Still, the Page Wizard can't be beat for speed and simplicity, and it offers a great way for new authors to get their Web feet wet before moving onto the more demanding (and powerful) authoring techniques described later in this book. Perhaps more important, you may choose to use the Page Wizard to create a page that will serve as the raw material ("Web clay") to be edited and expanded with the techniques you'll learn as this book progresses.

At the end of the hour, you will be able to answer the following questions:

- What's the Wizard, and how do I start it up?
- Is the Wizard the right way to go for me?
- How do I create a new page—text, pictures, and all—in the Wizard?
- What do I do with the page when I'm done?

What (and Where) Is the Page Wizard?

The Netscape Page Wizard is like the Wizard of Oz: It's called a wizard and pretends to be one, but it really isn't one. However, in the end (also like Oz), the Page Wizard delivers what you came for.

You're familiar with wizards. They're the friendly, automated routines that lead you step by step through otherwise complicated tasks, such as installing Windows, creating shortcuts, or installing Communicator. The Page Wizard technically is not a Windows wizard, and it doesn't look or act like one. It serves the same purpose, though. It leads you through the creation of a basic, custom-built home page.

The Page Wizard is a Web page stored at the following address:

```
http://home.netscape.com/home/gold4.0_wizard.html
```

Should I Use the Page Wizard?

When you fill in the blanks in the Page Wizard, your entries are automatically plugged into the appropriate spots in a Web page *template*. The template used is a very simple, straightforward home page—no more, no less.

NEW TERM   **Template.** A template is a finished Web page file that you can edit and customize to create a new page of your own much more quickly than starting from scratch. See Hour 4, "Making a Fast, Fancy Page with a Template."

Although different entries result in different content, the organization of the page remains the same, regardless of what you type in the Page Wizard. The Page Wizard offers you the ability to dress up the look of the page by choosing a background texture, custom colors for text, and stylized bullets and horizontal lines (although these formatting choices have drawbacks, as you'll see later in this chapter). But the layout of the text elements on the page remains unchanged, no matter what you do. All pages created with the Wizard look essentially the same—only the content changes (see Figure 3.1).

The template used by the Page Wizard is designed for a personal home page and is effective in that regard, even if it is a little short and overly simple. By making a few creative choices when filling in the blanks and then tweaking the page a bit in Composer, you can also use the Page Wizard to create a simple business page.

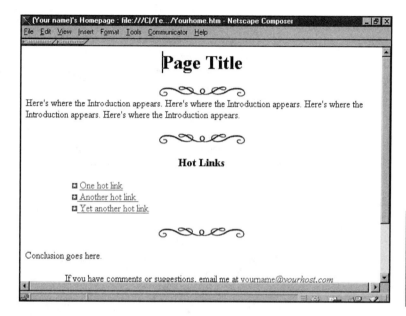

FIGURE 3.1.

A sample home page produced by the Netscape Page Wizard.

You can use the Page Wizard to quickly cobble together a basic page, and then you can enhance and expand that page in Composer.

Whether you should use the Page Wizard depends on whether the overall organization of the resulting page is reasonably close to what you want to achieve. If you want a dramatically different look for your page, or if you plan to build an elaborate Web document made up of multiple linked pages and files, you're probably better off skipping ahead to the next hour of this book.

Running the Wizard

Running the Page Wizard is an online affair. You can't simply download the Page Wizard page and then use it offline because the Page Wizard creates your page by taking entries you make in online forms and running those entries through a script processor that resides on Netscape's server.

Note that even though you're authoring, you run the Page Wizard in Navigator, not Composer. You do not need to open Composer until you save the finished page, as described later in this chapter.

As you follow the instructions for creating a page, you'll come across various names for elements the page may include—title, headings, paragraphs, and so on. For the purposes of running the Wizard, these elements are largely self-explanatory, and you needn't know a lot about what the names mean in order to create your page.

However, when you move on to Part II of this book, "Titles, Text, and Tables," you'll discover that each element in a Web page plays a very specific, unique role, and mastering the names and uses of the page elements is an important part of learning to compose and edit Web pages.

Like a growing number of Web pages, the page on which you run the Wizard is divided up into frames. Each frame acts like its own little independent window. You'll learn how to create your own frames-based Web pages in Hour 18, "Dividing a Page into Frames."

To Do: Start the Wizard

1. Open Navigator and connect to the Internet.

When you perform step 2, it doesn't matter what page you're on— Netscape's home page, another page, a blank page—just as long as Navigator is open and you're connected to the Internet.

2. In Navigator, choose **File**, **New**, Page From **Wizard**. This instructs the browser to connect to the Page Wizard. A screen appears like the one shown in Figure 3.2.

3. In the active frame (upper–right corner), scroll down past Netscape's cheery introductory copy to display the START button.

4. Click the START button in the upper-right frame. The page appears as shown in Figure 3.3.

As Figure 3.3 shows, the Wizard page is split into three frames:

- The upper-left frame, INSTRUCTIONS, describes each element you will create. Within each description are links that, when clicked, display a form or list of choices in the bottom frame.

- The bottom frame, CHOICES, is where you will type text in forms (to create page content) or choose aspects of the look of your page from lists of choices.

▼   • The upper-right frame, PREVIEW, shows a preview of your page. As you complete
           each form or selection in the CHOICES (bottom) frame, the preview is updated to
           show you the result. (After the first few forms, you'll need to scroll down in the
           PREVIEW frame to see the area of the page you've just created.)

FIGURE 3.2.

*The opening screen in
the Page Wizard.*

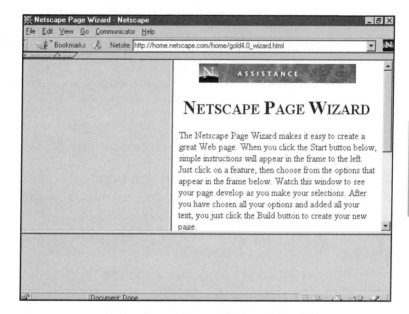

3

FIGURE 3.3.

*The first form in the
Page Wizard.*

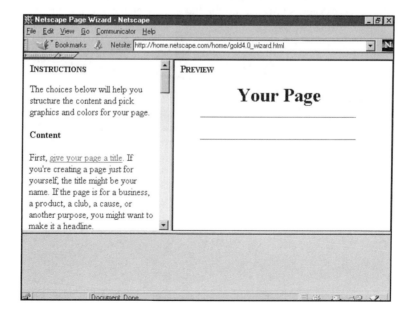

▼

The next several sections of this task describe how to complete all of the forms and make all of the selections required to complete your page. The forms and choices are discussed here in the order in which you encounter them in the INSTRUCTIONS (upper-left) frame.

You don't need to make your entries and choices in order. You may scroll ahead in the INSTRUCTIONS frame and make later choices and entries before making earlier ones. You may also scroll forward or backward in the INSTRUCTIONS frame at any time to revisit earlier entries (and change or delete them if you want to.

Finally, keep in mind that you needn't fill in every blank in the Page Wizard. If you leave a form empty, the wizard simply deletes that element of the page and any text used to label it. If you don't bother making a selection under the "Looks" portion of the Page Wizard, defaults are used.

To Do: Fill in the content of the page

In the Content section of the INSTRUCTIONS frame, you choose links that open text-entry forms in the CHOICES frame. Follow these steps:

1. Scroll the INSTRUCTIONS frame until you see the link *give your page a title* (see Figure 3.4).

2. Click the link. A form appears in the CHOICES frame, as shown in Figure 3.4.

3. Delete the descriptive text that appears in the form and type a title for your page. The Page Wizard uses this as the document title (which appears in the title bar of a visitor's browser, not on the page itself) and as a large, bold heading at the top of the page itself.

4. Click Apply. The new title appears in the PREVIEW frame, centered at the top of the page (see Figure 3.5).

The Page Wizard inserts a horizontal line above and below the introduction. Later, you'll get a chance to customize the look of that rule.

FIGURE 3.4.

Entering a title.

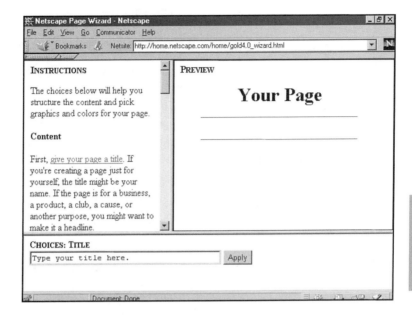

FIGURE 3.5.

A finished title (in the PREVIEW frame) and the CHOICES frame ready for your Introduction.

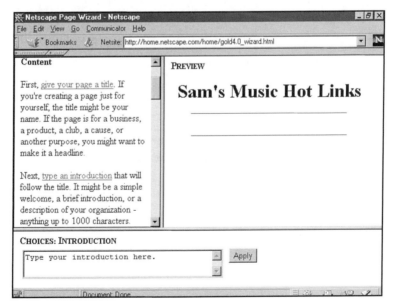

▼ 5. Scroll the INSTRUCTIONS frame until you see the link *type an introduction* (see Figure 3.5).

6. Click the link. A form appears in the CHOICES frame, as shown in Figure 3.5.

7. Delete the descriptive text that appears in the form and type an introduction of up to 1,000 characters for your page. When typing the introduction, you can press Enter to break lines or create a blank line. That way, you can create an introduction that is several paragraphs long (up to 1,000 characters total).

The Page Wizard inserts your introduction as a normal paragraph, left-aligned, following the title (see Figure 3.6).

FIGURE 3.6.

A finished introduction (in the PREVIEW frame) and the CHOICES frame ready for your Hot Links.

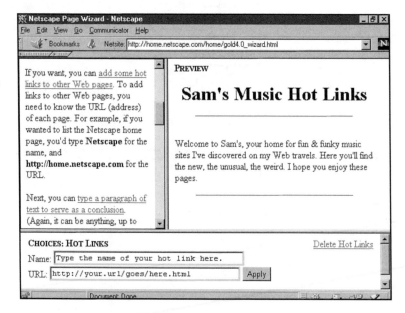

8. Click Apply. The new introduction appears in the PREVIEW frame.

9. Scroll the INSTRUCTIONS until you see the link *add some hot links* (see Figure 3.6).

10. Click the link. A form appears in the CHOICES frame, as shown in Figure 3.6.

11. The CHOICES: HOT LINKS form allows you to create a bulleted list of links to other pages or documents. Creating each link in the list takes three steps:

    • Delete the descriptive text that appears in the Name line of the form and type the text you want to appear in your page as the link source (the text to click to activate the link).

▼

- Delete the descriptive text that appears in the URL line of the form and type the complete URL to which visitors should be taken if they click the text entered in Name.
- Click Apply.

> The Page Wizard formats your hot links in a bulleted list. Later, you'll get a chance to customize the look of the bullets.

The Page Wizard inserts the Name text as one item in a bulleted list under a centered heading Hot Links (see the PREVIEW frame in Figure 3.7). You may now add to the list by entering another hot link (repeat step 11) or move on. (It makes sense to use at least two hot links or none at all; a bulleted list with only one item looks a little silly.)

FIGURE 3.7.

Finished hot links in the PREVIEW frame.

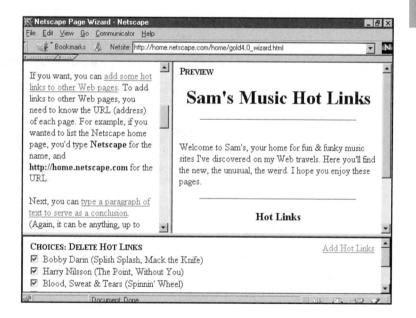

> If you apply a hot link and decide later you don't want it anymore, scroll the INSTRUCTIONS frame to the link for hot links (*add some hot links*) and click the link to reopen the CHOICES: HOT LINKS form. Then click Delete Hot Links. A new CHOICES form opens, as shown in Figure 3.7.

> The check marks appearing next to each link in the list indicate that the link
> is to remain in the document. To delete a link, click its check box. The link
> instantly disappears from the list and from the PREVIEW frame.

12. Scroll the INSTRUCTIONS frame until you see the link *type a paragraph of text
    to serve as a conclusion.*

13. Click the link. The CHOICES: CONCLUSION form appears in the CHOICES
    frame.

14. Delete the descriptive text that appears in the form and type a conclusion of up to
    1,000 characters for your page. Just as in the introduction, you can press Enter to
    break lines or create a blank line.

    The Page Wizard inserts your conclusion as a normal paragraph, left-aligned, fol-
    lowing the hot links (see Figure 3.15, later in this chapter).

15. Scroll the INSTRUCTIONS frame until you see the link add an email link (see
    Figure 3.8).

FIGURE 3.8.

Entering a signature.

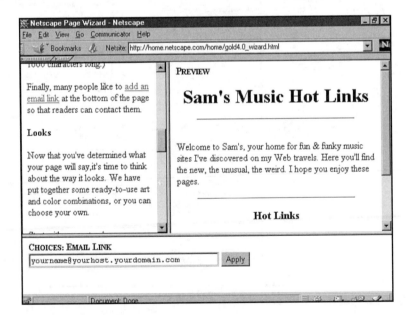

16. Click the link. A form appears in the CHOICES frame, as shown in Figure 3.8.

17. The CHOICES: EMAIL LINK form allows you to create a signature for the bot-
    tom of your page (see Figure 3.15, later in this chapter), including a mailto link

▼   that allows visitors to conveniently send your email. Delete the descriptive text that appears in the form and fill in your complete Internet email address.

18. Click Apply.

The Page Wizard builds a signature at the bottom of the page. In the signature,
▲   your email address appears as a mailto link.

To Do: Choose looks for your page

In the Looks portion of the Page Wizard, you can customize the look of your page in four ways:

- Choose a background color or pattern
- Choose custom colors for text, links, and visited links
- Choose customized bullets (for the bulleted list of hot links)
- Choose customized rules (horizontal lines)

Note that you do not have to make any of these selections. If you ignore the Look choices, your page will use no background color or pattern, the default text/link/visited link colors for each browser, and ordinary, default bullets and rules.

1. Scroll the INSTRUCTIONS frame until you see the link *a preset color combination* (see Figure 3.9). This link allows you to choose in one step a complete set of color selections that already work well together, so you needn't select each color (background, text, link, visited link) separately. (If you'd rather choose each color separately, skip to step 4.)

FIGURE 3.9.

Choosing a preset color combination.

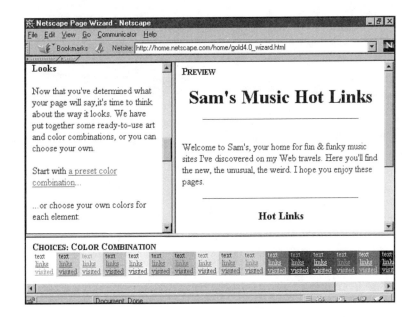

3

> It's usually best not to use a custom color for *visited links*. Web surfers have conditioned responses; they expect a visited link to appear in their browser's default color everywhere.

2. Click the link. A row of color choices appears in the bottom frame, as shown in Figure 3.9. Each choice includes a text color, link color, and visited link color all set against a square of background color. The four colors are all properly color coordinated.

3. Choose a color combination by clicking it. (There is no Apply button.)

4. If you did not choose a preset color combination or if you want to change any of the colors within your selection for preset colors, scroll the INSTRUCTIONS frame to the list of links beginning with *background color*.

5. Click any item (other than *background pattern*) to display a row of color choices like the one shown for BACKGROUND COLOR in Figure 3.10.

FIGURE 3.10.

Choosing colors.

6. Click a color block to choose the color.

7. To choose a background pattern, click the link *background pattern*. A row of choices appears in the CHOICES frame, as shown in Figure 3.11.

When choosing colors, try to contrast text, link, and background colors so that links are easy to spot. Also, keep your eye on your background selection to make sure the text and links will stand out from the background but not clash with it. (If you happen to be color blind, like me, leave the defaults; they know better than we do.)

Choosing a background pattern overrides any selection for background color but does not affect your color choices for text, links, and visited links.

FIGURE 3.11.

Choosing a background pattern.

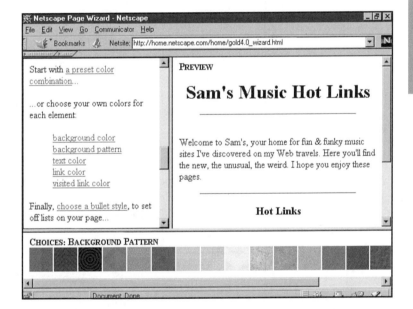

8. Click the desired background pattern. After a few moments, the results appear in the PREVIEW frame.

9. Scroll the INSTRUCTIONS frame to reveal the link *choose a bullet style*, as shown in Figure 3.12. Your selection for bullet style decorates the bulleted list of hot links created earlier.

10. Click the link. A row of custom bullets appears in the CHOICES frame, as shown in Figure 3.12. (The first choice, a solid circle, is not a custom bullet. It's the default choice, a standard HTML bullet.)

11. Click a bullet style to select it.

FIGURE **3.12.**

*Choosing a bullet
style.*

12. Scroll the INSTRUCTIONS frame to reveal the link for *choose a horizontal rule
    style*, as shown in Figure 3.13. Your selection of a rule style affects all the rules
    that the Wizard inserts automatically to divide up the sections of the page.

FIGURE **3.13.**

Choosing a rule style.

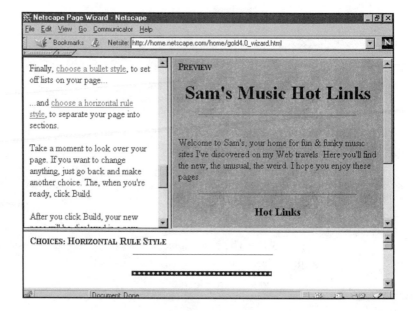

13. Click the link. A row of custom rules appears in the CHOICES frame, as shown in Figure 3.13. (The first choice, a simple line, is not a custom rule. It's the default choice, a standard HTML rule.)

14. Click a rule style to select it.

> When making bullet and rule selections, keep your eyes on the PREVIEW frame and evaluate carefully your previous choices for background texture and text/link colors. Rules and bullets must stand out against the background but not clash with the background, text, or links—nor should they clash with each other. When in doubt, use the default choices (the far left bullet choice and the top rule choice).

To Do: Create the completed home page

1. Scroll up and down through the PREVIEW frame and review your choices and entries. Have you said all you want to say? Are you satisfied with your page's "look?" Are your email address and any URLs you've entered complete and accurate (don't forget to double-check capitalization on URLs). Also, howz yer speling?

2. After checking your entries and making any changes or corrections, scroll to the bottom of the INSTRUCTIONS frame, as shown in Figure 3.14, where you will see buttons labeled Build and Start Over.

FIGURE 3.14.

Finishing up.

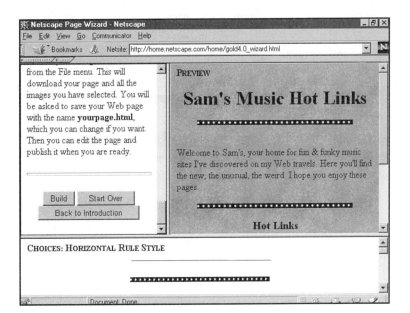

▼   3. Click Build. This button activates a script that takes your entries and selections,
        plugs them into a template, and opens the finished page in the browser, as shown in
        Figure 3.15.

FIGURE 3.15.

*The finished home
page.*

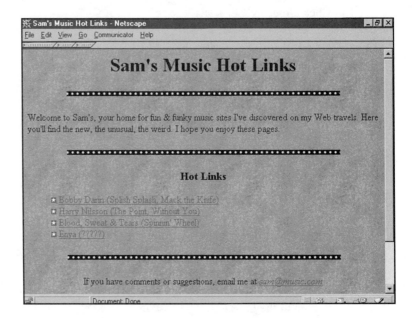

You must save the page when finished (as described in the next section), or
you'll lose it when you close Navigator. You must save using the Composer
rather than simply choosing File, Save **As** in Navigator because only
Composer will save the image files for the background pattern, custom bullets, and rules.

▲

To Do: Save the completed home page

1. From Navigator's menu bar, choose **F**ile, **E**dit Page. Composer opens, displaying
   your new home page, as shown in Figure 3.16.

Remember from Hour 2, "Getting Started with a Web Authoring Program,"
that although you can include spaces in Windows filenames, you cannot in
Web page filenames. A Web page filename must be all one word, include
no punctuation, and use the extension .htm or .html (for example,
ThisNameIsOK.htm.)

▼

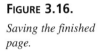

FIGURE 3.16.

Saving the finished page.

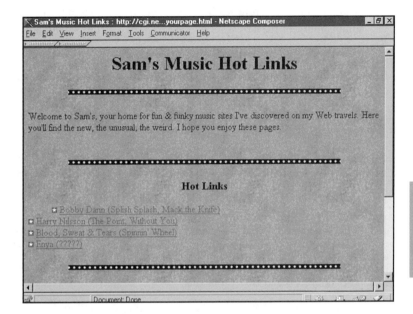

2. Click the Save button on Composer's toolbar (or choose **F**ile, **S**ave) to open a standard Windows Save dialog box. From here you may select a folder and filename for your page. The page is given a default filename of YOURPAGE.HTML. You can change this name to anything you like, but make sure the file extension remains .htm or .html. Click OK to save the file.

Your page is complete, and the files that comprise it—including one file for the page text and formatting instructions and separate image files for the graphical rules, bullets, and background pattern—are all stored on your PC.

Understanding Publishing

Your page is ready for publishing (unless you intend to edit or enhance it first in Composer). In a nutshell, publishing a Web page is a simple matter of uploading all of the files that make up the page into a designated directory on a Web server (or intranet server, if you intend your document to be used just by folks within a local intranet).

NEW TERM **Upload.** To upload is to send files from your computer to a server computer, such as a Web server (It's the opposite of downloading—receiving files from a server). When you publish a Web page, you upload its files to a Web server.

Most servers—whether Web or intranet—are guarded by security systems that prevent unauthorized users from storing files there. In order to publish, you must contact the administrator of the server on which you want to publish and obtain the following:

- Permission to upload files to the server
- The name and path of the directory in which the administrator wants you to store your files
- The specific steps required for uploading files to the server (the exact procedure varies somewhat)
- A username and password that you will use while uploading to identify yourself properly to the server's security system (so it will permit you to copy the files)

When you are ready to upload files, you will do so through a *communications protocol* supported by the server. The required protocol is almost always either of the same two protocols most often used for downloading files on the Internet: FTP (used for downloading files from an FTP server) or HTTP (used for downloading Web pages and other files from Web and intranet servers to browsers). Communicator's publishing system supports both FTP and HTTP uploads.

In fact, Composer includes a Publish button on its toolbar that enables you to publish (or update) your work with a single click. (Well, it really takes more than just one click, but it's still pretty easy.)

 You learn in detail how to use Composer's publishing features—and other techniques for publishing and testing your work—in Hour 21, "Publishing Your Page."

Summary

The Page Wizard offers a quick, easy way to build a complete, properly designed Web page. It's ideal for building a first personal home page and for creating a basic page you'll later enhance and expand with Composer.

To make the most of the Page Wizard, you must make carefully considered entries in each form field. You also must consider the effect of all of your choices together. It's not uncommon for new authors to become so enamored of fancy backgrounds and colors that the resulting page is an eyesore. Also, of course, you must consider how your page will look in browsers other than Netscape Navigator.

Workshop

Q&A

Q I see that little Netscape slogan along with a Netscape Now! button at the bottom of every page that I make with the Page Wizard. What gives?

A Like any living thing, Netscape wants to procreate. To that end, the company pollinates every page created using the Page Wizard with the Netscape Now! button, which is an inline image and also a link. The link connects to a page at Netscape that allows visitors to conveniently select and download a version of Netscape Navigator for their system.

From a practical standpoint, there's a good reason for this. Visitors to your page who don't use Netscape Navigator (or another browser that understands Netscape's HTML extensions) can't view your page in its full, extension-rich glory.

On the other hand, you might object to allowing your home page to serve as a free billboard for Netscape Communications Corp. If so, you can easily delete the plug. Hour 6, "Adding and Editing Text," shows you how to delete the text "This page was created with Netscape," and Hour 14, "Adding Pictures and Picture Backgrounds," shows you how to delete the button image and underlying link.

Can't wait? What the heck—here's how to do it. Open your new Wizard-built home page in Composer, click the Netscape Now! button to highlight it, and then press Delete. Position the mouse pointer to the left of the text and double-click to highlight it. Click Delete again. *Finito*.

Quiz

Take the following quiz to see how much you have learned.

Questions

1. The template upon which the Page Wizard is based is best suited to creating:

    a. Another template

    b. A disaster

    c. Harmony

    d. A basic personal home page

2. After building a Wizard page in Navigator, you must do what to finish up?

    a.   Spell-check.

    b.   Choose File, Edit Page and save the finished file in Composer.

    c.   Choose File, Print to print the page to the Internet.

    d.   Say a short prayer of thanks.

3. True or False: To publish your page, you upload it to a Web server.

Answers

1. (d)

2. (b) Choice d is optional.

3. True.

Activity

Open your Wizard-built page in Composer and try to edit it as you would a word-processing document. For example, click on some text, and then type are you changing the text? You'll learn how to edit pages soon enough, but a little experimentation can show you how easy editing a Web page really is.

HOUR 4

Making a Fast, Fancy Page with a Template

Time is tight for you—it's an issue. How do I know this about you? Well, of all the beginner's Web-authoring books out there, you picked up the one that promised to deliver within a specific time frame. Given what I know about you, I'm placing special emphasis on anything that can get you a great Web page quicker.

Aside from the Page Wizard you discovered in the last hour, nothing saves time better than using a template. In this hour, you'll discover templates and the ways they can get you a beautiful page in a snap. At the end of the hour, you will be able to answer the following questions:

- What's a template, and where do I find templates?
- How can I use any template to create a new Web page of my very own?
- How can I use any page on the Web as a template (maybe)?

Working with Templates

If Web pages were waffles, templates would be Bisquick.

NEW TERM **Template.** A ready-made Web page you can simply edit—replacing the template's text with your own—to quickly create a new, custom Web page that retains some design elements of the template.

As a head start to Web pages, templates offer a quicker and easier way to build Web pages than starting from scratch, but they also allow you greater flexibility in the design of your document than is possible with the Page Wizard.

Templates are especially valuable when you need to create a rather complicated page— perhaps one that you feel exceeds your own authoring skills—and aren't quite sure how to approach it. Figure 4.1 shows one of Netscape's cool templates.

FIGURE 4.1.

One of Netscape's cool templates.

 You can find all of the template files used in the examples in this hour in the Netscape Templates page at

`http://home.netscape.com/home/gold4.0_templates.html`

What's a Template?

A template is simply an HTML file filled mostly with meaningless, boilerplate content instead of the real thing. The prefabricated file has already been organized and formatted with paragraph properties, horizontal rules, and other bells and whistles. It also includes the basic elements of a Web page: title, headings, body, signature, appropriate links, and so on. (If you don't recognize these parts of a page, review Hour 1, "Understanding Web Authoring.")

By replacing the boilerplate content with your own content, you can quickly create an attractive, effective Web page without fussing over its organization or formatting. Of course, if you decide you want to change the formatting or organization of a page created from a template, you can, just as you can edit any HTML file in Composer.

Figure 4.2 shows a template for a Human Resources department page (hr2.html) from the Netscape Templates page. Figure 4.3 shows a page I created by replacing PERS1.HTML's text with my own. Compare the figures and observe that the only difference between the two is text content. Notice how I was able to take advantage of the template's organization, fancy horizontal lines, and character formatting while still making it my own.

The boilerplate content you see in most templates can take one of two forms. Sometimes, as in Figure 4.2, it represents content; that is, the phony content in the template looks and seems real, but it isn't. This approach gives you a clear model to follow in developing your own content. All the Netscape templates use this approach.

4

FIGURE 4.2.

An unedited template viewed in the browser window.

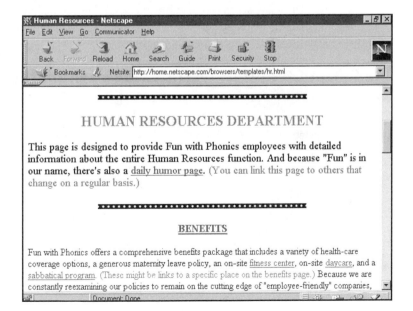

FIGURE 4.3.

The template edited into a real page with the addition of real content.

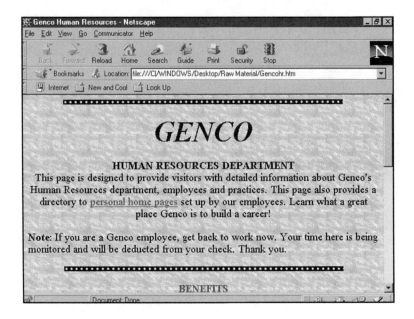

In other templates, descriptions are used where content should go. Often set in italics and surrounded by carets (< >), these built-in instructions offer specific suggestions and other guidance to help you determine what type of content to use and how to present it.

Often, this guidance is based on accepted principles of effective Web design or on emerging traditions for how pages with certain purposes—personal pages, business announcements, and so on—should be organized. Thus, templates not only save beginning authors time, but they also help ensure that their work conforms to accepted standards and principles for style and content.

Setting Preferences for Online Templates

The settings in the Preferences dialog box's Publishing category, as shown in Figure 4.4, pertain mainly to the publishing of your document, and they are therefore covered in greater detail in Hour 21, "Publishing Your Page." But before accessing any template files online, you should make sure that the check box for Keep Images with Page is checked. (It's checked by default, so unless you've unchecked it previously, Preferences is already properly configured for template access.)

A check mark next to Keep Images with Page instructs Composer to save any inline images along with the HTML file when you save a page (a template or any other page) that you've accessed online. This ensures that you'll have copies of any images on your PC, if you choose to keep any of the template's image files in your document. (The image files are saved in the same directory in which you save the HTML file.) This same check mark also ensures that when you send your document to a server to publish it, the images tag along.

FIGURE 4.4.

The Publishing category of Composer Preferences.

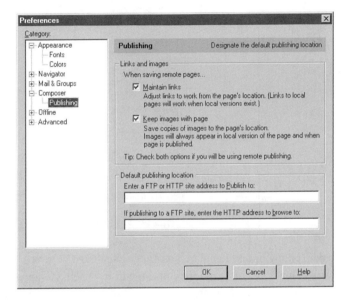

Where to Find Templates

Netscape's default template page contains a well-varied set of templates, with most of the major page purposes represented somewhere among them, as shown in Figure 4.5. However, you can find templates many places.

The set of templates set up by Netscape offers some specific advantages. The templates are specifically designed for use with Communicator and feature such built-in enhancements as

- The use of Netscape extensions and HTML 3 tags such as text centering, custom colors, backgrounds, and more.
- Handy *scripts* (see Hour 19, "Designing Interactive Forms") for common requirements, such as displaying the current date and time on a Web page.
- The Netscape Now! button, an image file linked to Netscape's FTP servers so that visitors to your page can easily download Netscape Navigator, install it, and then revisit your page to view your page formatting and run your scripts. (You can easily delete the Netscape Now! image if you want to.)

4

FIGURE 4.5.

The Netscape Templates page showing links to template files.

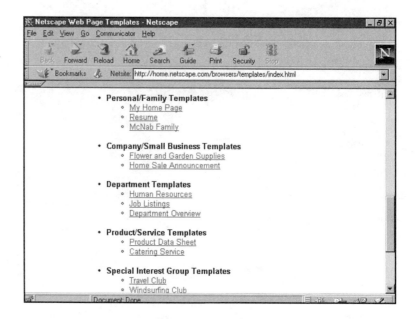

Note that a copy of any template you find online must be saved to your hard disk (by Composer, not Navigator) before you can edit it. When a template is already stored on your hard disk, you can simply open it in Composer and edit away.

Besides Netscape's templates, you can find dozens of other free templates all over the Web. Because these aren't Netscape's, you open them in Composer a little differently (see "Using Any Page as a Template," later in this hour). But once it's open, changing one template is the same as changing any other.

How Do I Choose the Right Template?

Most templates are designed to match popular approaches to certain types of Web pages. For example, the Netscape Templates page groups templates according to type or purpose, as shown earlier in Figure 4.5.

Before beginning to work with a specific template, open and examine a few different choices that seem to be likely candidates. If the available templates seem too far removed from what you want to accomplish, you might be better off finding and using as a template a page that more closely matches what you want to achieve. Your goal is to save yourself time and trouble by choosing a template that requires as little reworking as possible.

Be aware, however, that every aspect of a template is editable. If you choose a template that requires your content, some reformatting, and reorganization, you might still save time and trouble by using it rather than starting with a blank page. Often, by the time an author finishes adapting a template into her own page, she ends up making so many alterations that the finished document bears no resemblance to the template that spawned it.

That doesn't mean the template didn't help; it gave the author a place to start, something to fiddle with, raw material. And many times, that's exactly what an author needs to stoke the creative fires.

To Do: Open and save a template

▼To Do

1. From Navigator or Composer, choose **F**ile, **N**ew, Page From **T**emplate. The New Page From Template dialog box opens, as shown in Figure 4.6.

2. In the text box, enter either

    *   The path and filename of a template on your hard disk (click Choose File to browse for a file on your disk)
    *   The URL of a template stored on the Web

> If you don't need to see an online template before choosing to edit it, right-click a link that points to the template file and then choose Open Link in Composer from the context menu.

Alternatively, click the Netscape **T**emplates button to jump to Netscape's Templates page (refer to Figure 4.5), where you may select a template by clicking a link.

3. If you selected a local file in step 2, the file opens in Composer (even if you started out in Navigator). If you selected an online template, the template opens in Navigator. Choose **F**ile, **E**dit Page to open the file in Composer.

4. You may now edit the file in Composer, applying any or all of the techniques you discover throughout this book. It's a good idea to start out by giving the new page a title in the Page Properties dialog box (**F**ormat, Pa**g**e Colors and Properties), and then saving it with a new, unique filename.

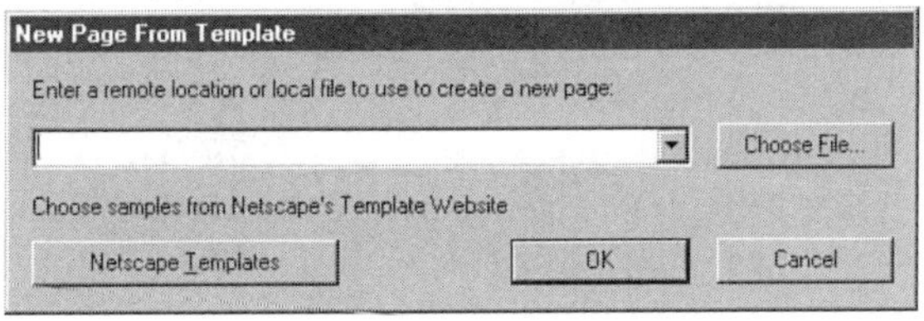

FIGURE 4.6.

The New Page From Template dialog box.

▲

New Page From Template

Enter a remote location or local file to use to create a new page:

[▼]   Choose File...

Choose samples from Netscape's Template Website

[Netscape Templates]   [OK]   [Cancel]

Editing a Template

Once a template has been saved on your hard disk, you can edit, expand, reformat, or delete any part of it. In some cases, you might find that you don't need to change anything; anywhere the template already says what you want to say, leave it alone.

Most of the text you'll see, however, must be replaced or deleted. Also, when you replace descriptive text (in templates that use it), you'll usually want to get rid of the italic character formatting.

When editing one of Netscape's templates (refer to Figure 4.5), your first task is to delete the instructions block at the top of the page. Just highlight it and press Delete.

You'll learn in detail how to edit Web pages in upcoming hours, but just to get you started (templates, after all, are for those who want to work quickly), here are a few quick editing techniques:

- To replace an entire paragraph, highlight the paragraph from beginning to end by moving the mouse pointer to the left of the paragraph and double-clicking. Then type your new content. The paragraph is instantly deleted and replaced with whatever you type. Your new paragraph takes on the same paragraph properties as the one you've replaced.

- To replace only a portion of a paragraph, highlight the portion you want to replace (click and hold at the start of the selection, drag to the end, and release), and then type your content. The highlighted section is deleted and replaced with what you type.

- To delete an image, click it once (to select it) and press the Delete key.

The only trick to editing a template is to change the content without screwing up the existing formatting. To that end, it's helpful to imagine that, between each set of paragraphs, there are hidden formatting instructions that must not be lost or corrupted during editing.

To make sure that you don't accidentally alter the formatting, avoid doing anything that would delete the space between paragraphs. For example,

- When the edit cursor (the tall vertical bar that appears whenever you type or edit text) appears at the very beginning of a block of text, do not press Backspace.

- When the edit cursor appears at the very end of a block of text, do not press the Delete key.
- If you do change the properties inadvertently, choose **E**dit, **U**ndo. If that doesn't do it, just click anywhere within the paragraph, choose **F**ormat, **P**aragraph, and then choose the appropriate paragraph properties from the submenu that appears. (See Hours 6, "Adding and Editing Text," and 7, "Formatting Text.")

Using Any Page as a Template

Choosing **F**ile, **E**dit Page from Navigator's menu bar has a special action: It opens Composer to edit the page that you are viewing in Navigator—even if that page is online (see Figure 4.7).

The principal use of the Edit Page option is to download and edit a Web page—a template file or other remote page—or to save a page created by the Page Wizard. Once the page is open in Composer, you can save it to your hard disk by choosing File, Save.

When you save a Web page file in Navigator (rather than Composer), you save only its text and text formatting—not its images or background pattern—so you haven't really captured the whole page for editing purposes. However, when you save the same file in Composer, you save all of it—text, images, background pattern, and any inline multimedia—so you can edit and adapt it in any way you want.

4

FIGURE 4.7.

Saving a page to use as a template.

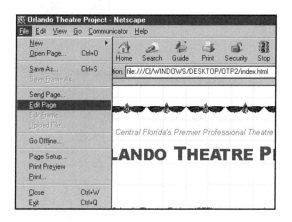

In effect, the Edit Page feature enables you to copy any page from the Web, edit it, and republish it as your own work.

Online templates are specifically designed for this purpose and are generally not copyrighted. Web pages that are not offered as templates, however, might be copyrighted, so copying and adapting them could be illegal. Even when the page itself is not copyrighted, it might contain copyrighted text, images, or other content. And even if nothing on a page is copyrighted, it's unethical to copy another author's work in this manner—and unnecessary because Composer makes creating your own page easy, especially with templates to help.

If you do choose to edit and adapt a Web page (other than one specifically offered as a template) for use as your own, you should replace all the content on that page with your own original content or content you know to be copyright free.

Summary

Talk about putting the cart before the horse! It's only four hours into the tutorial, and you have yet to learn the basics of putting text, pictures, and links into a Web page. But you already know two ways—the Wizard and templates—to crank out a pretty respectable page.

Since you've already experienced the rush of instant gratification, the next four hours provide an opportunity to settle down and work closely with the most important part of any Web page: the words.

Workshop

Q&A

Q Can I make my own templates?

A Sure. In fact, doing so can save you a lot of time if you create many similar pages.

To make your own templates, just build a page containing the elements that you tend to reuse from project to project. Create new pages by opening and editing that template file, making sure to save the creations with new filenames (using File, Save As) so that the template itself remains unaltered and ready to serve up the next new page.

Quiz

Take the following quiz to see how much you have learned.

Questions

1. True or False: If you use Composer, you can only use Netscape's templates.

2. To save a copy of a page you're viewing online in Navigator—including the page's text and pictures—do which of the following:

   a. Choose File, Save.

   b. Choose File, Save Page.

   c. Choose Edit, Page (to switch to Composer), then choose File, Save.

   d. Choose Edit, Page (to switch to Composer), then choose File, Save Page.

3. To remove instruction blocks or other objects from templates when making your own pages, highlight the block, and then

   a. Type to replace its text with your own, or press Delete to delete the block.

   b. Press Esc to "Escape" the block.

   c. Press the Spacebar to send the block to space.

   d. Press the Spacebar to send the block to a bar.

Answers

1. False. You can use any template you find.

2. (c)

3. (a)

Activity

The next time you're surfing the Web, flip to Appendix C of this book to the section called "Templates." There you'll find the addresses of some template sources. Check 'em out.

4

PART II
Titles, Text, and Tables

Hour

HOUR 5

Choosing a Title, Colors, and Other Page Properties

There's the forest, and then there's the trees.

In Web authoring, the trees are the content details—the words, the pictures, the links. But before you start planting pines, it's smart to deal with a few quick, easy elements that affect your page at a higher level: the title, color scheme, and other stuff that defines the shape of the forest.

At the end of this hour, you will be able to answer the following questions:

- What are Composer's "page properties," and where do you create and choose them?
- How do I apply a custom color scheme to my page?
- How do I add a color background?

About Page Properties

Everything you see in a Web page (and some things you don't see), you enter directly into Composer's document window. But one other standard part of an HTML file—the page title—is entered separately in the Page Properties dialog box, along with other descriptive information about the page.

In Composer, you'll use the Page Properties dialog box, as shown in Figure 5.1, to give your page a title, to enter descriptive information that will help people searching the Web locate your page, and to choose a color scheme and optional color background.

FIGURE 5.1.

The General tab of the Page Properties dialog box.

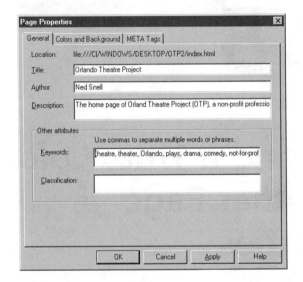

Why a Good Title Matters!

While every Web page must have a title, entering one in Composer is not required; if you don't supply one, Composer automatically uses the page's filename as its title. It's important that you enter a title, however, because the title describes your page to the Web.

For example, when a visitor to your page creates a bookmark for it in his or her browser, the title typically becomes the name of the bookmark, as shown in Figure 5.2. Also, Web directories (such as Yahoo) and crawlers (programs that build Web directories by search-ing the Web and cataloging its contents) use the title as the primary reference for what the page is about.

When people use Yahoo, Excite, and other Web-searching tools, you want them to find your page when your page really matches what they want and not to find your page when it's not a good match. Entering a good, descriptive title (and other page properties) helps make that happen.

FIGURE 5.2.

Page titles become bookmark names in most browsers.

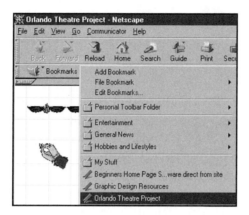

Don't confuse the title with the big, bold heading that often tops a Web page and serves as its apparent title. Remember, by the time a visitor sees that top-level heading, he or she has already arrived at your page and is presumably already interested in its subject. So that top heading can be more creative than the page title, or even subtle. But the true title must be descriptive, not clever.

Remember: The title entered in Page Properties does not appear on the page itself, but in windowing browsers (like most for Windows, Macintosh, and X Window systems); the title appears in the title bar of the window in which the page is displayed.

An effective true title should accurately describe the contents or purpose of your page. It should also be fairly short—no more than six to eight words—and its most descriptive words should appear first. Remember, in a bookmark list or Web directory, there's often room for only the first few words of a title, so your title needs to be short, and those first few words must be meaningful.

Here are some good titles:

Sammy's Racquetball Directory

The Video Store Online

All About Trout Fishing

Marvin C. Able's Awesome Home Page

New Jersey Events for July

In these good examples, notice that the most specific, important descriptor appears within the first three words: Racquetball, Video, Trout, Marvin C. Able, and New Jersey Events.

Notice also that the fewest possible words are used to nail down the page. In the first example, you learn in three words that this page is a directory of racquetball-related information and that it's Sammy's directory (to distinguish it from any other racquetball directories). What more do you need to know?

Here, for comparison, are some lousy titles:

My Home Page

Things to Do

Schedule of Events

A Catalog of Links and Documents Provided as a Public Service for Persons Researching Population Trends

In the first three crummy examples above, the titles are nondescript; they contain nothing about the specific contents of the page. The last example, although containing some useful information at the end, would be trimmed down to its first four or five words in a bookmark list, and those first few words say nothing useful.

You can add other descriptive elements besides the title in the Page Properties dialog box; these entries serve mostly to describe your page to crawlers and Web searches. Unlike the title, the other entries are optional, and none of them is as important as the title.

But if you supply these items and word them carefully, you'll increase your chances of drawing visitors interested in what you have to say. In other words, when a potential visitor conducts a Web search using any search term that might relate to the topic of your page, the visitor is much more likely to hit on your page if you've used a good, descriptive classification, description, and keywords.

To Do: Enter page properties

1. Open or create the file for which you are entering the page properties.

2. In Composer, choose Format, Page Colors and Properties. A dialog box like the one in Figure 5.3 appears.

FIGURE 5.3.

Entering page properties.

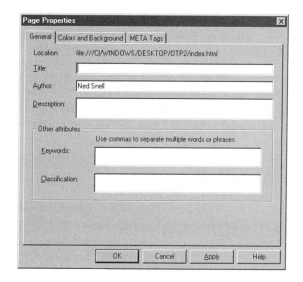

3. On the General tab, enter a title in the Title box. Be careful to capitalize and spell it exactly as you want it to appear in a title bar or bookmark list. Don't bother trying to use character formatting, such as bold or italic, in the title. No character formatting is possible within the text-entry areas in the Page Properties dialog box, and even if it were, it wouldn't show up anywhere titles typically appear.

4. Enter your name in Author. You can enter whatever you feel is most descriptive of you as an author: your name and title, your company name, or even your email address.

> The Author field is filled in automatically with the name used in the Author field in the Composer category of Communicator's Preferences dialog box. You may change the Author name in Page Properties, if you want to.
>
> You can change the name used automatically by choosing Edit, Preferences and changing the Author Name shown in the Preferences dialog box.

5

▼   5. Fill in any of the remaining fields that you want defined (all are optional); these are
       used by various Web directories and search engines as matches for categories or
       search terms, or to describe your page in the list of search hits.

       Description—A brief description of your page. Keep it short, and describe your
       page simply and accurately. Some Web search engines display the description—
       along with the title and URL of your page—in the list of search hits.

       Keywords—A list of words (separated by commas) descriptive of, or related to, the
       subject of your page.

       Classification—A list of words (separated by commas) that generally describe the
       subject of your page. Classification is similar to keywords, except it's used by dif-
       ferent search engines. The words used for classification should describe the overall
       subject of your page, whereas keywords might pertain to only one aspect or section
       of the Web page.

    6. Click OK. The properties you entered are saved as part of the HTML file. You can
▲   change them any time you like by returning to the Page Properties dialog box.

Choosing Custom Colors for a Whole Page

In general, a visitor's browser chooses the colors for the text and background of a page.
Netscape Navigator is no different. In the Preferences dialog box, you can choose
display colors for Navigator. (The settings are in the Color subcategory of the
Appearance category.)

When you apply *custom colors* to a Web page, you add to it instructions that tell the
browser to use the colors you've assigned instead of the browser's default colors.

> Unless you're careful when choosing colors, you could select text and back-
> ground colors that clash, or even choose a background color that's so close
> to a text color that the text becomes difficult to read or see. Using one of
> the color schemes (described shortly) is a great way to avoid this.

You can assign custom colors separately for each of the following page elements:

- *Normal text*—All text in the page that is not a link, including normal paragraphs,
  headings, list items, and so on.
- *Link text*—All links that are not active or followed links.
- *Active Link text*—Immediately after a link has been clicked by the visitor, it may
  remain visible for a few moments while the browser retrieves the file to which the

link points. While the link remains visible, it changes color to indicate that it has been activated.

- *Followed Link text*—Links that the visitor has previously used.
- *Background*—The entire background area of the page can be a solid custom color. The background color always sits behind text or images in the page, never covering them, obscuring them, or affecting their color.

To Do: Assign custom colors

1. In Composer, choose Format, Page Colors and Properties to open the Page Properties dialog box.
2. Choose the Colors and Background tab, as shown in Figure 5.4.
3. Click the radio button next to Use Custom Colors.

> Instead of using the menu bar, you can open the Page Properties dialog box by right-clicking anywhere in the page and choosing Page Properties from the context menu.

FIGURE 5.4.

Choosing page colors.

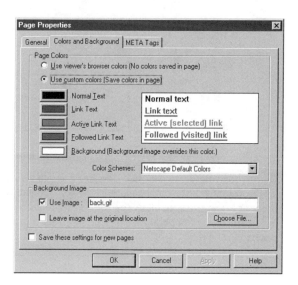

4. Choose a color for each page element. You can do this in two ways:
   - Click the colored rectangle next to the name of any page element whose color you want to change. A dialog box opens like the one shown in

Figure 5.5. Click the color you want, or click the Other button to open a dialog box in which you can create a new color using a standard Windows color
spectrum (see Figure 5.6).

- Choose one of the color schemes from the drop-down list. The color schemes
  are combinations of colors that look good together.

> After choosing a color scheme, you can optionally change the color of any
> page element if the scheme does not match precisely what you want.

FIGURE 5.5.

*Choosing a color for a
single page element.*

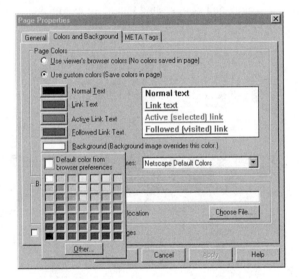

> On the box where you choose a color for a single element (refer to Figure
> 5.5), you can click the color square at the top, labeled Default Color from
> Browser Preferences, to allow the color of the element to be determined
> automatically by the default color settings of each browser used to view
> the page.

FIGURE 5.6.

Creating a new color.

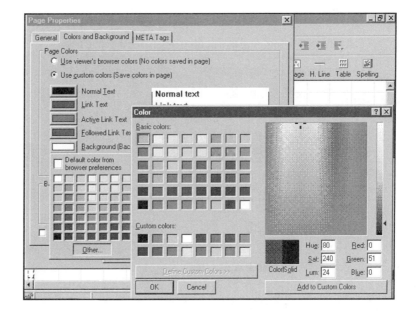

Summary

Choosing your page properties is a snap, and it's also important. Doing it not only starts defining your page's appearance and purpose, but also forces you to begin thinking more clearly about those aspects. There's nothing like thinking up a title to help you focus your plans for your page.

Workshop

Q&A

Q I've seen these cool backgrounds online, some that look like marble or other textures, and others that are pictures. How do I do those?

A Easy. Instead of using a background color, you can use an image file to create a graphical background for a page, as you learn to do in Hour 14, "Adding Pictures and Picture Backgrounds."

Note that if you do use an image for the background, the background color setting is irrelevant—an image background overrides a background color.

Quiz

Take the following quiz to see how much you have learned.

Questions

1. True or False: If you choose custom colors, they will show up in any browser.
2. Which of the following is the best title:

   a. John's Page

   b. John's Film Guide

   c. The Film Noir Links Site

   d. A Complete and Unabridged Directory to Pages About Film Noir

Answers

1. False. Custom colors only show up in compatible browsers, and then only if the visitor has not disabled them.
2. (c) Choices a and b are too vague, while d is too long and puts the relevant information at the end.

Activity

Start title-watching when you're online. Keep an eye on your browser's title bar and read the title of any page you visit. Which titles are effective? Which are not?

HOUR 6

Adding and Editing Text

Somebody once said to me, "Writing isn't so tough: All you have to do is find a quiet spot and open a vein."

That's true, actually, but to the extent that writing a Web page can be made less immediately life-threatening, a WYSIWYG editor does just that. The principal job in creating the text of a Web page involves two main tasks: getting the text into the file (by typing it, copying it, or importing it) and assigning paragraph properties to each block of text. The properties tell browsers how to present that text.

In this hour, you'll learn how to get text into your Web page files, format it by assigning properties, and edit it—including the all-important spell-checking. Dealing with the text first is usually the best way to build a Web page; it forces you to think about and resolve issues related to the organization and flow of content. At the end of the hour, you will be able to answer the following questions:

- What are the basics of entering, editing, and formatting the text elements of a Web page?

- How can I save time and typing with cut and paste, copy, and other text-entry tips?
- How can I make sure my spelling is perfect?

Understanding Paragraphs and Their Properties

What makes a particular paragraph a heading or something else are the properties with which you endow the paragraph. Assigning properties to a paragraph is no different than assigning a style in a word processor, and usually it's just as easy. In a nutshell, you type a line or block of text, and then assign properties to that paragraph to identify it as a heading, text paragraph, or whatever. *Voilà.*

NEW TERM **Paragraph.** Composer calls each discrete chunk of text—all the text between paragraph marks (the character you type when you press Enter)—a *paragraph*, whether it's a heading, one line in a list, a multiline paragraph, or just a bunch of words.

There are two parts to paragraph properties: paragraph styles and optional, additional styles, or *attributes*, within each style. You'll learn how the styles and attributes work together later in this hour in the section "About Attributes."

Note that paragraph properties apply only to entire paragraphs. For example, you cannot format two words in the middle of a paragraph as an address and the rest of the paragraph as a heading. Either the whole paragraph is one thing, or the whole paragraph is something else.

What Each Paragraph Property Does

The basic paragraph properties are described in the following sections and are shown in Navigator as they appear in Figures 6.1 and 6.2.

Normal

Use *normal* for general-purpose text—like what you're reading right now. Most browsers display normal paragraphs in a plain font with no special emphasis (such as bold or special color). Normal is the meat and potatoes of your Web page.

Headings

Use headings the way you see them used in this book: to divide and label the logical sections of the page or document. There are six levels of headings, ranging in relative importance from 1 (most important or prominent) to 6 (least important or prominent).

Because the level 1 heading is the most prominent, it is often reserved for the apparent title of your page—the one that appears within the page itself (not to be confused with the document title entered in Page Properties).

In most browsers, a level 1 heading is displayed as the biggest, boldest text on the page. Level 2 headings are smaller and not bold, or they are de-emphasized in some other way. Level 3 gets less emphasis than 2 but more than 4, and so on. (Six levels require a lot of variation, and in some browsers, the difference between headings only one level apart is barely distinguishable, as you can see in Figure 6.1.)

Text-based browsers, which can't display varying font sizes, use bold, underline, or even numbers to show the varying heading levels.

FIGURE 6.1.

Paragraphs and their properties: headings, normal text, and addresses.

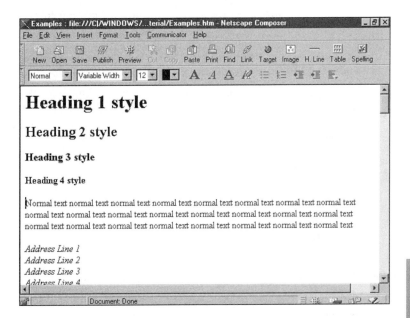

You can use whatever heading levels you want, but in general, obey the numbers. Subheadings within a section should have a higher level number than the heading for the section. For example, a section that begins with a level 2 heading might have level 3 sub-headings under it. The subsections under the level 3 heads might be level 4 heads, and so on.

Address

Use *Address* for creating an *address block*—a line or many lines identifying someone, which usually lists an email address, a snail mail address, or other contact information.

The Address property is used most often for the signature at the bottom of the page, but it can be used to give any address information on your page a unique style that sets it apart from other text. Navigator, for example, displays address blocks in italic; address blocks are the only page element automatically italicized by Navigator.

> Assigning the Address property to an email address on your page does not, by itself, make the address a mailto link that a visitor can click to send email. However, an email address with the Address property can be a mail-to link— you just have to make it one.
>
> To learn how to create a mailto link, see Hour 10, "Making Links."

Formatted

Formatted might seem like a misnomer because text assigned the *Formatted* property is in fact less formatted by the browser than any other kind. What *formatted* means in this context is *preformatted*—you have already lined up and spaced the text in a particular way, and you want browsers to leave that formatting alone.

Typically, browsers capable of displaying *proportionally spaced* fonts (such as TrueType's Arial, or even the snappy font you're reading now) use those fonts for most text because they look better than typewriter-style *monospaced* fonts (such as Courier New). Also, browsers ignore tabs, extra spaces, and blank lines (extra paragraph marks) in HTML files.

Suppose that you want to show a text chart or table on your page, or words arranged in a certain way. Tabs are *verboten*, so you need to use spaces and a monospaced font to make the words line up right. But if browsers are permitted to do their regular thing with that text, they will strip out the extra spaces, display the text in a proportional font, and generally screw up your lovely alignment job.

> You can use the Formatted property to create the effect of tables in your document, but you can also create real tables that look much better (see Hour 8, "Organizing Text with Tables and Rules."

For example, observe the careful alignment of columns and the use of a monospaced font in the simple table shown in Figure 6.2. This table uses the Formatted property. Notice how the browser's display font and regularity of spacing differs in the formatted table from the other text in the figure.

FIGURE 6.2.

Paragraphs and their properties: formatted text, description titles, and description text.

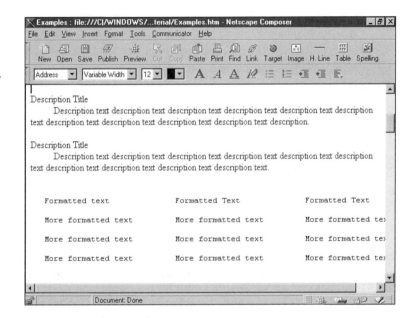

List Item

The *List Item* property formats lists on your page: bulleted lists, numbered lists, and other types of lists, as well. Each item in a list is a separate paragraph. To build a list, type each item on a separate line (really, a separate paragraph) and assign the List Item property to all the lines.

> You can assign List Item as the paragraph property and choose a bulleted list or a numbered list by clicking the Bullet List or Numbered List button on the toolbar.

6

Composer gives you a wide range of ways to format lists, including numbered lists with different numbering schemes, bulleted lists with different bullet types, nested lists, and more. For more about lists, see Hour 7, "Formatting Text."

Description Title and Description Text

The description properties apply HTML styles called *Definition Term* and *Definition Definition*. The HTML names come from the fact that using this property is a great way to build the effect of onscreen glossary entries. Just as in a glossary or dictionary entry, each description (or definition) is made up of two paragraphs: a description title, such as the word or phrase being defined, and description text, the definition. In Navigator, the description text is indented underneath the description title. Other browsers use similar techniques to put the title and text together nicely, so it's clear that they go together as a set.

Although glossary entries are the obvious application for the description properties, they aren't the only application: You can use the description properties any time you need to associate a word or phrase with a longer description or definition.

You can apply paragraph properties in whatever way suits you. (There are no HTML police—at least not yet....) But it's good practice to think of these properties as a way to determine the role a paragraph plays in your page, *not* its appearance.

For example, there's no technical reason that you can't write a lengthy paragraph and make it a heading, rather than normal text, to make it stand out on the page. But different browsers use different methods to make a heading look like a heading; some make headings big and bold, others underline headings, and some even number headings according to their levels. Some Web search engines catalog pages according to heading contents because headings generally contain subject information. Putting ordinary paragraph information into a heading might generate some screwy hits on your page from Web searches.

Use properties conservatively, according to their designated roles. Save your artistry for character formatting, images, backgrounds, and other ways you can spice up a page.

Entering Text and Assigning Properties

You can add text to a page and assign properties to that text in several different ways, all of which are described in the following sections.

Entering Paragraphs by Typing

When you create a new document, the edit cursor appears automatically at the very top of the document. Type away. To correct mistakes and make changes as you go, use the

Backspace, Delete, and Insert keys just as you would in any document. To end a paragraph and start a new paragraph, press Enter.

By default, your paragraphs are all set as normal text (unless you select a different paragraph property before you begin typing a paragraph). You can change them to other paragraph properties at any time, as described in the section titled "Assigning Paragraph Properties to Existing Text" later in this hour.

To Do: Enter text with copy and paste

To Do

This To Do describes how to copy text from another document in Windows—such as a word processing file and spreadsheet file—and place it in Composer so that it can be incorporated into your Web page. This is a convenient way to use pre-existing text, such as your résumé or a description of your business, in your Web page without retyping it.

1. Open the application normally used to edit or display the document from which you want to copy, and open the document.

2. Highlight the desired text. (To copy an entire document into your Web page, choose **E**dit, Select All in the application used to open the document.)

3. Press Ctrl+Insert to copy the selection to the Windows Clipboard. (Alternatively, you can click the Copy button on the toolbar or choose **E**dit, **C**opy.)

4. Open Composer and open (or create) the Web document into which you want to copy the text.

5. Click the spot on the page where you want to copy the text. If you've just created the document, the text must be copied to the top of the document where the edit cursor is already located. In a document that already has text, you can click at the start or end of any paragraph to add the selection to that paragraph, or press Enter between paragraphs to start a new paragraph for the selection.

6. Press Shift+Insert to copy the selection into the page. (Alternatively, you can click the Paste button on Composer's toolbar or choose **E**dit, **P**aste.)

6

When pasted into a blank document, the text is automatically assigned the Normal paragraph property. You can then change it to any other paragraph property.

When pasted into a document with other paragraphs in it, the text is automatically assigned the same property as the paragraph it is inserted into or adjacent to.

Assigning Paragraph Properties to Existing Text

There are two steps to assigning properties. First, you select the paragraph or paragraphs, and then you choose the properties.

- To select one paragraph, position the edit cursor anywhere within it (either by clicking within the paragraph or by pressing the arrow keys until the cursor arrives within the paragraph). Note that positioning the cursor within the paragraph is sufficient; you don't need to highlight the whole paragraph.

If working *sans mouse*, you can select multiple paragraphs by positioning the edit cursor anywhere in the first paragraph and holding down the Shift key while using the arrow keys to move to anywhere in the last paragraph in the selection.

- To select two or more paragraphs, click anywhere in the first paragraph, drag to anywhere in the last paragraph, and release, as shown in Figure 6.3.

FIGURE 6.3.

Selecting multiple paragraphs to assign them all the same paragraph property.

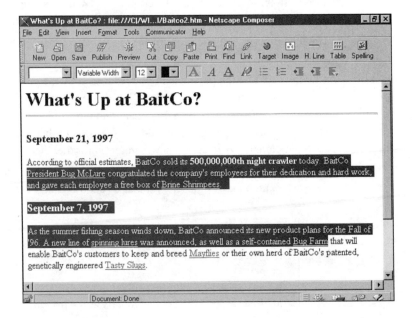

After the paragraph or paragraphs are selected, you can assign a paragraph property in any of four ways:

- Click the Paragraph Style drop-down list (at the left end of the Formatting toolbar) and select a paragraph style.

- Choose Format, Paragraph to display a submenu of paragraph styles. Click the name of the desired style to apply it to the selection. (If the style you want is a heading style, don't choose Format, Paragraph. Instead, choose Format, Heading, and then choose a heading level from the submenu that appears.)

- Choose Format, Character Properties to open the Character Properties dialog box (see Figure 6.4). Click the Paragraph tab and choose a style from the list provided.

FIGURE 6.4.

Choosing paragraph properties from the Paragraph tab of the Character Properties dialog box.

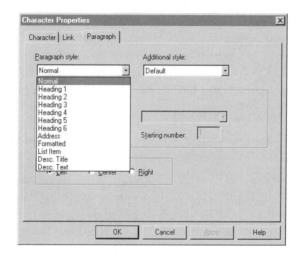

- Right-click the selection to display a context menu (see Figure 6.5), and then choose Paragraph/List Properties to display the Paragraph tab of the Character Properties dialog box (refer to Figure 6.4).

FIGURE 6.5.

Choosing paragraph properties from a context menu.

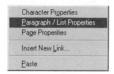

6

To Do: Assign properties and attributes as you type

Although there's a certain logic in entering your paragraphs and then assigning properties, you can do the opposite. To assign properties as you type a paragraph:

1. Click the spot you want the paragraph to go.

2. Click the Paragraph Style drop-down list on the Formatting toolbar and select a paragraph style.

▼   3. Type your paragraph. It will appear on the page as you type it, showing the proper-
        ties you selected. If you press Enter (to end the paragraph and start a new one), the
▲   new paragraph will take on your selected properties as well.

About Attributes

Choosing a paragraph style is not all you can do to a paragraph in the Paragraph tab of
the Character Properties dialog box. You can also choose an additional style from the
Additional Style drop-down list. When List Item is selected as the paragraph style, you
can choose from different list styles as well.

The additional style selections apply HTML *attributes*, special codes that modify the
effects of some HTML tags. When you select a paragraph style, you apply the HTML
tags for that style to the selection. When you choose an additional style or list style,
you're applying attributes that modify the effect of the HTML paragraph style tags.

Under Additional Style, you'll find three choices:

- *Default*—The default style. This option adds no attributes to the selected paragraph
  style, so the paragraph appears in its regular way.

- *List*—List is available as an additional style only if the paragraph style is List Item.
  The List additional style is fairly pointless, except that it enables the List style
  drop-down list in the Paragraph Properties dialog box. The List style drop-down
  list lets you choose a type of bullet for bulleted lists or a type of number for numbered lists.

> To learn the details of creating and formatting lists, see Hour 7.

- *Block Quote*—Block Quote identifies the selected paragraph as a block quote, a
  quote long enough that it needs to be set apart from other text. When you select
  Block Quote, the selected paragraph retains the paragraph style you set for it, but it
  is displayed in most browsers in a slightly different way from other paragraphs of
  the same style. Most browsers indent a block quote, just as block quotes are traditionally indented in books. Figure 6.6 shows two block quotes: The first, by
  Shakespeare, is in the heading 3 style, and the second, by Walt Kelly, uses normal
  text. But both use the Block Quote additional style.

FIGURE 6.6.

Two block quotes—the first in heading 3 style and the second in normal paragraph style—that both use the Block Quote additional style.

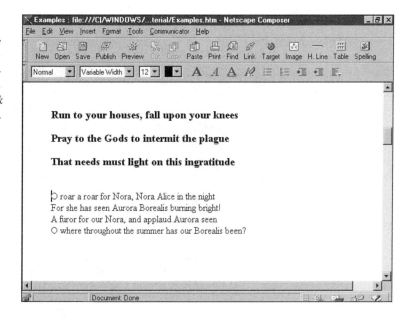

Aligning and Indenting Text

On the right end of the Formatting toolbar, you'll find the Alignment button. The Alignment button drops down three alignment options for aligning paragraphs to the left side of the page, to the right, or to the center. The Paragraph tab of the Character Properties dialog box offers radio buttons for the same choices (refer to Figure 6.4, earlier in this hour). These options can be applied to any paragraph in any style; you can select normal text, paragraphs, headings, or lists and center them on the page or align them to the left or right side (see Figure 6.7).

Left alignment is the default selection for all paragraph styles. You'll need to select left alignment only when undoing another alignment selection.

6

When applying alignment, restrain yourself. Center and align right are enabled by HTML 3 tags; in browsers that don't support HTML 3, your centered or right-aligned text will appear left-aligned anyway.

More importantly, our eyes are accustomed to left-aligned text, especially for *body copy,* or normal text. A big centered heading looks good on some pages, and right alignment can create a nice effect when text is put to the right of a graphic (see Hour 14, "Adding

Pictures and Picture Backgrounds"). However, centered normal text paragraphs can appear a bit odd, and centered lists look downright strange.

FIGURE 6.7.

*Left- (the default), cen-
ter-, and right-aligned
text.*

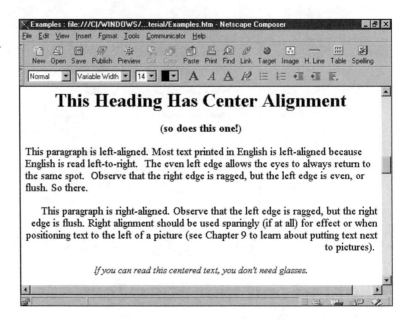

Indenting is enabled by a Netscape extension. In browsers that don't support indenting, the selection appears left-aligned.

Besides choosing the alignment of paragraphs, you can *indent* them, pushing them away from the left margin just as you would in a word processor. This capability is most useful when nesting lists (see Hour 7), but you can indent any paragraph. Composer supports multiple indent levels; you can increase the indent several times to push the paragraph farther away from the left margin. Decreasing the indent pulls the text back toward the margin.

As with alignment, don't go overboard with indents. Many browsers don't support indenting, so whatever structural or aesthetic impression you achieve with indents will be lost to many visitors. It's far better to select paragraph styles or attributes that are naturally indented, such as description text or a block quote. In browsers that don't support indenting, such paragraphs will still be set off in some unique way, so some of your intention might be preserved.

Note that the Character Properties dialog box has no indenting options. To indent, use buttons on the Formatting toolbar or options on the Format menu.

To indent a paragraph, select it and do any of the following. (Repeat the procedure to indent farther or to decrease the indent.)

To indent to the right (choose any one):

- Click the Increase Indent button on the Formatting toolbar.
- Press Ctrl+=.
- Choose Format, Increase Indent.

To decrease the indent (choose any one):

- Click the Decrease Indent button on the Formatting toolbar.
- Press Ctrl+-.
- Choose Format, Decrease Indent.

About Spacing

Composer is pretty smart in the way it handles extra paragraph marks within a page and extra character spaces within a paragraph—so smart, in fact, that experienced Web authors might find Composer's approach confusing, while newbies will find it completely natural.

Except within the Formatted paragraph style, HTML does not recognize paragraph marks in the HTML file as blank lines or extra blank spaces as extra blank spaces. Thus, browsers generally ignore these characters when displaying a page. In order to create extra white space between paragraphs or extra spaces in a line, Web authors must use the HTML tags for line breaks and non-breaking spaces, respectively.

Composer, however, figures that when you press Enter multiple times, you want to add white space—so it automatically inserts the appropriate tags. Similarly, extra spaces in a line are automatically recorded as non-breaking spaces and show up as blank spaces when the file is viewed through a browser.

To display all the paragraph marks so that you can evaluate the spacing and breaks you've applied, choose View, Show Paragraph Marks.

Checking Your Spelling

If you have any experience with Windows-based word processors, you'll find using Composer's spell-checker a snap.

 To check spelling within only a selected portion of the document, select the desired portion before starting the spell-checker.

To check spelling, you can begin with the edit cursor located anywhere within the current file—the spell-checker begins checking from the top of the file, no matter where the cursor is located. However, make sure that no text is selected (see "Editing Your Text," later in this hour) before you begin to check spelling; when any text is selected, Composer checks spelling only within the selection and ignores the rest of the document.

When ready, click the Spelling button on the Composition toolbar (or choose **T**ools, Check **S**pelling). Starting at the top, the spell-checker begins searching through the file, looking for words that are not in its dictionary (which might be misspellings or correctly spelled words that simply aren't in the dictionary, such as most proper names).

When the spell-checker encounters a word that's not in the dictionary, a dialog box like the one in Figure 6.8 opens. In the Word box at the top of the dialog, the word in question appears. In the Suggestions box, Composer displays a list of words it predicts might be the one you intended (if it can think of any).

FIGURE 6.8.

Checking spelling.

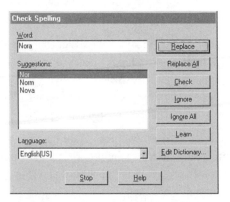

You can deal with each offending word in any of several ways. If what you typed is in fact correct (just not in the dictionary):

- Click Learn to automatically add the word to the dictionary so that the spell-checker will not stop on it in this or any other page you compose. (You're telling Composer to "learn" the word for future reference.) It's a good idea to add names and other words you use often to the dictionary so that the spell-checker will ignore them.

- Click Ignore All to ignore all instances of that word in the file. If this one instance is correct but others might not be, click Ignore to ignore the current instance but to call others to your attention when the spell-checker comes to them.

> You can stop spell-checking mid-file by clicking the Stop button in the Check Spelling dialog. Note that any changes you made before clicking Stop are still in effect; to undo the changes, you must close the file without saving it (select File, Close).

If what you typed is incorrect:

- If a correct entry appears among the suggestions, click it and then click Replace (to change only the current instance of the word to the selected suggestion) or Replace All (to change all instances of the word to the selected suggestion).

- If no correct suggestion appears, edit (or replace) the word in the Word box until what appears there is correct, and then click Replace or Replace All.

> After typing or editing the word in the Word box, you may click the Check button on the dialog to make the spell-checker look for the word in the dictionary. If the spell-checker cannot find the word in its dictionary, but you're sure it's correct, click Learn to add the word to the dictionary.

6

After you deal with a word questioned by the spell-checker in any of the ways just described, the spell-checker continues searching through the file until it comes to the next word that is not in the dictionary. When it reaches the end of the file, a dialog box appears to report that the spell-check is complete.

If you find that the spell-checker's dictionary is missing many words you need, or that it spells some words differently from the way you want them spelled ("color" instead of "colour," and that sort of thing), you may want to edit the dictionary. To edit the dictionary, click the Edit Dictionary button on the Check Spelling dialog. The Personal Dictionary dialog opens, as shown in Figure 6.9. Make your changes as follows:

- To add a new word, type it in the New Word box and click the Add button.
- To edit an existing word, select it in the list of Words, type its replacement in the New Word box, and then click the Replace button.
- To delete a word from the dictionary, select it in the list of Words and click the Remove button.

Actually, if "colour" and other British spellings are what you want, there's an easier way to add them to the dictionary. On the Check Spelling dialog, open the list at the bottom labeled Language and choose English(UK).

FIGURE 6.9.

Editing the spell-checker's dictionary.

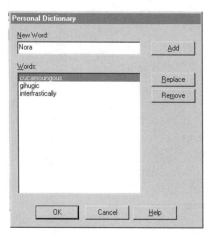

Editing Your Text

Editing a Web page is straightforward, very much like editing any word processing document. To do almost anything, highlight the text you want to change, and then make the change. You can also search for a text string using Composer's Find in Page tool.

Highlighting Text

To highlight text with your mouse, position the cursor at the start of the area you want to highlight, and then click and hold the left mouse button. Drag to the end of the selection and release the mouse button. Note that you can select as much text as you want in this way: a few characters, a word, a whole paragraph, or a group of paragraphs.

When you drag through an area that includes both text and images, only the text is selected. Images must be selected separately (see Hour 14).

You can also highlight a selection for editing in other ways:

- Double-click a word to select it.
- Double-click at the very beginning of a line to select the first word.
- Double-click at the very end of a line to select the last word.
- Position the pointer to the left of a paragraph and double-click to select the entire paragraph, or single-click to select just the line the cursor is next to.

Replacing Selected Text

When text is selected, begin typing. The selection is deleted immediately and replaced with whatever you type. Any surrounding text that was not highlighted remains unaffected.

You can also replace a highlighted selection with the contents of the Clipboard by clicking the Paste button on the toolbar or by choosing **E**dit, **P**aste. (Of course, you must previously have cut or copied something to the Clipboard; see the section titled "Copying or Moving Selected Text," later in this hour.)

Deleting Selected Text

Press the Delete key to delete the selection.

You can right-click selected text to display a context menu with choices for changing properties, for creating links, and for cutting, copying, and pasting (refer to Figure 6.5).

6

To delete the selection from its current location but copy it to the Windows Clipboard so that it can be pasted elsewhere in the page (or into another page or another Windows document), click the Cut button on the toolbar or choose **E**dit, C**u**t.

Copying or Moving Selected Text

To copy a highlighted selection, click the Copy button on the toolbar or choose **E**dit, **C**opy. Then click in the location where you want the copy to go and click the Paste button or choose **E**dit, **P**aste.

To move a highlighted selection, click the Cut button on the toolbar or choose **Edit**, **Cut**. Then click in the location where you want the selection moved and click the Paste button or choose **Edit**, **P**aste.

To Do: Find text

When you've composed or imported a particularly long page, you might need to quickly locate specific words or passages while editing. Composer includes a Find facility for this purpose. (Note that Composer does not feature a Find and Replace capability. Replacing is up to you.)

To find a text string anywhere within your Web document:

1. Choose **Edit**, **F**ind in Page. The Find dialog box opens, as shown in Figure 6.10.

FIGURE 6.10.

The Find dialog box.

2. In the Find what box, enter the exact text string you want to find.

3. To search for text that matches not only the text string but also its precise capitalization, check the Match case check box. To search from the spot where the edit cursor is located back to the beginning of the page, click the Up radio button. To search from the spot where the edit cursor is located to the end of the page, click the Down radio button.

4. Click Find Next.

Undoing Edits ("Goofs")

If you goof on any edit and wish you hadn't done it, you can undo it. To undo the last edit you made, choose **Edit**, **U**ndo or press Ctrl+Z.

Tips for Good Text Design

It's your page, and far be it from me to tell you what it should look like. However, if you are interested in some of the accumulated wisdom of the Webmasters, here are a few things to keep in mind when working with text on your page:

- Write clearly and be brief. Web surfers are an immediate-gratification, fast-food–type lot. To hold them, you must dole out your message in quick, efficient bites.

- Break up your message into pages of reasonable length, and break up pages into at least two or three sections (three is best) delineated by headings, pictures, or horizontal lines (see Hour 7). This makes your page more attractive and inviting and also allows visitors to scan your page easily for items of interest.

- Don't overdo emphasis. Look through your page and watch for overuse of bold, italic, and custom font sizes and colors. Watch also for the use of headings, block quotes, or other properties used to pump up a paragraph that really belongs in normal text. Let your page's organization (and pictures) create visual interest and let your choice of words emphasize important ideas. Use bold to light up a word or two and use italic for things that belong in italic, such as book titles or foreign phrases.

- Even though you have the spell-checker, proofread carefully on your own before publishing. In addition, have someone else check your spelling and critique your writing and layout.

- Always use a signature (see Hour 10).

Summary

Composer provides simple toolbar buttons, dialog boxes, and menus for applying properties to paragraphs—the most important activity in building a Web page.

When you apply properties to a paragraph, you're actually surrounding the paragraph with the appropriate HTML tags in the underlying HTML source file. The menus and dialog boxes save you the trouble of remembering what all the tags are and apply those tags conveniently and accurately.

Workshop

Q&A

Q **If text I want to add to my page already exists in a word processing (or plain text) file, how can I get it into Composer without retyping it?**

A Copy and paste (or cut and paste) is the most effective way to copy text or pictures from any Windows document into Composer. Copy and paste is quick and easy, and it prevents compatibility problems by stripping the text of any extraneous formatting not supported in Composer. But there are other options.

More and more, application developers are endowing their programs with the ability to save files in HTML format for import to the Web. For example, Microsoft Office 97 applications—Word 97, Excel 97, PowerPoint 97, and Access 97—can

6

all save files in HTML format. You can open a document in Word 97, save it in HTML format, and then edit it and tune it up in Composer. Because Word can import many different file types, you can use it as a conversion tool to change most other document file types to HTML. Just import the file from its native format to Word, and then save the file in Word in HTML format.

You can also pick up utilities (often for free) that can convert files in various word processing or other formats into HTML, often preserving some of the page formatting. For example, Microsoft offers Internet Assistant, a free add-in to earlier versions of Word (before Word 97) that gives those versions the same save-as-HTML capability found in Word 97. Similar utilities are available for WordPerfect and other applications.

Quiz

Take the following quiz to see how much you have learned.

Questions

1. True or False: You can make one word in a sentence into a heading (to make it stand out) and the rest into a normal paragraph.

2. To stop the spell-checker from thinking your name is a misspelling:
   a. When the spell-checker is stopped on your name, click the Learn button on the Check Spelling dialog to add your name to the dictionary.
   b. Click the Edit Dictionary button on the Check Spelling dialog and type your name into the dictionary.
   c. Either a or b.

3. To make sure columns of text line up neatly, you can:
   a. Apply the Formatted property to them.
   b. Make the text into a table (see Hour 8).
   c. Use tabs to align the columns.
   d. Either a or b.

Answers

1. False. Paragraph styles always affect a whole paragraph, never just a part of it.

2. (c)

3. (d) Either a or b would work, but not c—you can't use tabs in a Web page.

Activity

If you haven't already done so, type (or cut and paste) a simple Web page in Composer for practice (your résumé is always a good practice document). Assign appropriate properties to the text, but don't worry yet about making it beautiful—that comes next.

6

HOUR 7

Formatting Text

It's easy—too easy, in fact—to begin thinking that a Web page is made up of three basic parts: text, images, and links. Although that's generally true, it tends to imply that text is for content, images are for show, and links are for action.

The facts are a little muddier than that. Text is first and foremost a vehicle for information, but when text is dressed up in a fancy font or cool color, it contributes to both content and design—feeding two brain hemispheres for the price of one. Similarly, organizing text into a bulleted or numbered list affects both content and style.

In this hour, you step beyond paragraph properties and into fancy text formatting. At the end of the hour, you will be able to answer the following questions:

- How do I make attractive lists?
- Can I choose the color of text?
- How do I choose the font and size for text, as I would in a word processor?

Working with Lists

In Hour 6, "Adding and Editing Text," you discovered that List Item is one of the paragraph styles you can apply to tell a browser how to format a block of text. Of course, there are different types of lists; so for any paragraph assigned the List Item paragraph style, you can choose from several different *list styles* generally supported by browsers (see Figure 7.1). These styles are as follows:

Unnumbered list—An ordinary, indented bulleted list.

> The numbers in numbered lists do not appear in Composer. Instead, place-holders (# for Arabic, *X* for Roman, *A* for uppercase, *a* for lowercase) appear. To see the actual numbering, click the Preview button.

Numbered list—A list whose items are numbered from top to bottom with Arabic numerals (1, 2, 3), Roman numerals (III, IV, V), or letters (A, B, C or a, b, c).

Directory list—A bulleted, unindented list of short items. The items must be short (a word or two) because some browsers wrap directory lists into columns.

Menu list—A bulleted, indented list of short items.

FIGURE 7.1.

List styles.

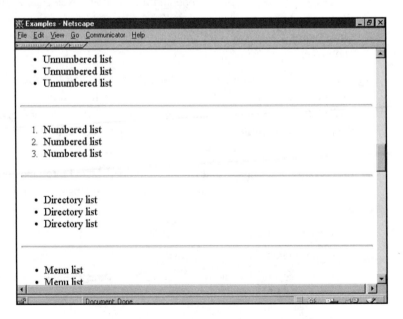

Description list—Longer items (even short paragraphs) formatted in an indented, bulleted list.

If the list style you use is either Unnumbered or Numbered, you can choose from among bullet styles or number styles (see Figure 7.2).

FIGURE 7.2.

Bullet and numbering styles.

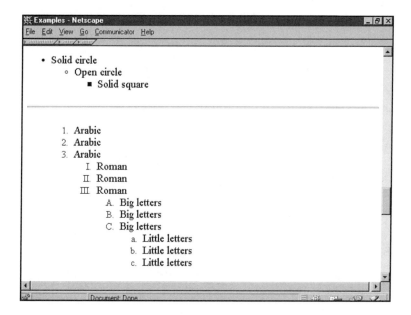

For an Unnumbered list, you can choose among the following bullet styles:

Automatic—Composer picks the bullet style; the default choice is the solid circle. See the section titled "Nesting Lists" later in this hour to learn when Automatic selects other bullet styles.

Solid circle—The default bullet type, an ordinary black dot.

Solid square—A filled-in square.

Open square—An empty square, like a check box.

In some pages you see online, and in pages built by the Page Wizard (see Hour 3, "Wizarding Up an Instant Web Page"), you see cool list bullets that are geometrical, multicolored, and even animated. These are not real bullets assigned by a bullet style attribute, but images inserted right before each line of text. See Hour 14, "Adding Pictures and Picture Backgrounds."

7

When you select Numbered list, you can choose from the following number styles:

Automatic—Composer picks the number style; the default choice is 1, 2, 3. See "Nesting Lists" later in this hour to learn when Automatic selects other number styles.

Arabic numerals—1, 2, 3, 4, and so on.

Roman numerals (uppercase only)—I, II, III, IV, and so on.

Uppercase letters—A, B, C, D, and so on.

Lowercase letters—a, b, c, d, and so on.

Creating and Formatting Lists

> You cannot change the list style (or bullet or number style) in the middle of a list, unless you *nest* (indent) the list items to which you want to apply a different style. See the section titled "Nesting Lists" later in this hour.

As with all other text formatting, you create a list by first entering the text of one or more list items; each item is a separate paragraph and may be as long or as short as you choose. You then select the list item paragraphs and apply properties in any of the following ways:

- On the Formatting toolbar, click the Bullet List button or the Numbered List button.
- Choose Format, List to display a submenu of all list styles, and then choose the desired style from the submenu.
- Open the Paragraph tab of the Character Properties dialog box, where you can assign the List Item paragraph style, additional list styles, and bullet and number styles.

Note that you can choose a Bullet style or Number style only on the Paragraph tab. When you create a bulleted or numbered list from the Formatting toolbar or List submenu, the Automatic bullet or number style is assigned by default.

To Do: Build a bulleted list

1. Type and then select the list item paragraph.
2. Click the Bullet List button on the Formatting toolbar. The list items are formatted as a bulleted list with the default bullet style (Automatic).
3. Open the Paragraph tab of the Character Properties dialog box (choose Format, Character Properties, Paragraph or right-click the selection and choose

▼ **P**aragraph/List Properties from the context menu). In Figure 7.3, observe that the Paragraph Style and List Style fields have already been filled in with List Item and Unnumbered List respectively.

FIGURE 7.3.

Formatting lists using the Paragraph tab of the Character Properties dialog box.

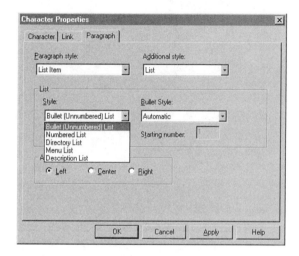

For a Numbered list, you can enter a starting number in the box under the Number style. (The default is 1.) Always use Arabic numerals to choose a starting number, even if you want the list to use letters or Roman numerals. For example, to begin a list with E, enter 5 as the starting number. For IV, enter 4.

4. Under Bullet Style, choose a style.

▲ 5. Click OK.

Nesting Lists

Composer gives you one more way to format lists. You can create multileveled, outline-style lists by *nesting* lists within lists, as shown in Figure 7.4.

To nest a list within a list, you simply indent the items to be nested. The easiest way to build a nested list is to enter all of the items in one flat list, and then go back and selectively indent the nested parts. To indent a group of items in a list, select them and click the Increase Indent button on the Formatting toolbar.

7

FIGURE 7.4.

Nested lists.

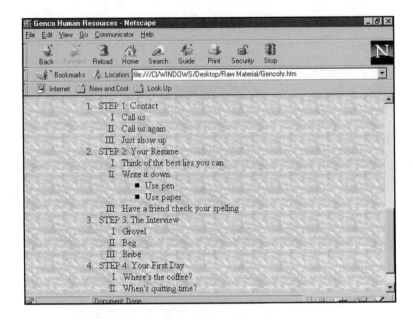

Composer forces all list entries at the same indent level to use the same list properties. For example, you cannot switch from bullets to numbers in the middle of a list unless you first indent the numbered section of the list. When you nest lists, you can switch list styles in the nested items, making them different from the unindented list. You can also change Bullet or Number styles in the nested lists.

 When you nest Numbered lists, each nested list is automatically renumbered starting with 1—the typical approach for an outline—unless you use the Paragraph tab of the Character Properties dialog box to specify a different starting number for each nested list.

When Automatic is selected as the Bullet or Number style, Composer automatically changes the bullet or number style for each indent level in the list. For example, if you nest items in a bulleted list with the solid circle bullet type, those nested items with the Automatic bullet type are assigned solid squares.

 In a nested list, you cannot use a higher level of Number or Bullet style than that of the list above. For example, if the main list used Roman numerals, a list nested within it would use uppercase or lowercase letters (not Arabic numbers).

If that nested list contains within it another nested list that uses the Automatic Bullet style, the innermost nested list automatically uses empty squares. The same happens with numbered lists nested and assigned the Automatic Number style. If the main list uses Arabic numerals (1, 2, 3), the first level of indenting automatically uses Roman numerals, the next level uses A, B, C, and so on.

Dressing Up Text with Character Properties

Paragraph properties always apply to a whole paragraph; for example, you cannot make part of a paragraph a heading and another part normal text. However, you can apply *character properties* to a single character in a paragraph, a few words, a whole paragraph, or a whole document. Character properties are optional settings you apply to text to change its appearance.

> Paragraph properties and character properties generally work together to define the look of a paragraph and the text within it. Keep in mind, however, that browsers apply some character formatting to text based on paragraph style alone. For example, they'll automatically show headings in large, bold type. When you apply character formatting, you override any default formatting the browser applies.

The most common use of character properties is to emphasize words by making them bold, italic, or underlined, just as you would when formatting a document in a word processor. But you can also change the color of characters, make them blink, change the *font face* (typeface) or size, and so on.

Font face and font size are the most advanced of the character properties that Composer supports. Most browsers support two of Composer's font choices: *variable width* and *fixed width*. When you assign the variable width font face to text, browsers display that text in their standard, proportionally spaced font. The fixed width font face instructs the browser to use a typewriter-style, monospaced font—the same font face applied automatically when you apply the Formatted paragraph property.

Composer's remaining choices for font face are specific fonts or typefaces. Choosing one of these instructs the browser to use the selected font (or, in a few cases, a font from the same family). The trick is that the font you choose must be installed on the visitor's computer (PC or Macintosh), or the visitor's browser must have a special built-in font viewer. For example, if you set text in Century Gothic, your visitors will see that font only if they happen to have Century Gothic installed on their computers (otherwise, the text reverts to the browser's variable-width font).

7

Among the font choices you can make in Composer, three choices are special: Arial, Times New Roman, and Courier. These three choices do not require that the visitor have these fonts; instead, they instruct the browser to use any available font of the same general family.

- Arial is a proportionally spaced *sans serif* font. (Sans serif means it lacks the decorative lips or bars that appear at the points of characters in serif fonts.) A browser on a computer lacking Arial may substitute another sans serif proportional font such as Helvetica.

- Times New Roman is a serif proportional font for which a similar font, such as Century Schoolbook, may be substituted.

- Courier is a monospaced font (like that used to display text in the fixed-width character property or Formatted paragraph property). Another monospaced font, such as Letter Gothic, may be substituted.

For font size, most browsers support the HTML *relative font scale*, in which the size of text is indicated not by points as it would be in a word processor, but by relative steps above or below the size of normal text, which is size 0. Text assigned a font size of +3 is three steps bigger than normal; text assigned –2 is two steps smaller than normal.

In addition to the HTML scale, Composer supports what might be called "Netscape point sizes" (although they're also supported by Internet Explorer). Netscape point sizes are specific font sizes, measured in points as in a word processor. Point sizes give you more precise control over the size of text when the page is viewed through a browser that supports point sizes.

When you want to create really exciting text effects, you might get better results by creating an image that also contains text—like a graphical logo—instead of fiddling with fonts. You'll have more creative freedom to shape and color the words, and the results will be supported by all graphical browsers (see Hour 14).

Besides font face and font size, you can apply two other character properties: style and font color. Style applies optional attributes to selected text, such as bold, italic, underline, or blinking. Color applies a custom color to selected text when you want that text to appear in a color other than the one assigned by the browser or by the colors assigned to the page.

Some character properties are based on extensions to HTML. As you might expect, anything you can do to text in Composer is fully supported by our popular friends, Internet Explorer and recent versions of Netscape Navigator. Among other browsers, however, you'll find a slippery slope of support levels.

Nearly all graphical browsers support relative font sizes. Most support character styles such as bold, italic, and underline; however, some browsers interpret these styles as merely "emphasis" and decide on their own how to show that emphasis. For example, text you make italic might show up underlined (and not italic) in a browser that makes its own rules for emphasizing text. Unusual styles such as superscript and blinking text are not often supported outside the Netscape and Microsoft camps. Text color is an offshoot of custom colors and is supported in any browser that supports custom colors (as long as the visitor has not disabled that support).

Font faces and Netscape point sizes are the least widely supported character properties. Many graphical browsers can deal with your assignment of fixed width or variable width as a font face, but specific font choices (such as Arial or Courier) and specific point sizes (as opposed to relative font sizes) are supported almost exclusively by the two leading browsers.

Configuring Navigator and Composer Font Preferences

Before working with character properties in general (and with fonts and sizes in particular), it's wise to configure two categories in the Preferences dialog box related to how Communicator deals with fonts. You open the Preferences dialog box by choosing Edit, Preferences.

The Encoding choice at the top of the dialog box shown in Figure 7.5 selects the character set (alphabet) used for displaying Web pages. If most pages you visit are in English, Western (the default) is the correct choice. Other Encoding selections enable character sets for showing text in other languages.

In the Preferences dialog box, choose the Appearance category, and then the subcategory Fonts (see Figure 7.5). Make sure the bottom radio button—Use document-specified fonts, including Dynamic Fonts—is selected to enable Navigator to show font face selections when you check your work in the browser and when you browse online. When a page includes no specific font settings, Navigator displays text in the fonts shown at the top of the dialog box.

FIGURE 7.5.

*Configuring
Navigator's font
settings.*

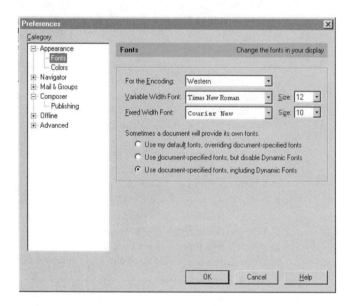

Next, choose the Composer category (see Figure 7.6). At the bottom of the dialog box, you can select a Font Size Mode:

- If you want to deal with font sizes exclusively in points, choose the top radio button. When showing a page that does not use point sizes, Composer will convert the relative font sizes to Netscape point sizes so that you can avoid the confusion of dealing with two different kinds of font size.

- If you want to deal with font sizes exclusively within the HTML font scale, choose the middle button. Use this choice only if you do not intend to use Netscape point sizes in any document.

- If you want the option to apply and see either type of font size, choose the bottom radio button.

Applying Character Properties

To apply character properties, you must always begin by selecting the exact block of characters to which the properties will be applied. You can select a single character, a word, a phrase, a whole paragraph, multiple paragraphs, or a whole page.

FIGURE 7.6.

*Configuring
Composer's font
preferences.*

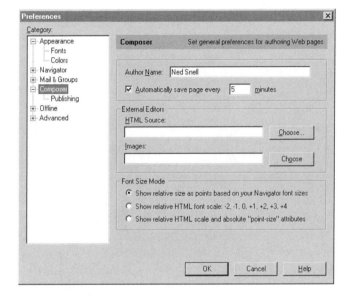

Once you've made your selection, you can apply character properties from buttons on the Formatting toolbar, the Format menu, or the Character tab of the Character Properties dialog box:

- On the Formatting toolbar, you'll find drop-down lists for choosing Font (which is really font face), Font Size, and Font Color. You'll also find buttons for applying the Bold, Italic, and Underline styles. As long as the selection remains highlighted, you can apply multiple properties. For example, you can select characters, choose a font, click the Bold button, and then choose a font color to apply three kinds of formatting in one operation.

- On the Format menu, choices for **F**ont, **S**tyle and **F**ont, **S**ize each open a submenu from which you can select properties. Also on the Format menu, **C**olor opens a dialog box for choosing font color.

- Choose F**o**rmat, Character Pr**o**perties to open the Character Properties dialog box (see Figure 7.7), which opens automatically to the Character tab. In the tab, use any combination of selections from drop-down lists and check boxes to apply the formatting you desire.

You can remove character properties in several ways, as well. When you remove character properties, the text's appearance reverts to the default formatting assigned by the browser (usually based on the assigned paragraph style).

7

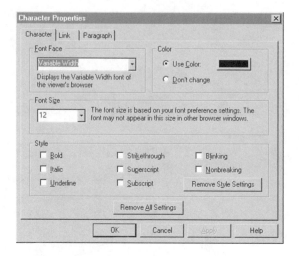

Figure 7.7.

*Formatting text with
the Character
Properties dialog box.*

Begin by selecting the text you want to remove properties from, then

- Remove Bold, Italic, or Underline styles by clicking the Bold, Italic, or Underline button on the Formatting toolbar.

- Remove all character properties—including font faces, sizes, styles, and color—by clicking the Remove All Styles button on the Formatting toolbar (or choosing Format, **R**emove All Styles, or clicking the Remove **A**ll Styles button on the Character tab of the Character Properties dialog box).

Summary

Still think images are the meat of a page's looks? You haven't entered a single image, and yet you've discovered an easy arsenal of techniques for dressing up a page, including list formatting and fonts.

Sure, you'll still want to use images, but as your pages evolve, always remember that you have these simple but effective design tools available to you.

Workshop

Q&A

Q **Because I can't know what fonts my visitors might have on their computers, shouldn't I steer clear of the Netscape font faces—especially considering that some browsers don't even support them?**

A Actually, Netscape fonts are a pretty safe bet. First, keep in mind that when you use Netscape fonts, nothing terrible will happen in browsers that can't support Netscape font faces—those browsers simply display the text in their default display fonts.

Second, Windows 3.1, 95, 98, and NT all come with a default set of TrueType fonts, and Macintoshes are equipped with a similar list. If you use fonts from these default lists, you've got a pretty good shot at getting your desired font displayed to most Netscape and Internet Explorer users on PCs and Macintoshes—and that's a majority of the Web surfers out there. You can better your odds by sticking with the three super fonts—Arial, Times New Roman, and Courier—so that computers lacking those fonts can substitute a similar font.

Quiz

Take the following quiz to see how much you have learned.

Questions

1. True or False: You can make one word in a sentence bold and leave the rest regular.

2. In a nested, bulleted list, Composer will vary the bullet style used for each level if you apply which of the following bullet styles?

    a. Variola

    b. Bullet-Matic

    c. Auto-Nesto

    d. Automatic

3. If you want a few words at the top of the page to be big and bold, what's the best way to format the text?

    a. Choose a big, bold font.

    b. Apply the Heading 1 paragraph style.

    c. Do nothing—browsers automatically make text at the top big and bold.

    d. Any of the above.

Answers

1. True. Character properties can be applied to all or only part of a paragraph.

2. (d)

3. (b) Using a standard HTML paragraph style ensures that all browsers will display that text with proper emphasis.

7

Activity

Using any sample or practice page, apply fun, unusual fonts to all text and print out the result. Then remove the fonts so that the text is formatted only by the paragraph styles and print the result. Compare the pages and consider how the fonts affect not only the appearance of the page, but also its readability.

HOUR 8

Organizing Text with Tables and Rules

Between text and pictures, there's a gray area. There are objects that affect the composition and organization of a Web page, but these objects aren't exactly text or pictures; they are lists tables, and horizontal lines.

Tables are a great way to organize text in a meaningful, attractive way. And horizontal lines divide pages up visually into meaningful sections, making the page both more appealing and easier to read. In this hour—before moving ahead to pictures in Part IV—you'll learn how to apply these "gray area" techniques to make the most of text. At the end of the hour, you will be able to answer the following questions:

- How do I insert horizontal lines in my page and control their appearance?
- How do I make a table?
- Can I customize table borders, headings, captions and other things that affect the table's appearance?

Adding Horizontal Lines

The simple, straight lines running horizontally across many Web pages (see Figure 8.2 later in this hour) have always been known in Web parlance as *horizontal rules* because they're created by the HTML tag <HR>—*HR* for *Horizontal Rule*.

Netscape apparently thinks the term *rule* is confusing, so in Composer, it's a horizontal *line*. (If you're trying to develop a non–Netscape-specific understanding of authoring terms, just remember that rules are rules, except in Composer, where rules are sometimes broken.) Creating a horizontal line in Composer inserts the <HR> tag into your document to draw a rule.

In some pages you see cool, graphical horizontal lines that zigzag, flash, or scroll. These are not real HTML "horizontal lines" but images inserted to achieve the same effect, only cooler. See Hour 14, "Adding Pictures and Picture Backgrounds."

Virtually any browser can handle a horizontal line because any computer system can draw one across the screen (even if it's only with underscores or dashes). Lines are a universal way to add some visual interest to your page and break up logical sections of a page or document to communicate more effectively.

To Do: Add a horizontal line

1. In your page, position the edit cursor where you want to insert the rule.
2. Click the H. Line button on the Composition toolbar or choose **Insert**, **Horizontal Line**.

The line appears at the insertion point. You can leave it like it is or change its appearance by choosing Horizontal Line Properties, as shown next.

To Do: Format a line

After inserting a line, you can change its appearance by editing its properties. Look ahead to Figure 8.2 to see the ways that the steps in this To Do can create different line styles.

1. Double-click the line to open the Horizontal Line Properties dialog box (see Figure 8.1).

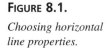

FIGURE 8.1.

Choosing horizontal line properties.

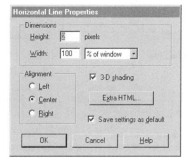

After choosing line properties in the Horizontal Line Properties dialog box, you can check the check box labeled Save settings as default. If you do, clicking the H. Line button inserts a line with the properties you just saved.

2. Under Dimensions, enter the Height (thickness) of the line in pixels. The default is 2 pixels, which creates a very fine, but clearly visible line (classy and understated). Then choose a line Width that's a percentage of the Navigator window's width. The default, 100%, draws a line across the entire window. A width of 50% draws a line half as wide as the window.

3. Under Align, choose and click a radio button to align the line along the left edge of the screen, center the line, or align it on the right (center usually looks best).

The Extra HTML button on the Horizontal Line Properties dialog box enables you to add advanced attributes to the line by editing the HTML code directly. See Hour 17, "Editing HTML."

4. To create a shadow below the line to give it a 3D look (see Figure 8.2), click the check box next to 3D *s*hading.

 5. Click OK.

About Tables

A table—regardless of the medium in which it appears—is chunks of information arranged in rows and columns. The grid of rows and columns form cells in which you can organize text.

FIGURE 8.2.

Horizontal lines with various properties.

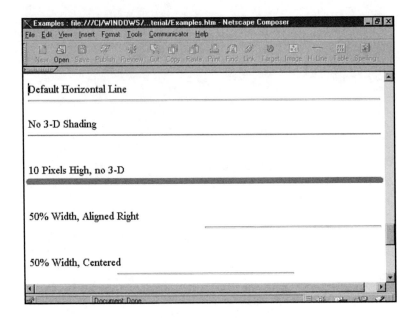

 NEW TERM **Cell.** In a table, the box made by the intersection of a column and a row is called a *cell*; cells contain the table content, or *data*.

> You can put text or pictures in a table cell. You learn how to put a picture in a table cell in Hour 14.

Although rows, columns, and data are the minimum requirements for any table, a more elaborate table contains additional elements (see Figure 8.3). It might have column or row headings and a caption above or below it. It might have solid lines, *borders*, appearing on all sides and between cells to form a grid. Note, however, that the borders may be omitted so that cell data is neatly organized in rows and columns, but not boxed up (see Figure 8.4).

Tables are transparent in that the page's background color or pattern shows through areas not covered by cell data or borders. However, a table may have its own background (see Figure 8.5), which does not cover the borders or cell data but does cover the page's background.

FIGURE 8.3.

Parts of a table (not all are required): Rows, Columns, Row Headings, Column Headings, Cells, Data, Borders, Caption.

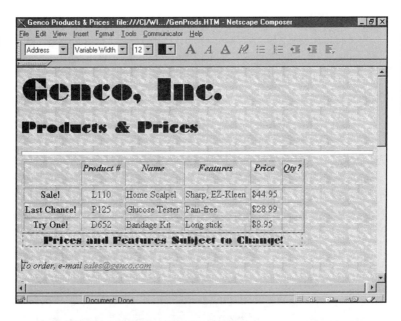

FIGURE 8.4.

A table with no visible borders.

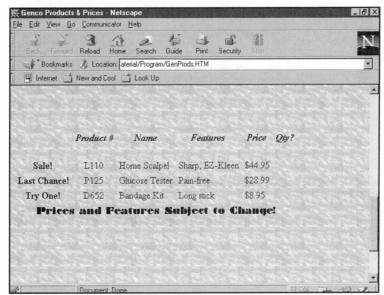

There's a lot you can do to format tables to your liking. But keep in mind that the precise formatting of your tables is greatly controlled by the browser displaying it. The height and width of cells is calculated automatically based on the number of columns and the length of the cell content. The width of a column is determined by the width necessary to contain the longest cell data in the column. When the data in a cell is long or when a table has many columns, the cell content may be wrapped automatically to allow the table to fit within the window.

FIGURE 8.5.

A table with its own background.

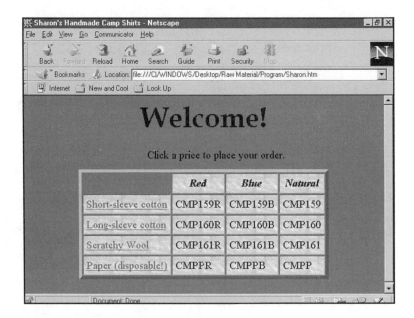

To Do: Create a table in Composer

1. Position the edit cursor at the spot in the document where you want a table.

2. On the Composition toolbar, click the Insert Table button (or choose **I**nsert, **T**able, **T**able). The New Table Properties dialog box opens (see Figure 8.6).

To delete a table, click anywhere on it and choose **Edit, Delete Table, Table.** The table and any data it contains are deleted.

The New Table Properties dialog box has defaults for all entries; you can simply press Enter to insert a simple, default table (one row, two columns), and then add more rows and columns and adjust formatting later.

▼

FIGURE 8.6.

Inserting a new table.

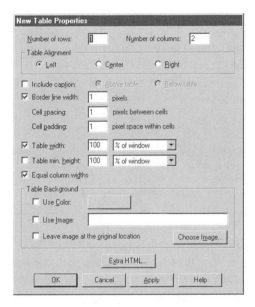

8

3. Choose the size and other aspects of the table by filling in the fields of the New Table Properties dialog box. (Note that you need not format the table perfectly now; you can change any aspect of the table, even the number of rows and columns, later, as described in the section title "Formatting a Table in Composer.") You may choose from the following:

Number of Rows/Number of Columns—Enter a number for each, from 1 to 100.

Table Alignment—Position the table on the page, aligned to the left, right, or center.

Include Caption—Check the check box to add a special text box above or below the table for a caption (click a radio button to choose Above Table or Below Table).

Border Line Width—Check the check box to display borders, or clear the check box to make the table borders invisible. If you choose to display borders, enter the number of pixels wide you want the border to be. A higher number will display a thicker, bolder border. By default, the outside border is *beveled* to give the table a dressy, 3D look.

As you develop your table, click the Apply button at any time to see the table as it would be created with the current settings. The Apply button does not close the dialog box, so you can continue to customize the table. When the table appears as you want it, click OK to close the dialog box.

▼ Cell Spacing/Cell Padding—*Cell spacing* is the width of the space between cells, whereas the *cell padding* is the space between the borders and the cell content (like margins). The default measurement for each of these (one pixel) usually works fine. But after you enter your cell data (as you learn to do in the next section), you might decide that the cell data appears cramped with too little space between cell entries. In such a case, increasing the cell spacing, cell padding, or both can "open up" the table, adding space between entries and cells.

You can express the table width and the table minimum height as a percentage of the window or as a number of pixels. But for reasons described in earlier hours, it's usually best to avoid pixel measurements, except for small items such as border and horizontal line thickness.

Table Width—By default, a table is spread out to fit the entire window in which it is browsed. If you want the table smaller than that, check the Table width check box and then enter a value less than 100 for % of window.

Table Min. Height—By default, a table's height is determined automatically by its contents; the longer the data in the cells, the longer the table. If you want the table to be a certain minimum height, even if its content would not require that height, check the Table min. height check box, and then enter a value for % of window. (You may enter a value of more than 100%, since visitors can scroll.)

Equal Column Widths—Browsers automatically adjust the width of each column as necessary to fit cell contents. In general, a column will be displayed as wide as necessary to accommodate the widest cell entry in the column. If you want your table to have a very regular appearance in which all columns are exactly the same width regardless of their contents, check this check box.

4. Make entries in the Table Background section of the New Table Properties dialog box to add a background to the table (which hides any portions of the page background that peek through the table). You may choose

You can't use a table background color and background image together. The image overrides the color.

Use Color—Puts a solid color behind the table. After checking this check box,
▼ click the rectangle to the right of the check box to drop down a menu of colors

▼ from which to choose. Click a color square or click the Other button to open a color palette for creating and selecting a custom color.

Use Image—Enter the path and filename of an image file to use as a table background (or click Choose Image to browse for an image file). If the image file's area is smaller than that of the table, the image will be tiled, repeated across the whole table background, just like a page background image. (To learn more about images, see Hour 13, "Getting (or Making) Pictures for Your Web Page.")

> When your new table appears, you'll notice a pattern of dashed lines indicating the table borders (if you did not choose to display borders) and a dashed box for the caption (if you chose to include one). These lines appear only in Composer to identify the table; they will not appear when the file is viewed through a browser.

5. After you complete the New Table Properties dialog box and click OK, an empty table appears in your document. Create the cell contents or format the table as
▲ described in the following sections.

Entering Data in a Table

After creating the rows and columns of your table, it's time to put data in it (and to enter its caption, if you chose to create one).

> If you enter nothing in a cell, it becomes a *blank cell*. A blank cell's borders don't show, and the table background doesn't appear behind it—it's as if the cell were not simply empty, but not even part of the table.
>
> Later in this hour, you'll discover creative ways to use blank cells to achieve certain table effects. But for now, simply be aware that you must enter something in every cell for all of the table's borders to display properly and for the table background to show through the whole table. If you have no specific data for a cell, just type a space in it so it's not empty.

Entering Text and Captions

To add text to a table cell, position the edit cursor there by single-clicking in the cell. Then type away—it's that simple. To add the caption, click in the dashed box Composer displays to represent the caption area; then type your intended caption. When you finish typing in a cell, press Tab to jump quickly to the next cell.

When the text you type exceeds the width of the column, it breaks between words and wraps to the next line, as if the cell were just a very small page. Note, however, that text can break only between words; if you type an especially long word in a cell, the cell width (and thus the width of the entire column) increases automatically to accommodate the word.

Actually, the text you type for the caption doesn't need to be an actual title or caption. It can be any text you want displayed directly above or below the table.

When typing in a cell or caption box, you can press Enter to start new paragraphs. You can also apply virtually any type of text formatting you would apply anywhere else in a Web page using the same selection techniques and formatting tools. Specifically, you can apply the following:

- Fonts and attributes (bold, italic, color, and so on)
- List formatting (bulleted, numbered, and nested)
- Alignment (left, right, center)
- Indenting

You can control the horizontal alignment—left, center, and right—of text in a cell by using the regular Composer text formatting tools (the Alignment button or Format, Align). However, you can also control the text's *vertical* position in a cell—top, middle, bottom—through the Table Properties dialog box.

The thing to keep in mind about alignment and indenting is that the formatting is relative to the *cell*, not the page or table. For example, if you apply center alignment to text in a cell, the text is positioned in the center of the cell, not the center of the table or page.

Formatting a Table in Composer

After creating your table and entering data, you might need to adjust its appearance by adding rows or columns, changing the border width, or customizing the table in other ways.

You accomplish most table formatting on the three tabs of the Table Properties dialog box (see Figures 8.7 through 8.9). To use the dialog box, begin by positioning the edit cursor within the table, row, or cell you want to format; then choose Format, Table Properties.

You can also open the Table Properties dialog box by pointing to the table, row, or cell you want to format, right-clicking, and choosing table properties from the context menu.

As you work with the Table Properties dialog box, click the Apply button at any time to see the table as it would appear with the current settings. The Apply button does not close the dialog box, so you can continue to customize the table.

In the Table tab (refer to Figure 8.7), you can change any of the choices you made when creating the table. The options on the Table tab are identical to those on the New Table Properties dialog box.

FIGURE 8.7.

The Table tab of the Table Properties dialog box.

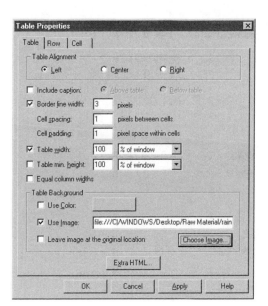

FIGURE 8.8.

The Row tab of the Table Properties dialog box.

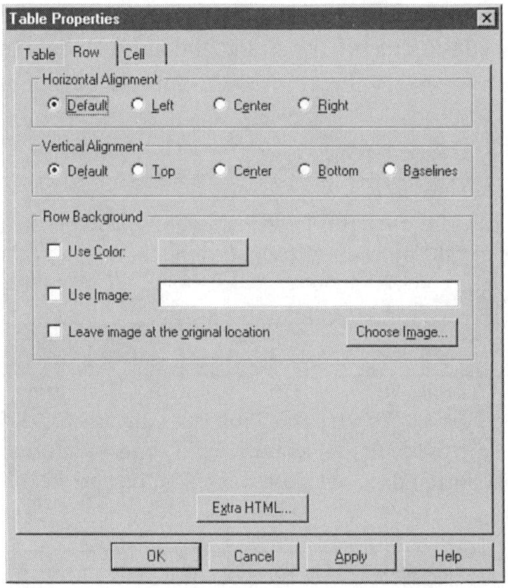

FIGURE 8.9.

The Cell tab of the Table Properties dialog box.

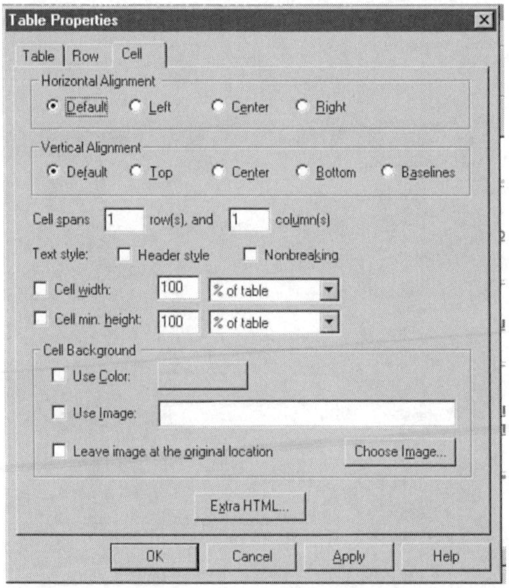

In the Row tab (refer to Figure 8.8), you can choose both Horizontal Alignment and Vertical Alignment for the contents of all cells in a row (including text and images). Horizontal alignment positions the data relative to the sides of the cell containing it; vertical alignment positions the cell relative to the top and bottom of the cell. Default, available for both types of alignment, simply leaves in place any existing alignment applied to the cell contents.

You can adjust a table's width with drag-and-drop. Point to the left or right border of the table so that the pointer becomes a two-headed arrow, and then click and drag to make the table wider or narrower.

In the Cell tab (refer to Figure 8.9), you can choose the alignment options for a cell without affecting the rest of the row. You can also set options for the following:

- Cell Spans—Allows you to make a single cell spread across multiple rows and columns (see the section titled "Creating Irregular Table Designs").

- Text Style—Use the check boxes to apply either (or both) of two optional, special text styles for table contents. Header Style applies bold formatting for row and column headings. Nonbreaking prevents browsers from breaking a line of text between words and wrapping to the next line; it forces the table to widen the column in order to show the text in a single line, even if it contains multiple words.

- Cell Width—By default, the width of all cells in a column is determined automatically by a browser, based on the widest cell contents in the column. By entering a cell width (in pixels or as a percentage of the overall table width), you can fix the width of the cell (and its column) to your chosen measurement, regardless of cell contents.

- Cell Min. Height—Specifies a minimum height (expressed in pixels or as a percentage of the table height) for the selected cell, regardless of its contents.

Creating Column and Row Headings

What's a heading, anyway? Well, it's text that's formatted differently from the rest of the table data, so that it is clearly not meant as table data, but as a descriptive label for a row or column (see Figure 8.10).

With that said, you can create column or row headings simply by applying unique formatting to the text in the top or bottom rows (column headings) or leftmost or rightmost columns (row headings). Applying bold or italic, making the font different, giving the cells containing the headings their own background, choosing a unique text color, or doing all of the above are easy ways to create headings.

> Using the Table Properties dialog box to assign the header style to cells does not preclude you from also applying any text formatting you wish to those cells.

If you want to get technical about it, you can use the Table Properties dialog box to apply the actual, legitimate table heading tags to these cells. Select a cell (or row) you want to use as a heading, open the Table Properties dialog box, choose the Cell tab, and check the check box next to Header Style.

FIGURE 8.10.

Column and row headings.

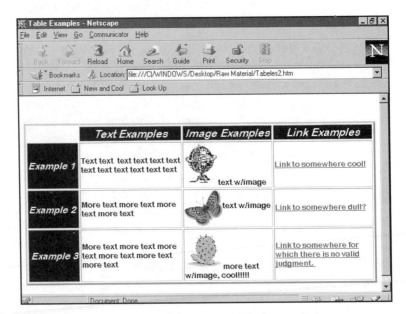

Working with Rows, Columns, and Cells

When you first create a table, as described earlier in this hour, you choose the number of rows and columns, and you get a table that's a nice, regular grid. Often, that'll be just what you want.

But sometimes, after entering some of your data, you'll find you need to add or delete rows or columns. Other times, you might need to create a complex or *irregular* table, one in which a single cell can spread across multiple rows or columns, or where one row has more or fewer cells than others.

In the next few sections, you learn how to manipulate rows, columns, and cells to create precisely the table you want.

Adding and Deleting Rows and Columns

When entering data, you can jump from cell to cell by pressing the Tab key. The Tab key moves among the cells like a reader's eyes, moving left to right across a row, and at the end of a row, it jumps to the leftmost cell in the row below.

But guess what? When you reach the end of the final row and press Tab, a new row appears with the edit cursor positioned in its leftmost cell, ready for a cell entry. This feature enables you to define your table without knowing exactly how many rows it will have. You can simply keep entering data and using Tab to move forward until all of the data has been entered. As you go, Composer keeps adding rows as they are needed.

Of course, you might sometimes want to add columns, or add new rows between existing rows, rather than at the bottom of the table.

> In Windows, you can also add rows and columns by pointing to a spot in the table, right-clicking, and choosing Insert, Table, **R**ow or Insert, Table, Column.

- To add a row, position the edit cursor in the row *above* the spot where you want the row added and choose **I**nsert, **T**able, **R**ow. A new row appears beneath the row containing the edit cursor.

- To add a column, position the edit cursor in the column *to the left of* the spot where you want the column added and choose **I**nsert, **T**able, Column. A new column appears to the right of the column containing the edit cursor.

To delete rows or columns, always begin by positioning the edit cursor anywhere in the row or column that you want to delete. Then choose **E**dit, Delete Table, **R**ow or Edit, Delete Table, Column. When you delete rows or columns, keep in mind the following:

- Any data in the deleted row or column is deleted too.

- When you delete a row, rows below shift up to fill the gap.

- When you delete a column, rows to the right shift left to fill the gap.

Creating Blank and Empty Cells for Effect

Cells containing absolutely no data—not even a space—are called *blank cells*. In Composer, a blank cell looks like any other cell, but with no data. But when you browse the table, the cell appears to drop out completely, showing no borders and omitting the table background (if any), allowing the page background to show through.

Like many Web authoring techniques, a blank cell can be called a "mistake" or a "nice touch," depending on how you look at it. For example, in a table that uses both row and column headings (see Figure 8.11), a blank cell is a nice way to deal with that pesky upper-left cell.

FIGURE 8.11.

A table containing a blank cell in the upper-left corner.

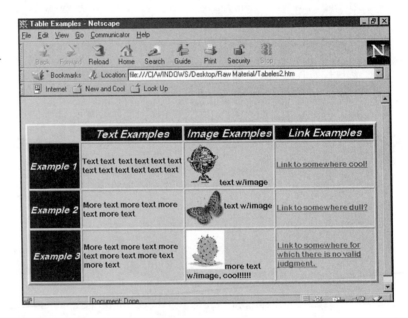

Creating Irregular Table Designs

We think of tables as regular grids, but they don't need to be. A cell can span multiple rows or columns in order to achieve certain effects, as shown in Figure 8.12.

To create a cell like those in Figure 8.12, click the cell, and then open the Cell tab of the Table Properties dialog box. In the Cell spans boxes, enter a number of rows for the cell to span or a number of columns, or both. For example, the large cell in the upper-left corner of Figure 8.12 spans two rows and two columns.

Another way to create irregular table formats is to add or delete cells.

FIGURE 8.12.

An irregular table design.

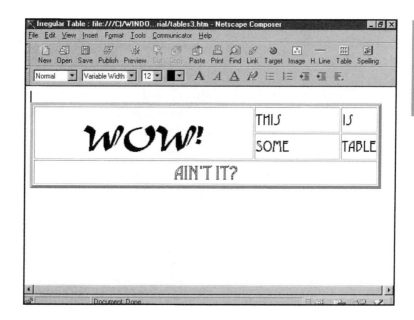

Summary

A simple table is a simple deal. And that's the best way to start—simple. Don't get wrapped up in long, complex tables too soon. Try sticking with simple tables of just a dozen cells or so, not just because it's a good way to learn, but because big hairy tables defeat their own purpose. They confuse visitors instead of informing them. Eventually, you'll move up the table growth curve to tougher, smarter table techniques.

Workshop

Q&A

Q I have stuff I want to put in a table, but I really don't want my table seen only by the HTML 3 world. Are there other options?

A There are several ways you can create the effect of a table without limiting its appearance to HTML 3–compatible browsers. First, you can simply type your table into the page (in Composer) using spaces to align the columns, and then apply the Formatted paragraph property to it. This instructs browsers to display the material in a monospaced font and to properly display all extra spaces. You won't get borders or fancy formatting, but virtually everyone—including folks without HTML 3 browsers (and even those with text-only browsers)—will see your table.

Alternatively, consider making your table into a picture. Some image editors (such as Paint Shop Pro, which is included on the CD-ROM accompanying this book) enable you to type text, dress it up, and save it as an image or as part of an image. Another way to do this is to create your table in a word processor or spreadsheet, and then use a screen-capture program to crop out the table and save it as an image. If your table is fairly simple, presenting it as a picture is a good way to put it out to virtually all graphical browser users.

Q Can I put a table inside a table?

A Certainly, and you can achieve some interesting effects by using a different border for the table inside (the "nested" table). You can even nest tables within tables within tables.

To nest a table, create the outside, or *parent*, table. Click the cell in which you want to nest a table, and then click the Insert Table button and create the table as usual. Observe that when creating and editing the nested table, some settings will work a little differently. For example, you choose table width not as a percentage of the window, but as a percentage of the *parent cell*, the cell holding the nested table.

Quiz

Take the following quiz to see how much you have learned.

Questions

1. True or False: A horizontal line and a horizontal rule are two different things.

2. A cell containing no data and whose borders don't show is
   a. A blank cell.
   b. A difficult cell.
   c. One that has a space character in it.
   d. A hard cell.

3. You control the look of text in a table cell using
   a. The special table-text formatting tools.
   b. The very same tools you use to format any other Web page text.
   c. Your mouse only.
   d. Nothing—you cannot format table text.

8

Answers

1. False. Two terms for the same thing.

2. (a) If (c) were true, the cell's borders would show because the cell isn't really empty. So there.

3. (b)

Activity

Look at the pages you've started. Where are the logical breaks in the text? Try inserting horizontal lines at the breaks and see what it does for the look and readability of the page.

PART III

Linking to Stuff

Hour

HOUR 9

Understanding Links

Links are one of the great mysteries of Web authoring. Everything else is upfront and visible; everything else just has to look right. A link, on the other hand, has to do something—it has to act right. Links are mysterious because what they do when they are activated is not immediately visible to the naked eye.

Fortunately, creating links is surprisingly simple. The only tricky part is correctly phrasing the underlying URL. With an eye toward the real linking pitfalls, this hour shows what links are all about. At the end of the hour, you'll be able to answer the following questions:

- What are the two parts in every link?
- What kinds of stuff can a link lead to?
- How do I properly phrase the URLs for linking to all types of remote Internet resources, including Web pages, email addresses, and so on?
- What's the difference between a *relative* link and an *absolute* link, and why does it matter?

What's in a Link?

Every link has two parts. Creating links is a simple matter of choosing a spot on the page for the link and then supplying both parts:

- The *link source*, the actual text (or graphic) that appears on the page to represent the link. When a visitor activates a link, he or she clicks the link source to activate the unseen URL below.

- The URL describing the page, file, or Internet service to be accessed when the link is activated.

You can create menus or directories of links like those in Figure 9.1 by making each link a separate line in the List Item paragraph property. Links don't have to be on separate lines, as Figure 9.1 shows. You can use any words or phrases in your page as links, including headings (or words in headings), words in normal paragraphs, list items, or even single characters in any paragraph property.

FIGURE 9.1.

Links (underlined) in text and by themselves in a menu.

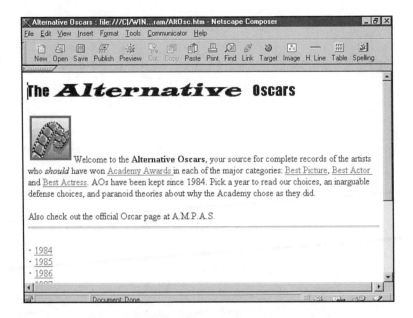

The link source takes on the paragraph properties of the text it is inserted into or closest to, but you can change the paragraph properties of the link source at any time, just as you would for any other text. The underlying link is undisturbed by such changes.

What's Linkable?

A link can point to any resource that can be expressed in a URL or to *local files* (files residing on the same server as the page containing the link). That includes not only remote Web pages and other pages and files residing on the same Web server as your document, but also newsgroups and articles within them, email messages, and Gopher and FTP servers. In your travels on the Web, you've already encountered links pointing to all such resources.

A link can point to a specific location within a Web page—even to a specific location within the same page containing the link. For example, in a long Web page, each entry in a table of contents can be a link pointing to a specific section of the page (see Figure 9.2). This allows visitors to navigate quickly and easily within the page. The spots within pages to which a link can point are called *targets*.

FIGURE 9.2.

A menu (table of contents) made up of links to targets within the same document.

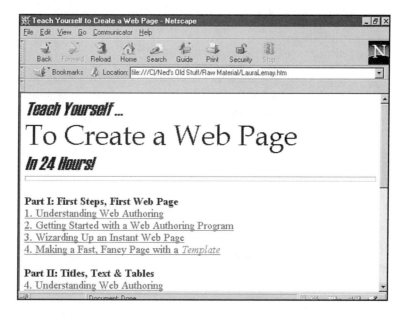

To create a link, you use the same procedure regardless of the type of resource the link points to. However, for each type of resource there are issues you must consider when composing the URL for the link. The next several sections describe in detail the special considerations for each type of URL.

Web Pages

Web pages are the most commonly linked resource, and for good reason: you can bet that anybody viewing your Web page can view any other Web page, so links to Web pages are a reliable way to provide information. Linking to Web pages also allows your visitors to apply a consistent set of navigation techniques; Gopher directories, for example, can be a little baffling to newer Web surfers.

> The easiest way to ensure that a URL is properly expressed is to copy it directly from the Web.

URLs pointing to Web pages always begin with the protocol designator `http://`. The protocol is followed by the Web server hostname, the directory path to the page file, and the actual HTML file of the page, as follows:

```
http://hostname/pathname/file.HTM
```

In some cases, you can omit the filename. Some Web servers have default files they display automatically whenever someone accesses the server or a directory without specifying a filename. For example,

```
http://www.mcp.com/
```

accesses the default page for the server `www.mcp.com`, and

```
http://www.mcp.com/publications/
```

accesses the default page for the directory `publications` on the server `www.mcp.com`.

Note that the preceding directory examples end in a slash. You should always use a slash to end an HTTP URL that does not end with a filename; the slash instructs the server to access the default file (usually `INDEX.HTML`). Some servers can still access the default file if you leave off the slash, but some won't. In a link, use the slash for safety's sake.

Finally, always be careful to follow the exact capitalization of the URL as it would appear in Navigator's Location box when you view the page. Many Web servers are case sensitive and won't recognize the directory or filename if it is not properly capitalized.

Targets in Pages (Anchors)

Web pages can contain predefined locations to which links can point. These spots are called *anchors* in HTML (and are created with the `<A>` tag—A for *anchor*). In Composer, they're called *targets*. You'd think Communicator, with its salty lighthouse and ship's wheel logos, would have kept the nicely nautical anchor nomenclature, but the target it is. Go with it.

You can add targets to your own Web pages and then link to those targets from elsewhere in the same page or from other pages you create. In addition, you can create links to point to any existing targets in other pages on the Web.

When you create a target (see Hour 11, "Linking to an Exact Spot in a Page"), give the target a name. You create links to targets as you do to a Web page, with one difference: you add the name of the target to the URL you enter for the link.

You can use a *relative pathname* to point to a target in another file stored on the same server (to link from one page of a multipage document to a target in another page in the document, for example). See the following section titled "Local Files."

Local Files

Just as you can link to resources on any server, you can also link to resources residing on the same server as your Web document. Obviously, this is what you would do when linking among the pages of a multipage presentation. But you might also choose to link to anything on your local Web server that relates to the topic of your page, such as another Web document or a text file containing related information.

Technically, the pathnames you enter to create links to local files are not URLs. When you're creating a link, however, you enter these pathnames in the same place you would enter a URL for linking to a remote resource. That's why I refer to them generically as URLs.

When you phrase the URLs to create links to local resources, you have to consider the differences between *relative* pathnames and *absolute* pathnames.

Relative Pathnames

Relative pathnames include only the information necessary to find the linked resource from the document containing the link. In other words, the path given to the file is *relative* to the file containing the link; from outside that file, the information supplied as the URL for the link is insufficient to locate the file.

If you use Composer's one-button publishing to publish your document on the server, don't worry much about relative and local pathnames. Composer takes care of that automatically, as explained in Hour 21, "Publishing Your Page." Still, to assert full control over your Web project and to be able to resolve any problems that might arise, it's important that you understand the principles behind these pathnames.

For example, suppose all of the pages of your multipage document share the same directory on the server and one of those pages is called FLORIDA.HTM. To link from any page in your document to FLORIDA.HTM, you need enter only the filename as the URL for the link. For example,

```
FLORIDA.HTM
```

Suppose all pages but the top page reside in a folder or directory called STATES, and that this folder is within the same folder containing the top page. To link from the top page to FLORIDA.HTM in the STATES directory, you would enter the directory and filename, separated by a slash. For example:

```
STATES/FLORIDA.HTM
```

This approach works as far into the folder hierarchy as you wish. Just be sure to separate each step in the path with a slash. For a file several levels beneath the file containing the link, you might enter

```
ENVIRO/US/STATES/FLORIDA.HTM
```

Now suppose you're linking from a page lower in the directory hierarchy to a page that's higher. To do this you must describe a path that moves up in the hierarchy. As in DOS (and in FTP servers), a double period (..) is used in a path to move up one level. For example, let's create a link from the FLORIDA page back to the top page (call it TOP.HTM), which we'll assume is one level above FLORIDA. For the URL portions of the link, you would enter

```
../TOP.HTM
```

If TOP.HTM were three levels above FLORIDA, you would type

```
../../../TOP.HTM
```

Use relative pathnames to link together the pages of a multipage document on your PC. Because the paths are relative, when you publish that document to a server the inter-page links will still work properly. See Hour 12, "Using Links to Build a Web Site."

Finally, suppose you want to link to a local file that resides in a folder that is not above or below the file containing the link but is elsewhere in the hierarchy. This would require a path that moves up the hierarchy and then down a different branch to the file. In such a case you use the double periods to move up and then specify the full directory path down to the file.

For example, suppose you want to link from

`ENVIRO/US/STATES/FLORIDA.HTM`

to

`ENVIRO/CANADA/PROVINCE/QUEBEC.HTM`

The phrasing you need is

`../../../CANADA/PROVINCE/QUEBEC.HTM`

The three sets of double periods move up to the `ENVIRO` directory; then the path down from `ENVIRO` to `QUEBEC.HTM` follows.

> On DOS and Windows systems, a relative or absolute path might include the letter of the hard disk, but it must be followed by a vertical bar (¦) rather than the standard colon. For example,
>
> `C¦/STATS/ENVIRO/CANADA/PROVINCE/QUEBEC.HTM`

Absolute Pathnames

Absolute pathnames give the complete path to a file, beginning with the top level of the directory hierarchy of the system. Absolute pathnames are not portable from one system to another. In other words, while composing a multipage document on your PC, you can use absolute pathnames in links among the pages. However, after you publish that document, all of the links become invalid because the server's directory hierarchy is not identical to your PC's.

In general, you'll use absolute pathnames only when linking to specific local resources (other than your own pages), such as FAQs, residing on the server where your page will be published.

Absolute pathnames are phrased just like relative pathnames, except that they always begin with a slash (/) and they always contain the full path from the top of the directory hierarchy to the file. For example:

`/STATS/ENVIRO/CANADA/PROVINCE/QUEBEC.HTM`

Other Internet Services

In addition to Web pages and their targets, links can point to any other browser-accessible servers. But before linking to anything other than a Web page or a target, keep in mind that not all browsers—hence not all visitors—can access all of these other server types.

Nearly all browsers can handle Gopher and FTP. Less common is mail access, and even less common is newsgroup access. Netscape Navigator has native support for both. Other browsers open helper applications for mail. For example, Internet Explorer opens Windows 95's Exchange mail client when a mailto link is activated. Still, many browsers have no news or mail access.

Gopher

Pointing straight to a Gopher server to display the main directory there is pretty simple. You simply build the URL out of the gopher:// protocol designator and the Gopher server hostname, as follows:

```
gopher://gopher.umn.edu
```

Beyond that, pointing to a specific file or subdirectory on a Gopher server gets tricky, often involving port numbers and a complex system of paths, so there's no simple set of rules for specifying the path to a Gopher file in a URL. Therefore, the best way to point a particular Gopher file is to use any of the following techniques:

- Explain in your Web page the menu choices required to navigate from the main directory to the file and then link only to the server.

- Using Navigator, connect to the Gopher server and click menu items to navigate all the way to the Gopher resource, then copy the link from the Location box to your document (as described in Hour 10, "Making Links").

- Search for a Web page that carries the same information as the Gopher resource (these are becoming increasingly common) so that you can avoid linking to the Gopher server at all.

FTP

Using a link to an FTP server, you can point to a directory or to a specific file. If the link points to a directory, clicking the link displays the list of files and subdirectories there (see Figure 9.3), and each listing is itself a link the visitor can click to navigate the directories or download a file. If the link points to a file, the file is downloaded to the visitor's PC when he or she activates the link.

If you create a link to an HTML file residing on an FTP server, clicking the link downloads the file and displays it, just as if it were on a Web server.

FIGURE 9.3.

An FTP directory.

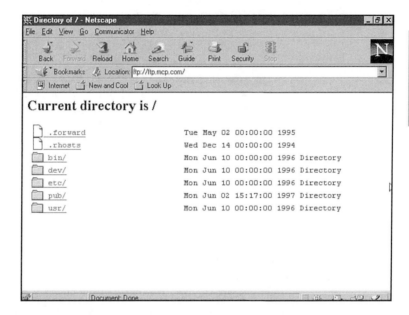

Observe that you do not end an FTP URL with a slash when linking to a directory. This differs from an HTTP URL, where a slash is always advisable except when accessing a specific HTML file.

To link to an anonymous FTP server, use the protocol designator ftp://, followed by the name of the FTP server, the path, and the filename (if you are linking to a file), as the following examples show:

ftp://ftp.mcp.com—Links to Macmillan's anonymous FTP server and displays the top-level directory.

ftp://ftp.mcp.com/pub—Links to Macmillan's anonymous FTP server and displays the contents of the pub directory.

ftp://ftp.mcp.com/pub/review.doc—Links to Macmillan's anonymous FTP server and downloads the file review.doc from the pub directory.

You can link to non-anonymous, password-protected FTP servers. However, in most cases such servers have been set up precisely to prevent public access. A URL to a non-anonymous FTP server includes a username and password for accessing that server, so anyone who accesses your page can access the FTP server—or read the URL activated by the link to learn the password.

Obviously, you should never create a link to a non-anonymous server unless you have express permission to do so from the server's administrators. And getting such permission is unlikely.

To link to a non-anonymous FTP server for which you have permission to publish a link, you phrase the URL exactly as you would for anonymous FTP, except that you insert the username and password (separated by a colon), and an @ sign, between the protocol and the path, as shown:

`ftp://username:password@ftp.mcp.com/pub/secrets.doc`

This URL downloads the file `secrets.doc` from a password-protected server for which the username and password in the URL are valid.

News

A link can open a newsgroup article list or point to a specific article within that list. Although both newsgroups and the articles they carry come and go, a link to the article list might be valid for years. On the other hand, a link to a specific article might be valid for only a few days—until the article ages past the server's time limit for newsgroup messages, when the article is automatically deleted from the server.

Thus, the best use of news links is to point to the article list of a newsgroup whose topic relates to that of the Web document. If a newsgroup contains an article that you want to make a long-term part of the page, copy it into a separate file and link to that file, or simply copy it into a Web page.

Before copying a news article into a page, check for copyright notices in the article. Whether it's copyrighted or not, email the author and request permission to use the article.

To link to a newsgroup to display the current article list, use the protocol designator `news:` followed by the name of the newsgroup. (Note that a news URL omits the double slashes used in HTTP, FTP, and Gopher URLs.) For example, the following are valid news links:

```
news:alt.video.laserdisc
```

or

```
news:news.announce.newusers
```

> Observe in Figure 9.4 that the newsgroup names and Message ID are under-
> lined in the article header. They're links and can be copied directly into a
> page in Composer with copy and paste or drag and drop.

9

To link to an article, find the message ID in the article's header; it's enclosed between
carats (< >) and labeled *message ID* by most newsreaders (including Collabra; see Figure
9.4). To phrase the URL, use the protocol designator news: followed by the message ID.
Note that you do not include the carats, and you do not need to include the newsgroup
name in the URL:

```
news:Do5D18.7Hs@deshaw.com
```

FIGURE 9.4.

*A news article header
(bottom pane) in
Collabra, showing the
newsgroups to which
the message is posted
and the message ID.*

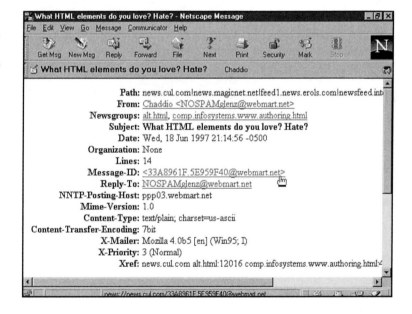

Mail

Mail URLs can be the most difficult to goof up. You enter `mailto:` followed by an email address. That's it. (Note that a mail URL omits the double slashes used in HTTP, FTP, and Gopher URLs.) For example:

```
mailto:nsnell@mailserver.com
```

 Before putting an email address other than your own in a link, ask permission from the addressee.

The most common use of `mailto:` links is in a signature at the bottom of a page. (You learn how to create a signature in Hour 10.) But you can use a `mailto:` link anywhere it makes sense to offer your readers a way to contact you or someone else.

To Do: Study links

Follow the steps below to explore the way the links you see online are phrased.

1. Connect to the Internet, and open your Web browser. (Use the Netscape Navigator browser included with this book, or Internet Explorer. These steps may not work with other browsers.)

2. Go to any page you like, and locate a link on it.

3. Point to the link (don't click), and then look in the status bar at the bottom of the browser window. The URL to which the link point appears there, shown exactly as it is phrased in the HTML file.

4. Explore other links this way. In Web pages you visit regularly, try to find links to:

   Other Web pages

   Targets

   Files

   FTP directories

   Email addresses

Summary

As you discover in the next three hours, creating links is pretty easy. In fact, making the link is the easiest part, especially if you copy the link from elsewhere. Phrasing the URL just right is the hardest part. Now that you understand the ins and outs of URLs, in the next hours you'll pick up some tips for ensuring you get 'em right when you make links.

Workshop

Q&A

Q I'm still fuzzy on this whole relative/absolute path business, and I have a headache. Can I just stay stupid on this one, and hope everything works out in the morning?

A To some extent, you can. Just trust Composer. When making links to local documents, use the Browse button in the Link Properties dialog box to choose files, so that Composer can phrase the path for you. Then use Composer's publishing features (see Hour 21) to publish your document instead of handling the uploading on your own. Composer automatically adjusts the local file links and uploads all the linked files so that the links still work on the server.

Quiz

Take the following quiz to see how much you have learned.

Questions

1. Which of the following can you link to?

    a. Another Web page.

    b. A file (a Word document, for example).

    c. An email address.

    d. All of the above.

2. What are the two parts of any link?

    a. The part the visitor sees (link sauce) and the address and/or file to which the link leads (Earl).

    b. The part the visitor sees (link sausage) and the address and/or file to which the link leads (ORL).

    c. The part the visitor sees (Lance Link) and the address and/or file to which the link leads (URN).

    d. The part the visitor sees (link source) and the address and/or file to which the link leads (URL).

3. When a visitor clicks a mail link:

    a. He or she receives email from you.

    b. His or her email program opens a new message, pre-addressed to the email address in the link.

   c. His or her computer prints a letter.

   d. Nothing happens—mailto links are a cheap gag.

Answers

1. (d)
2. (d)
3. (b)

Activity

On your Web travels, watch for pages for which you'd like to create a link in your own creations. When you're on such a page, create a bookmark (if you browse with Navigator) or a Favorite (if you browse with Internet Explorer) for the page. As you'll see in Hour 10, doing this not only makes creating the link easier but also ensures that you'll phrase the URL accurately.

HOUR 10

Making Links

By design, this is an easy hour. The only hard part about making links is understanding how they work, and getting the URL right—and you learned all about that in Hour 9, "Understanding Links." In this hour, you'll put that knowledge to work.

But I haven't given up making things easy yet. You're also about to discover a variety of ways to make picking up the URLs for your links quicker, easier, and more accurate. At the end of the hour, you'll be able to answer the following questions:

- How can I make linking easier and more accurate by copying and pasting URLs?
- How do I create a new link?
- Can I create a signature for my page, so visitors can conveniently send me email?
- How do I get rid of a link?

As you know, links can be attached to text or pictures. However, you won't learn how to add pictures to your pages until Hour 14, "Adding Pictures and Picture Backgrounds."

Although most of what you learn in this hour applies to both text and pictures, you won't pick up the specifics of making picture links until Hour 14.

Copying Links from Other Pages

Anywhere you see a link, you can easily copy it into your page using either of two popular techniques found in both Windows and Mac systems: copy and paste or drag and drop. For example, you can copy the URL of a page you're currently viewing on the Web—call it the *source document*—and paste it as a link into your page in Composer—the *target document.*

In fact, a page you've just accessed on the Web makes the most reliable source for a link. If you copy the URL of a file while viewing it and paste it as a link into a page you're creating, you can trust that the link will probably work properly (until and unless the page or other resource is moved or removed).

In other places where you can pick up links, the links might be accurate and up-to-date, or they might not be. Obviously, if the link is faulty where you get it, it won't work in your page, either. Test, test, test. (See Hour 23, "Testing and Maintaining Your Page Online.")

Sources for copying links include

- Navigator's Location box (where the URL of the current page appears)
- The Bookmarks folder (in Navigator) or the Favorites folder (in Internet Explorer)
- The header of a news article in your Internet newsreader program
- The header of a mail message in your email program
- Any link appearing in a Web page seen through Navigator

When copying a link into your page, keep in mind the following:

- Except when you copy from Navigator's Bookmarks list, the link source is not copied; instead, the link source that appears in Composer is the URL itself. To give the link a name to appear instead of its URL, edit the Link Properties as described later in this hour. (When you copy a bookmark as a link, the link source is the name of the bookmark.)

- The link takes on the paragraph properties of the paragraph it is inserted into or closest to. Remember, though, that a link can accept any paragraph properties or character properties—though in most browsers, the character properties cannot override the default way links are displayed. That's a good thing, actually, because you don't want your formatting to disguise the fact that a link is a link.

To Copy and Paste a Link

Copying and pasting, in case you've forgotten, is a two-part deal. First, you copy something to the Windows Clipboard and then you paste it from the Clipboard into the place you want it to go. You can accomplish each half of the job in several ways. There are several ways to copy, and several to paste, and you can combine any copy method with any paste method and get the same results.

10

From the following lists, pick a copy method you like, pick a paste method you like, and put 'em together.

To copy

- A link to the Web page currently appearing in Navigator: Right-click the URL in the Location box, then choose Copy from the context menu.

- A link shown in a Web page: Right-click the link, and choose Copy Link Location from the context menu (see Figure 10.1).

- A link appearing in Navigator's Bookmarks list: Open the list in Navigator by clicking the Bookmarks button and then choosing Edit Bookmarks. Right-click the desired bookmark and choose Copy Link Location from the context menu.

- A link appearing in Internet Explorer's Favorites menu: Choose Favorites, Organize Favorites from the menu bar. In the Organize Favorites dialog box, right-click the Favorite you want to copy, and choose Properties from the menu that appears. Then press Ctrl+Insert to copy the URL to the Clipboard.

- A link appearing in the header of a news or mail message: Open the message and locate the desired link in the message header. Right-click the link, and choose Copy Link Location.

To paste a link from the Clipboard into your page, do the following:

1. In the open page in Composer, click the spot where you want to insert the link.

2. Choose **E**dit, **P**aste (or press Shift+Insert).

FIGURE 10.1.

Copying a link to the Clipboard by right-clicking.

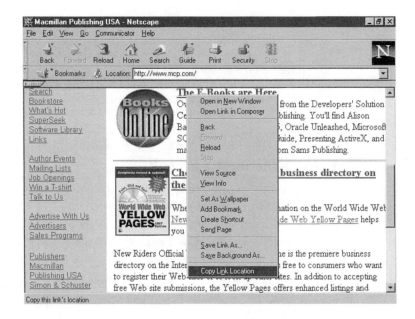

Alternatively, you can right-click the spot where you want to paste the link and then choose **P**aste Link from the context menu.

To Do: Drag and drop a link

1. In Navigator, open the page (local or remote) containing the desired link, or open the Bookmark folder or news or mail message containing the link.

2. Open the target document in Composer.

3. Position the open windows so that both are visible on the Windows desktop. One way is to right-click an open spot on the Windows 95 taskbar and choose one of the two "Tile" options (see Figure 10.2).

> To drag and drop a link to the page currently open in Navigator, drag the page proxy icon in the Location bar to the Composer window.

▼   4. Scroll in the Navigator (or folder) window until the desired link is visible.

Figure 10.2.

Windows tiled for dragging and dropping a link.

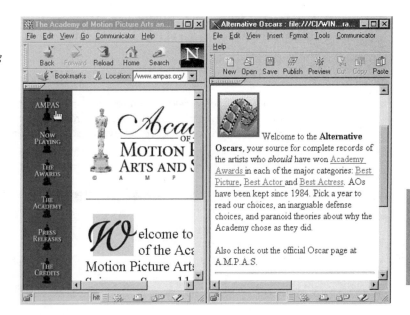

You can edit the character properties of link source text, making them bold or italic, for example. However, most browsers override such formatting to keep links identifiable. Most browsers show the formatting but always insist on underlining links, no matter what else is done to them. That's good—it ensures that your visitors will always be able to easily identify links in your pages.

5. Click and hold the left mouse button on the link and drag it to the Composer window. As you drag, the pointer becomes a link pointer, to indicate that you're dragging a link.

6. When the chain pointer moves into the Composer window, the edit cursor follows its movements. If you drag to any edge of the window, the window scrolls in that direction. Pull the mouse through the page until the edit cursor arrives at the spot where you want to insert the link.

▲   7. Release the mouse button to drop the link.

Inserting a New Link

1. In Composer, click at the spot in the page where you want the link to appear.

2. Click the Insert Link button on the Composition toolbar. (Alternatively, you can choose **Insert**, **L**ink or right-click the spot and choose **I**nsert New Link from the context menu.) The Link tab of the Character Properties dialog box opens, as shown in Figure 10.3.

> When you insert a new link, make sure nothing is highlighted before you open the Link Properties dialog box. Any highlighted text becomes the link source (see the section titled "Making Existing Text into a Link" later in this hour).

FIGURE 10.3.

Inserting a new link.

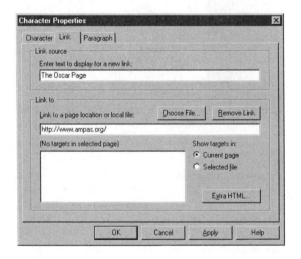

3. Fill in the Link source (the words you want to appear on the page to represent the link). If you leave Link source blank, the URL will appear in the page as the link source.

4. Under Link to a page location or local file, fill in either the URL of a remote resource or a local pathname. You can also click **C**hoose File to browse for a local file.

5. Click OK. The link source appears in the page at the edit point. The link source is underlined and displayed in the page's link text color.

Making Existing Text into a Link

To make an existing paragraph or any text within a paragraph (including normal text, a heading, a list item, and so on) into a link, follow these steps:

1. In the page, highlight the words you want to use as the link source.

2. Open the Link tab of the Character Properties dialog by right-clicking the high-lighted text and choosing Create Link Using Selected, as shown in Figure 10.4. (Alternatively, you can open the dialog box using any of the methods described in the section titled "Inserting a New Link.")

FIGURE 10.4.

Using a context menu to create a link from existing text.

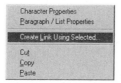

When the Link tab of the dialog box opens, note that the selected text appears as the Link source (see Figure 10.5).

10

FIGURE 10.5.

Link properties for a link made from existing text.

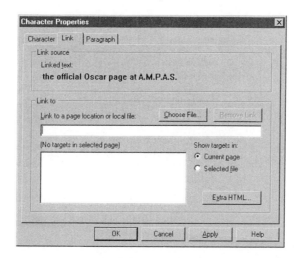

3. Complete the URL or pathname in the Link to a Page Location or File box, and click OK.

Creating a Signature

A signature is really nothing more than some sort of generic sign-off message that has an email address embedded within it. A few stock wording choices—in popular flavors—are

Inviting: Comments? Questions? E-mail me at nsnell@mailserver.com

Formal: If you have any comments or questions regarding this page, contact `nsnell@mailserver.com`

Efficient: Feedback: `nsnell@mailserver.com`

Traditionally, the paragraph containing the signature uses the `Address` property, though that is not required. The email address itself is also a mailto: link, in addition to being part of the address paragraph.

To Do: Create a signature

1. Click where you want the signature to be located (usually at or near the very end of the page, and only on the top page of a multipage page).

2. Type the signature message, including the email address.

3. Choose paragraph properties for the signature. (In Figure 10.6, the *Address* property is used, according to standard practice.)

FIGURE **10.6.**

A signature, with a mailto link under the email address.

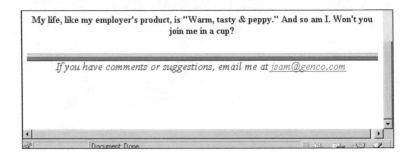

4. Highlight just the email address and click the Link button on the toolbar.

5. In the Link to a Page Location or File box, enter the mailto link. For example:

   `mailto:nsnell@mailserver.com`

6. Click OK.

De-Linking Text

Suppose you want to remove a link from your page but keep its link source text on the page. You could simply delete the link and retype the text. That's a solution for a link or two, but if you want to kill all the links in a large section or entire page, you'd find all the retyping tedious.

Instead, you can highlight the text and choose **E**dit, Remove Lin**k**. This works even if you highlight entire blocks of text or complete pages. All the text, including words or paragraphs that were once link sources, remains. But the link beneath is removed, as is the link color and underlining.

Summary

Just because you can link everywhere doesn't mean you should. Pages with extraneous links are no more useful than linkless ones. Carefully check out each place you'll link to. Is it really useful to your readers? Does it provide something new, or simply duplicate material your other links already lead to? Does it appear to be on a reliable server, or one that's often inaccessible or slow?

Your goal should be to provide your readers not with as many links as possible, but with a choice selection. And it goes without saying that you must check, update, and add to your links often. Do that and your visitors will return often.

10

Workshop

Q&A

Q If I want to offer quick access to other resources related to my page, can I link directly to a category listing in a Web directory, such as Yahoo or the WWW Virtual Library?

A Sure, and many people do that. As always, it's proper to email the Webmaster of any directory you link to and request permission.

Also, try not to get too specific; link at the most general point in a directory's hierarchy that pertains to your topic, and let the visitor navigate down to the specifics. Broad categories in directories are fairly stable and remain in place for years. Very specific directory listings low in the hierarchy might disappear or change names, invalidating any links to them.

Quiz

Take the following quiz to see how much you have learned.

Questions

1. True or False: You must assign the Address paragraph property to the text of a mailto link.

2. To create a link in Composer, you can:

   a. Point to an empty spot, click the Insert Link button, and enter both the link source and URL in the dialog box.

      b. Highlight existing text, click the Insert Link button, and enter just the URL in the dialog box.

      c. Read Hour 14 to learn how to add a picture and make it into a link.

      d. Any of the above.

3. The best way to ensure that the URL of a link is accurate and up to date is to:

      a. Avoid linking to any page unless you visit it every day to verify its continued existence.

      b. Create the link by copying & pasting the URL from the page itself.

      c. Spell check the URL.

      d. Any of the above.

Answers

1. False. The text of a mailto link can be formatted any way you like.

2. (d)

3. (b)

Activity

In Navigator, create a new Bookmark folder specifically for bookmarks to pages you may want to use one day as links. While surfing, whenever you come across such a page, save a bookmark in the folder so it's easy to find later when you're adding links to your creations.

Hour 11

Linking to an Exact Spot in a Page

If Web pages were books and links were a card catalog, targets would be thumbtabs.

Let me explain. Just like a card catalog entry, a link takes you only to a whole document—a Web page—not to any particular place *within* that document. That makes links great for broad surfing, getting into the general ballpark of what you want.

But sometimes you want to take your visitors not just to a particular page, but to an exact spot within that page. That's the job of *targets*, sometimes called *anchors* in Web authoring programs other than Composer.

At the end of the hour, you'll be able to answer the following questions:

- Where and why would I use targets?
- How do I create a target in a page?
- How do I create a link that takes the visitor to a particular spot within the page he's viewing?

- How do I create a link that takes the visitor from one page to a particular spot in another page?

Understanding Targets

A target is a hidden HTML tag—hidden in that it is not visible to the visitor, but it is visible within the HTML file when not viewed through a browser, as shown in Figure 11.1.

Target

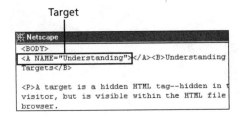

FIGURE 11.1.

Target code in an HTML file.

The code marks an exact spot within the page to which a link can point. A single Web page can have many targets, each one with a unique name so that a link can point to one and only one particular target.

Unlike links, targets are not connected to any words or pictures appearing on the page—they have no link source. Instead, they mark a spot *between* words or paragraphs. Targets have names, but again, the name does not appear on the page; it's used only as a reference for links.

> Of course, you can create the effect of an on-page target name by copying for the target name the text that the target is next to. I can create a target called "Chapter 1" right next to the heading, "Chapter 1."

Why use targets? Well, there are three basic scenarios, all involving long Web pages where, without targets, the visitor would have to do a lot of scrolling to locate particular information on a page:

- At the top of a very long Web page (such as a Frequently Asked Questions, or *FAQ*, file), you can include a list of links, each of which points to a different part of the file. The links enable the visitor to jump easily to any part of the file, instead of scrolling through it.

In Hour 12, "Using Links to Build a Web Site," you learn how to create a long Web page using links, targets, and other techniques to make the page easy to navigate.

- You may wish to use targets when links on one page refer to particular parts of another page that happens to be a long one. The links can point to parts of the long page, not just the page itself.

- In a frames-based page (see Hour 18, "Dividing a Page into Frames"), links in one frame can bring up particular parts of a file displayed in another frame. Like the other techniques, this reduces the visitor's need to scroll, making the page easier to navigate.

I've already said this, but it's important: In HTML code (see Hour 17, "Editing HTML") and in other Web authoring programs (see Hour 24, "Developing Your Authoring Skills"), targets are called *anchors*. As long as you use Composer, you don't need to know that. But when you move to other Web authoring tools, you'll need to remember that target = anchor.

Creating Targets in a Page

Before you can begin linking to targets, you must create those targets in the page. The following To Do shows how to insert targets in a page in Composer.

To Do: Add a target to a page

1. Open or create a page in which targets may be useful—typically a long, text-heavy page with many different subject headings, as shown in Figure 11.2.

2. Click a spot in the page where a link pointing to the target should take a visitor. In a page like the one shown in Figure 11.2, immediately before each heading is a good spot for a target.

3. Click the Target button on the Composition toolbar. (Alternatively, choose Insert, Target from the menu bar.) The Target Properties dialog box opens, as shown in Figure 11.3.

4. Type a name for the target. The name doesn't have to be long, but it must be different from the name of any other target in the file.

11

FIGURE 11.2.

Targets are most useful in long Web pages logically divided up into sections.

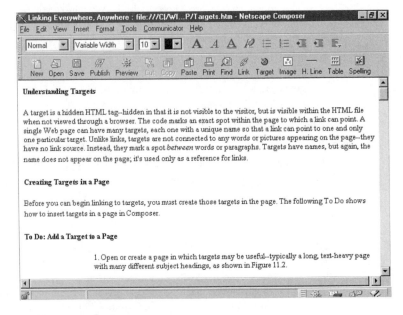

FIGURE 11.3.

The Target Properties dialog box.

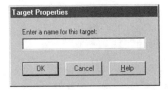

To create the target name automatically out of existing text, highlight the text before opening the Target Properties dialog box. The text will appear in the dialog box as the name, and the target will be positioned immediately following the selected text.

This is a very effective technique to use when targets are associated with headings in a page. Use the heading text as the target name, and that will make creating the links (as you learn to do later in this hour) much easier.

5. Click OK. A target icon appears in the document, as shown in Figure 11.4, to show you where the target is. (The target icon is visible in Composer, but not through Navigator or any other browser.)

To delete a target, just click it to select it, then press Delete. The icon disappears from the page in Composer.

FIGURE 11.4.

The finished target, as seen through Composer. (The icon won't appear in the page when seen through a browser.)

Target Icons

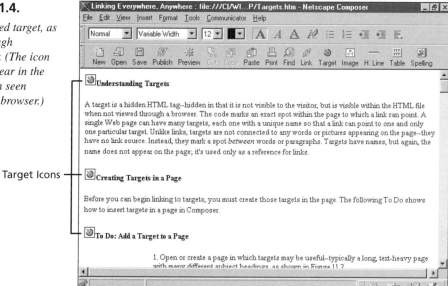

11

Linking to Targets

You can create two kinds of links that point to targets:

- A link within the same page as the target to which it points.
- A link in one page that points to a target in another page, either a page you created or another page online.

In the next two To Dos, you learn how to create both types of links. Following the To Dos, you discover some special steps for linking to pages that are not your own.

To Do: Link to targets in the same page

1. Create the page and insert its targets. Use meaningful target names to help you create the links.

2. Create the link source text for a link that will point to a target, and then select the text.

In Hour 14, "Adding Pictures and Picture Backgrounds," you'll learn not only how to add pictures to your pages, but also how to use a picture as a link source.

It's jumping ahead a little, therefore, to get into pictures here, but I should tell you now that links using any type of link source—text, pictures, or even multi-link imagemaps (see Hour 20,"Putting Multiple Links in One Picture")—can point to targets.

3. Click the Insert Link button on the Composition toolbar. The Link tab of the Character Properties dialog box opens.

4. Leave the Link to a Page Location or Local File box empty and click the radio button next to Current **P**age. A list of the target names in the current file appears, shown in the same order in which they appear in the document (see Figure 11.5).

FIGURE 11.5.

Composer lists the available targets in a page, so you can choose which one to link to.

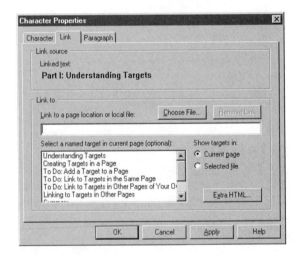

5. In the list, click the desired target. Its name appears in the Link to a Page Location or Local File box, preceded by a # (pound), as shown in Figure 11.6. Click OK.

6. To test the link, preview the page in Navigator.

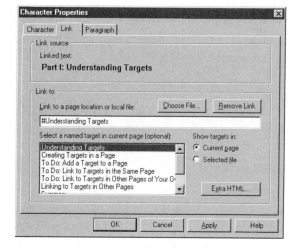

FIGURE 11.6.

The URL of a link to a target includes the target name preceded by a pound sign.

To Do: Link to targets in other pages of your own

To Do

1. Create the page containing the targets and insert its targets. Use meaningful target names to help you create the links.

2. Create the page containing the links, including the link sources you will use to point to targets. Store the page file in the same folder as the page containing the targets.

11

For the links to work, it's important that both the page containing the links and the page containing the targets are published in the same server directory online (see Hour 21, "Publishing Your Page").

3. Click the Insert Link button on the Composition toolbar. The Link tab of the Character Properties dialog box opens.

4. In Link to a Page Location or Local File box, enter the filename of the page containing the targets, and then click the radio button next to Selected File. A list of the target names in the selected file appears, shown in the same order in which they appear in the document.

5. Click the desired target. Its name appears in the Link to a Page Location or Local File box preceded by a pound sign. Click OK.

Linking to Targets in Other Pages Online

Although it can be done, it's a little tricky to create links to targets in a page that is not your own, but rather a page that's already online.

The best way to link to a target in other pages online is first to learn the target's exact URL, which is made up of the page's URL, a pound sign, and the target name (refer back to Figure 11.6). For example, the URL

```
http://www.test.com/sample.htm#target1
```

points to a target named `target1` in a page file called `sample.htm` on a server called `www.test.com`.

The easiest way to learn the URLs of targets in an online document is to browse to the document in Navigator and find the links in that document that point to the targets. When you point to a link (don't click), the status bar at the bottom of the Navigator window shows the full URL to which that link points—including the target.

Once you know the complete URL, you can create a link to it like any other link to a Web page, adding it to the Link to page location or local file box in the Link Properties tab. (You can ignore all the target stuff on the Link Properties tab; just enter the complete URL and target, and you're done.)

As always, when linking to pages that are not your own, you should email the Webmaster of the page to which you want to link and ask if it's OK.

Note that some Webmasters may say it's okay to link to the page, but not to targets within the page. This may happen when the page contains advertising or other information the Webmaster wants all visitors to see; linking to targets would allow them to bypass such stuff.

Summary

You probably won't use targets often; if you feel you need targets, you should first consider breaking up the page into several smaller pages. But when it makes sense to publish a lot of information in one file, targets help your visitors wade around in all that info conveniently.

Workshop

Q&A

Q   **Should I finish the rest of my page before adding targets to it? I'm wondering what happens to the targets if I do a lot of editing and formatting to the file after I've added them.**

A   In general, it makes sense to complete most other aspects of your page before adding targets. That way, the targets won't get all shuffled around to the wrong spots if you do heavy editing on the page later, such as adding, moving, or replacing large blocks of material.

However, note that most formatting activities don't hurt targets. If a block of text that includes a target has its font or alignment changed, for example, the target will still work (though the icon will appear to take on any alignment changes or indents you apply to the adjacent text).

Quiz

Take the following quiz to see how much you have learned.

11

Questions

1. True or False: Targets are tied to specific blocks of text or pictures, just like links.

2. What's another name for a target?

    a. Bullseye

    b. Public figure

    c. Anchor

    d. Buoy

Answers

1. False. Targets go between other objects in a page and do not require a "source" the way a link does.

2. (c)

Activity

Review any pages you've been working on. Consider whether any might best be reworked as pages containing targets. When online, pay special attention to any page containing targets (when you click a link and jump elsewhere in the same page, you've found 'em!). Why are targets used in the page? Do you think the targets are useful?

HOUR 12

Using Links to Build a Web Site

There are pages, and then there are *sites*—groups of pages linked together. (The term "Web site" is also used to refer to the server on which those pages are published; see Hour 21, "Publishing Your Page.")

Without carefully created links and targets, a set of Web pages is no site— it's just a bunch of individual, unrelated pages. Link those pages together in just the right way, and they become a cohesive site your visitors can explore to enjoy all that's offered on every page.

In this hour, you'll revisit the various ways a Web site can be structured (first introduced in Hour 1, "Understanding Web Authoring") and learn how and when to deploy each method in your own projects. At the end of the hour, you will be able to answer the following questions:

- How do I choose when and whether to build my site as a linear, hierarchical, Web, or other site structure?

- For each type of structure, what links (and sometimes targets) do I need to insert in order to link my pages together properly?

- What tips should I apply to make sure that my site is attractive, logical, and easy to use?

Building a Multi-Page Linear Site

In a multi-page linear site, the pages and links are set up in a way that encourages the reader to read a group of pages in a particular order, start to finish (see Figure 12.1).

This design makes sense when the content your site delivers is made up mostly of medium-sized blocks of text (around one screen) that should be read in a particular sequential order, beginning to end. (Some people call this structure "slide show" because the visitor steps through the pages in order, as in a slide show.)

FIGURE 12.1.

*The structure of a
multi-page linear site.*

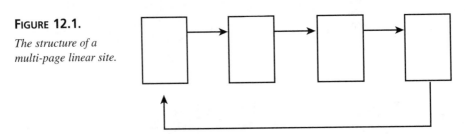

For example, suppose this book were converted into a Web site. Its "hours" serve the reader best when read in order because each chapter builds on material from the ones before it. So to encourage the reader to proceed in order, the site would be designed so that the natural flow from page to page (or hour to hour) follows the proper order. Other content that fits this design includes a story that's too long to fit on one page, or lengthy step-by-step instructions.

Each page in a multi-page linear site features a prominent link, often labeled "Next" or "Continue," that leads only to the next page in order. Other links may be offered as well, but be careful about offering too many links in such pages—they enable the reader to stray from the order, defeating the purpose of the design.

Tips for Multi-Page Linear Site Design

When developing a multi-page linear Web site, keep in mind the following tips for good design:

- Try to divide the material into pages on which there's just enough content (text and images) to fill the screen. Since the visitor is moving sequentially through the pages, he or she should not have to scroll, too. Putting just the right amount of text on each page enables visitors to conveniently explore the whole site just by clicking the "Next" link that you provide.

- A "Next" link on each page is the only link that's required, and often, the only one you'll want. However, if you can do so without cluttering up the design too much, it's nice to offer a "Back" link (pointing to the preceding page) on each page after the first so that the reader can review, if necessary. Also handy is a "Back to Start" link that points to the very first page, so that the reader can conveniently jump from any page to the beginning.

- The very last page in the order should always contain a link back to the very first page, even if you choose not to provide such a link elsewhere.

To Do: Create a simple multi-page linear site

1. Start a new page. If you want, add some sample text to it.

2. At the top of the page, type Next.

3. Apply the Heading 2 style to the Next (to make it big and bold) and give it right alignment (to position it in the upper-right corner of the page).

4. Save the new page as Page1.htm.

5. Choose File, Save As and save the file again as Page2.htm (a new page that's identical to Page1.htm).

6. Repeat step 5 to create Page3.htm, Page4.htm, and Page5.htm.

7. Open Page1.htm, select Next, and click the Insert Link button.

8. For the link URL, choose Page2.htm.

9. In Page2.htm, make Next link to Page3. In Page3.htm, make it link to Page4. In Page4.htm, make it link to Page5.

10. In Page5.htm, change the word "Next" to "Start Over." Then make Start Over link to Page1.htm.

11. Preview Page1.htm in Navigator. Use Next to step through the pages. Your basic five-page linear site is done. Fill in the pages any way you want to.

Working with One-Page Linear Pages

When 1) you have a lot of text to deliver, 2) that text is naturally divided into many small sections, and 3) you want to deliver it in an efficient way, a one-page linear design is a terrific (and often overlooked) approach (see Figure 12.2).

This structure is often applied to lengthy reference material provided as one part of a larger, multi-page site, but a well-designed one-pager can actually serve as your whole site.

FIGURE 12.2.

A sample one-page linear design.

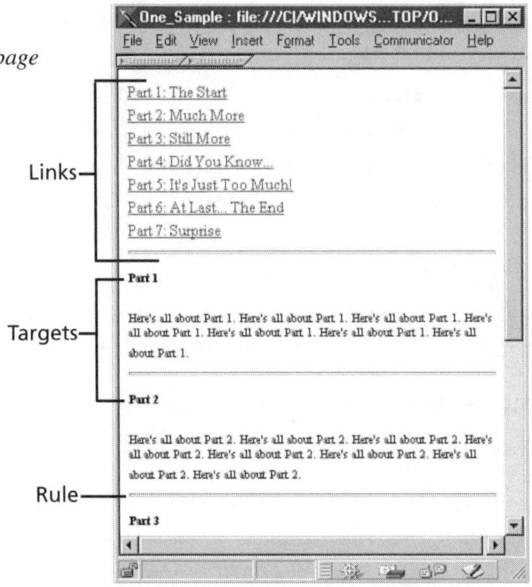

Links—

Targets—

Rule—

Readers can always scroll through the entire page, but typically, the very top of the page shows a list of links—a table of contents or index of sorts. Each link points to a target (see Hour 11, "Linking to an Exact Spot in a Page") somewhere down in the page. The links help readers quickly find particular information without having to scroll for it.

The longer the page and the more separate sections it has, the more important the table of links at the top.

If a page is only three or four screens long, the visitor can pretty easily explore it by scrolling. Five screens or longer, and you owe your visitors the assistance of some links.

Tips for One-Page Linear Design

When developing a one-page linear design, keep in mind the following tips for good design:

- At the very top of the page, or adjacent to the table of contents, insert a target. Between each logical section of the page, insert a "Back to Top" link that points to the target at the top. This enables the reader to conveniently return to the TOC after reading any section.

- Limit pictures (see Hour 14, "Adding Pictures and Picture Backgrounds"). The danger of this design is that the long page will contain so much data that it will take a long time to download to the visitor's browser. But text—even a lot of text—moves through the Net pretty quickly. So if you limit yourself to an image or two, usually at the top of the page, you can lend some visual interest while still enabling the page to download quickly.

- Scroll through the page. If the total page exceeds 15 screens, consider breaking it up into a hierarchical or multi-page sequential design.

- Use horizontal rules (see Hour 8, "Organizing Text with Tables and Rules") to divide sections of the text visually.

To Do: Create an indexed, one-page linear page

▼ To Do

1. Start with any practice page, preferably one with a lot of text. (You can make such a page by simply copying the text that's there over and over and over.)

2. Insert a horizontal line every two or three paragraphs.

3. Just above each horizontal line, insert a target. Name the targets Part1, Part2, and so on.

4. At the top of the page, create a list with the following text:

   Part 1

   Part 2

   Part 3

5. Highlight the top item in the list, "Part 1," and click the Insert Link button. Make the link point to the target with the matching name.

6. Repeat step 5 for Part 2 and Part 3.

▲ 7. Preview the page in Navigator and test the links.

12

Making a Web-Style Site

In a Web structure, anything goes (see Figure 12.3). Any page can link to any other page, or to all other pages. This structure makes sense when the various pages contain information that is related to information on other pages, but there's no logical order or sequence to that information.

In a Web-style site, there may be a "top" page provided as a starting point (as in a hierarchical site, described later in this hour), but from there, readers can wander around the site in no particular path. Web structures are best suited to fun, recreational subjects, or to subjects that defy any kind of sequential or hierarchical breakdown.

FIGURE 12.3.

A Web-style structure.

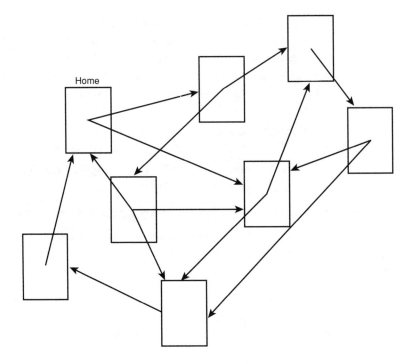

Typically, each page of a Web-style site contains a block of links—often in a column along one side of the page or in a block at the bottom—that lead to every other page in the site (see Figure 12.4).

Tips for Web-Style Design

When developing a Web-style site, keep in mind the following tips for good design:

- Before you resort to a Web structure, make sure your message really calls for one—you might just be having trouble recognizing the logical organization of your content.

- It's easy for visitors to get lost in a Web-style site. I recommend always including a "top" page that serves as an all-purpose starting point, then making sure every page in the site contains an easily identifiable link back to the top page. That way, lost visitors can easily get back to a landmark from which to set off down a new path.

FIGURE 12.4.

FIGURE 12.4.

Each page in a Web-style site typically contains a block of links to all other pages in the site, if there aren't too many.

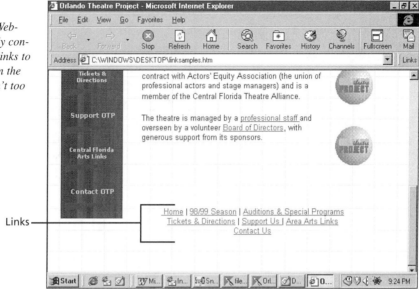

Links

Making a Hierarchical Site

The most well-organized design (see Figure 12.5), a hierarchical Web site, starts out with a general, "top" page which leads to several second-level pages containing more specific information. Each of these second-level pages leads to third-level pages containing more specific info about the second-level page to which they are linked, and so on, and so on.

The careful organization of a hierarchical site is not for the mere sake of neatness. The structure of the page actually helps the visitor find what he or she wants, especially when the site carries a lot of detailed information.

For example, suppose the site sells clothes, and I want a dress shirt. The top page might show links to Women's clothes and Men's clothes. I choose Men's and arrive at a second-level page offering links to shirts, pants, and shoes. I choose shirts, and I see a third-level page offering dress and casual. I choose dress, and I'm there. The structure of the page made my search easy, even though the site offers hundreds of items.

Tips for Hierarchical Design

When developing a hierarchical site, keep in mind the following tips for good design:

- As in a Web-style design, be sure that every page in the site contains an easily identifiable link back to the top page, so visitors can easily get back to the top without having to struggle up the hierarchy a level at a time.

12

FIGURE 12.5.

A hierarchical structure.

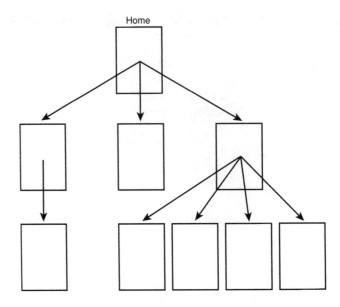

- More than with any other design, a hierarchical structure demands that you think and plan the content of each page and the organization of the pages very carefully so that the site flows logically. As with my shirt example, visitors should be able to drill intuitively down through the hierarchy to find specific information.

- Keep in mind that you have many levels available to you. Don't try to link the top page to a dozen second-level pages—doing so suggests you have not really figured out the organization. Ideally, each page should lead to no fewer than two pages and no more than seven or eight, in the level below it. Then again, don't follow arbitrary rules. Just be sure the page organization and the natural organization of the content match.

Summary

The organization of pages in a site is not really a Web-authoring challenge: It's a content-management issue. Understand exactly what you're trying to say and how to say it best, and the correct site structure will become immediately apparent to you. All that's left is adding some links (and maybe targets), and you know how to do that already, don't you?

Workshop

Q&A

Q **What if I'm planning to use some content that's naturally sequential, some that's naturally hierarchical, and some that's random? How do I make it all fit one model?**

A You don't have to. For more elaborate Web sites, a *hybrid* approach is called for.

A hybrid approach generally starts out hierarchical, with an overview top page to serve as a starting point. But at the second level, that top page might link down to a one-page linear, or to the top page of what will then spread out into a Web structure, or to the first page of a multi-page linear slide show, or to the top of a whole new hierarchy.

With a hybrid approach, you can make content at the second and lower levels conform to whatever structure suits it, while still using the top page to hold the whole affair neatly together.

Quiz

Take the following quiz to see how much you have learned.

Questions

1. At last, you've finished your children's story, and you want to put it online. The story has six short parts, each with an illustration. Which is the best design type for it?

    a.   one-page linear

    b.   multi-page linear

    c.   hierarchical

    d.   herbivorous

2. You want to publish a site about your team with a separate bio/photo page for each member: There's Phyllis, the president; under Phyllis, there are the three VPs; and under each VP, there are four drones. What's a good way to organize these 16 pages into a logical site?

    a.   one-page linear

    b.   multi-page linear

    c.   hierarchical

    d.   cantankerous

12

Answers

1. (b)

2. (c) Choice (a) might seem like a possibility, but the content contains too many photos to download promptly, and it also fails to reflect the team dynamics the way (c) does.

Activity

Stop looking at pages for awhile and look instead at sites. How are the sites you enjoy organized? Can you tell right away when you arrive at a site what its structure is? Can you tell from the type of content offered why the author chose to use the particular design he or she chose? And did he or she make the right choice?

PART IV

Adding Pizzazz with Multimedia

Hour

HOUR 13

Getting (or Making) Pictures for Your Page

In Hour 14, "Adding Pictures and Picture Backgrounds," you'll begin adding pictures to your page. But the trickiest part of adding pictures isn't the adding—it's getting the pictures in the first place, and getting them in the proper format. In this hour, you'll learn how, where, and why to get pictures for your page.

At the end of the hour, you will be able to answer the following questions:

- Where can I get pictures for my Web page?
- How can I create pictures of my own?
- What rules—file type, resolution, and other factors—must my picture files follow to appear in a Web page?

About Inline Images

Inline images are those that automatically appear within the layout of the page when the page is accessed by a graphical browser.

Don't confuse inline images with *external* media: images, video clips, sound clips, and most animations. These usually display or play only when the visitor activates a link; they're not part of the layout of the page. External media—including external images—are covered in Hour 15, "Snazzing Up with Sound and Video."

Computer image files come in many types. Common types include .pcx and .bmp files, which are used most often in Windows, and TIFF (.tif) files, which are often used on Macintoshes and in publishing. However, the most common type of image file used for inline images is GIF (pronounced *jif* and using the file extension .gif). The next most popular type is JPEG (with a .jpg file extension in most systems).

 Although images in file types other than GIF or JPEG are inappropriate for use as inline images, other file types can be used as external images (see Hour 15).

GIF files offer certain advantages (see the sections titled "Understanding Interlacing" and "Understanding Transparency" later in this hour), but they are limited to 256 colors (or 256 shades of gray in black-and-white images). For most graphics, especially those originally drawn on a computer, this "8-bit" color is plenty. But for photographs, paintings, and other images taken from life, 256 colors do not permit enough variation in color or shade to present a realistically shaded image; the results can look computerish.

However, GIF's 256-color limitation is not necessarily a big disadvantage. This is true for two reasons:

- Images in 16-bit color (65,000 colors) or 24-bit *true color* (16 million colors) tend to occupy much larger files than 256-color graphics—so much so that they might be inappropriate as inline images because they'll take too long to download to the visitor's browser. (See the section titled "File Size" later in this hour.)
- The majority of your audience will be running their browsers in 256-color mode anyway, which cannot display the extra color depth and detail possible in 16-bit and 24-bit color graphics. The picture will still show up, but it will look no better than a 256-color image.

However, if you want or need to display more than 256 colors or grays, a JPEG file can handle it.

All graphical Web browsers can display inline GIF images, and a few can display only GIF images. The most popular browsers—Navigator and Internet Explorer—can also display JPEG images. So all of your inline graphics should be GIF or JPEG files, and you should favor GIF when you have the choice.

Creating and Acquiring Image Files

Where can you get images? You can make (or acquire them) in the following ways. The important issue is not where they come from, but their file type, size, and other factors.

Often, the best way to get your images is to make them. Doing so is easier than you might think. If you can work a Web browser, you can use a draw or paint program:

Paint/Draw—You can use a paint or draw program to create your inline graphics. Ideally, the program should be able to save your picture as a GIF (or, optionally, JPEG) graphic. If not, you can *convert...*

Convert—If you have existing graphics you want to use in your page that are not in GIF or JPEG format, you can convert them to GIF or JPEG using a paint program or conversion utility.

> The software that comes with many scanners, digital cameras, and video capture devices can save images in GIF or JPEG format; when it cannot save in these formats, you can almost always save the file in TIFF format and then use another program such as Paint Shop Pro (included on the CD) to convert to GIF or JPEG.

Scan—Using a hand scanner, sheetfed scanner, or flatbed scanner, you can scan photographs or other images and save them (using the scanning software) as GIF or JPEG images.

Shoot—Using a digital camera or video capture device, you can capture an image from life.

Note, however, that you don't have to create your own images—you can pick up existing images for a wide range of purposes. Collections of *clip art* are available on the Web and in commercial and shareware software packages.

13

NEW TERM **Clip art.** Image files (and sometimes other kinds of media files, such as animations or sound clips) that you did not create but which are made available to you for use in your Web pages or other documents. Clip art libraries can be found on the Web bundled with some software packages and on CD or disk at your local software store.

As a rule, clip art is offered copyright-free, and you can use it any way you want. Some clip art collections are copyright-protected for some uses; be sure to read any copyright notices accompanying any clip art before you publish it in a Web page.

The CD-ROM includes a collection of clip art images for creating list bullets, bars, and backgrounds, which you learn to add in Hour 14.

Also, Appendix C, "Online Resources for Web Authors," shows the addresses of a variety of great clip art libraries online.

Clip art collections on the Web generally offer their wares by displaying the images in a Web page. You can copy these images directly from the Web page into your page using the steps shown in the following To Do.

To Do: Copy clip art from the Web into your page

1. Using Navigator as your browser, visit one of the clip art sites described in Appendix C.

2. Browse around the site until a picture you want to use appears on your screen.

3. Viewing the page in Navigator, right-click the desired image and choose Save Image As from the context menu, as shown in Figure 13.1. A Save As dialog box opens.

4. Save the file using the path and filename desired. (The image's current filename has been supplied for you, but you can change it. Do not change the extension, which informs browsers of the image's type.)

5. Switch to Composer and insert the image into your page as described in Hour 14.

You can use the same procedure to download any image you see in any page on the Web. But be careful not to download and publish copyrighted images.

Important Stuff to Know About Inline Images

Before inserting an image into your page, consider the following issues.

File Type

As a rule, try to use GIF files whenever possible. Doing so ensures that almost any visitor using a graphical browser can see the image.

When you want to publish a more photo-realistic image, or if you have a JPEG file you can't get converted to GIF, you can use a JPEG file as an inline image. If you do, be aware that you're hiding that picture from the folks using browsers that don't support JPEG (who are few).

FIGURE **13.1.**

*Clipping an image file
from the Web.*

With either GIF or JPEG, your image editor gives you a choice of color model and resolution. Choose RGB as the color model and 72 dpi as the resolution. These settings offer the best balance between appearance and file size.

File Size

In theory, it takes fewer than 10 seconds for a 20KB image file to travel from a server to a browser over a 28.8Kbps Internet connection. But a host of other factors affect the speed with which an image makes it to a visitor's optic nerve, including the disc access speed of the server, processor speed and available memory in the client PC, performance of the browser software, and multitasking speed.

Still, the one-second-per-2KB rule of thumb is a good way to estimate the speed with which your page will materialize on most visitors' screens. Given that, consider how long you want to make visitors wait to see your whole creation. Popular wisdom says a typical Web surfer won't wait even 30 seconds before moving on—and, of course, popular wisdom is usually wrong. Unless visitors are highly motivated, they might depart early if your page takes as few as 15 to 20 seconds to shape up.

13

Add up the size of your HTML file and all the inline images you plan to add to it. The recommended maximum is 30KB—such a page appears, images and all, in 30 seconds or less. Realistically, though, it's wise to try to keep the whole package to around 20KB (not counting images and other files supplied through external files, which you'll learn about in Hour 15).

The obvious solution is to use fewer images. Other than that, here are some ways to keep your page compact:

Use images that take up less area on the page—Smaller pictures generally mean smaller files.

Use fewer colors—When drawing or painting an image, use as few colors as you can to achieve the desired effect. When working with clip art or scanned images that contain many colors, use an image editor to reduce the number of colors or the size of the *color palette*. Most editors offer options for making color images black and white, or for posterizing a photograph to give it a graphical look. Either of these options tends to reduce file size dramatically and can result in some nifty effects.

Create text-only alternative Web pages—When your page is heavily graphical, create a second set of all pages beyond the top page, using the same general content but no graphics. On the top page, provide a link to this text-only version of your page. Visitors with text-only browsers and others who simply don't care to wait for images can use the text version instead.

Use thumbnails and external media—Instead of displaying large GIF or JPEG images inline, use inline thumbnails (see Figure 13.2) or text as link sources to external versions of the images. That way, visitors have the option of viewing or ignoring the images. Visitors wait more patiently for images they choose to view.

Copyrights

The ease with which images can be scanned, converted, copied, or even captured from the Web itself is a natural invitation to copyright infringement—and, in fact, the Web today is rampant with copyright violations. Smart authors are getting better about inserting copyright notices (see Figure 13.3) prominently on their pages to remind visitors that the work they see is not free for copying.

Regardless of whether it was accompanied by a copyright notice, do not publish any image unless

- You created it yourself by drawing or painting it or by photographing it with a digital camera. (Note however that publishing a photograph of copyrighted artwork—

such as a snapshot of a copyrighted painting in a museum—might violate the copyright.)

FIGURE **13.2.**

Thumbnails, small versions of images.

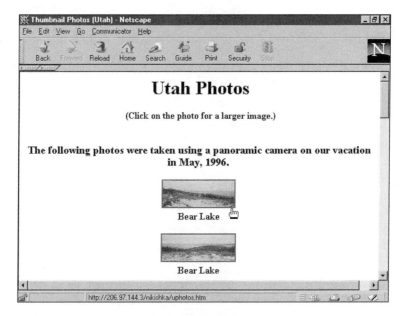

- You scanned it from artwork you created or artwork you know to be copyright free.
- You acquired it from a clip art collection whose copyright notice specifically calls the images contained therein "copyright-free" or states clearly that you are authorized to publish the images. (If the copyright notice requires that you label the image with information about its creator, do it.)

If you publish your own artwork on the Web, include on your page a link to a copyright notice in which you reserve the rights to your artwork.

13

Understanding Interlacing

Interlacing your GIF images is one way to speed up the apparent display of images on your page. Interlacing doesn't affect the final look of the image in your page at all and requires no changes to the steps used to insert or format the image in your page. But interlacing does change the way the image materializes on the screen in some browsers.

FIGURE 13.3.

A copyright notice on a clip art page.

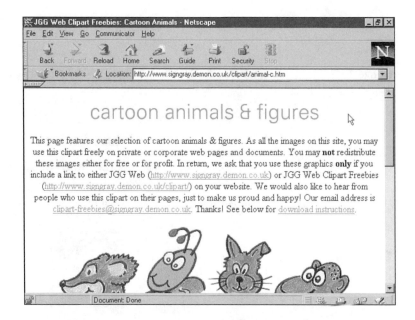

When it's retrieving a non-interlaced GIF image, a browser typically displays an image placeholder until the entire GIF image has been downloaded, and then it displays the image. If you save your GIF image in interlaced format, browsers that support interlacing can begin to display the image while downloading it. As the image is retrieved, it appears quickly as a blurry rendition of itself and then incrementally sharpens up as more of the image is retrieved.

Interlacing allows visitors to your page to get an idea of what your images look like before they've finished downloading. If the visitor sees what he or she needs to see before the image comes into focus, the visitor can move on without waiting for the finished graphic.

The program you use to create a GIF image might permit you to save the image either as an interlaced GIF or as a non-interlaced GIF. If the program saves only non-interlaced GIF files, you can use a program such as Paint Shop Pro to convert the file to an interlaced GIF.

In the section titled "Creating Images in Paint Shop Pro" later in this hour, you'll learn how to save a file in interlaced GIF format.

Understanding Low-Res Versions

Another way to give visitors something to look at before the graphics show up is to use your image editor to save an alternate version of the image in a very low resolution (and with a different name from the high-resolution version). You can then define the *low-resolution version* as the image alternative representation when choosing Image Properties for the high-resolution version (as described in Hour 14).

In browsers that support alternative representations, the low-res, alternative image displays first, and it appears quickly because decreasing resolution makes the image file smaller. Although the visitor examines the low-res version, Navigator loads the full resolution image in the background and prepares it for display. When the full resolution image is ready, it replaces the low resolution version on the page. Like interlacing GIF images, this technique allows visitors to get an idea of what the image represents well before the final image shows up. You can use low-res alternatives for both GIF and JPEG images.

Obviously, the larger the file size of your images, the more important interlacing and low-res alternatives become.

Understanding Transparency

In a GIF image, you have the option to make one color within the image *transparent*. In a Web page, the transparent parts of the image don't show, so whatever is behind the picture—usually a background color or pattern—shows through.

You'll have to deal with transparency more often than you might think. For example, when you paint a picture in most paint programs (including Paint Shop Pro), the file you create contains not only the parts you paint or draw, but also a white or colored background of a particular size. If you insert the picture in a Web page, the background shows up as a colored square or rectangle behind the parts you painted (see Figure 13.4). However, if you select the image's background color as the transparent color, the background square or rectangle is invisible in a Web page, allowing the page's background to show through.

Composer offers no built-in control of transparency; you must select the transparent color when you're creating or editing the image. In the next section, you'll learn how to create images in Paint Shop Pro, including how to choose the transparency color. Many other programs also let you select the GIF transparency color. If your favorite paint program does not, you can simply create an image in that program, then open it in Paint Shop Pro to choose the transparency color (see "Converting Other File Types to GIF or JPEG" later in this hour).

13

FIGURE 13.4.

In the bottom sample, the image background color is the GIF transparent color, so the page background shows through.

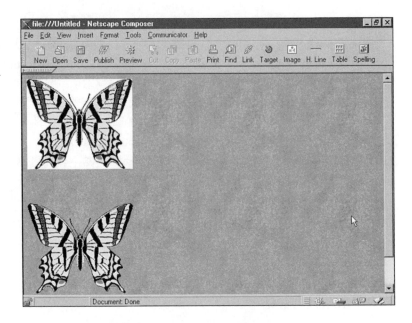

Creating Images in Paint Shop Pro

The CD-ROM bundled with this book includes a trial version of Paint Shop Pro, a full-featured paint program you can use to create, edit, and convert images for your Web pages.

In fact, Paint Shop Pro is so sophisticated that I could devote a whole book to it. But you and I have Web pages to write, and truthfully, if I just give you the basics to get you started, you'll discover the rest of Paint Shop Pro pretty easily on your own.

The next several pages explain the basics of using Paint Shop Pro to create, edit, and format images for use in Composer.

Creating and Editing an Image File

To create a new image, open Paint Shop Pro and start a new image file by clicking the New Image button on the toolbar or choosing **File**, **New**. The New Image dialog box opens, as shown in Figure 13.5.

In Paint Shop Pro, you don't choose the file type (GIF, JPEG, etc.) when creating the image, but when saving it.

In the dialog, the Width and Height fields define (in pixels) the width and height of the image you will create; you can edit these to your liking or ignore them and adjust the size of the image later. The Image Type drop-down list offers three choices—256 colors, 256 grays (grayscale), or 16.7 million colors. Choose 256 colors or 256 grays to create an 8-bit image. Steer clear of the other option (see the section titled "File Size" earlier in this hour).

Figure 13.5.

New Image dialog box.

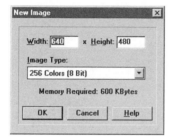

Note that after you've made your selections in Width, Height, and Image Type, the dialog reports the approximate size of the file in bytes (Memory Required).

After completing the New Image dialog box, click OK to begin painting. An empty window opens (see Figure 13.6), flanked by the toolboxes you will use to paint and edit your new image:

Select—This toolbox contains buttons for defining and selecting different areas of the image, and for choosing colors.

Paint—This toolbox contains buttons for selecting the tools you can use—a pen, paintbrush, chalk, and so on. Each tool creates a different effect when you use it, and you can apply any number of different tools to create a variety of effects within a single image.

To Do: Explore Paint Shop Pro

▼ To Do

The best way to learn Paint Shop Pro is to play around with it. To help you explore, here are a few steps you can try.

1. At the bottom of the Select toolbox, locate the overlapping squares for Foreground Color and Background Color. You can use as many different foreground colors in an image as you like, but just one background color.

2. Double-click the Foreground Color box. The dialog box shown in Figure 13.7 appears. Choose a color by clicking it and then click OK.

▼

13

FIGURE 13.6.

New Image window and toolboxes.

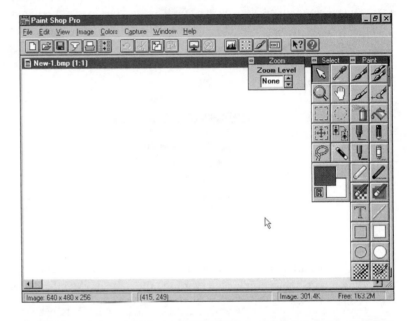

FIGURE 13.7.

Choosing a color to paint with.

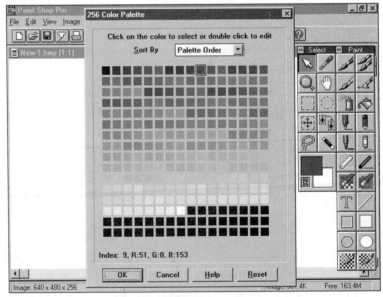

3. Now you'll choose a paint tool to apply the color you just selected. In the Paint toolbox, click the Rectangle button. The pointer becomes a rectangle.

> You operate all of Paint Shop Pro's shape tools—Rectangle, Filled Rectangle, Oval, and Filled Oval—in the same way: choose the tool, click and hold, then drag to define the shape.

4. Point to a spot in the empty window. Click and hold the mouse button, and drag. As you drag, a rectangle appears. By changing the distance and angle at which you drag, you can adjust the shape and size of the rectangle. When it appears as you want it, release the button. A rectangle appears, its outline the color you selected in step 2.

5. In the Paint toolbox, click the Color Chalk button. The pointer becomes a piece of chalk. Click and hold in the image area and move the mouse to draw a heavy, rough chalk line. Observe that you can draw right over the rectangle (see Figure 13.8).

6. Double-click the Foreground Color box again and choose a new color—one that's much lighter or darker than the one you've been using.

7. In the Paint toolbox, click the Flood Fill button. This tool fills up a selected shape with the current foreground color.

8. Click inside the rectangle. The rectangle is filled with color. (If your chalk line cuts across the rectangle, only the part of the rectangle marked off by the chalk line might be filled.)

Got the idea? Try out all of the paint tools, one by one, to see how each works. Try switching Foreground Colors between each tool selection to make your new work visible where it overlaps what you've already done. Then move on to the next section to learn how to add text to your images.

Making Text into Art

Art often includes words. Think of logos, for example. Look at the animated Netscape logo in the upper-right corner of the Navigator window. It blends text (a big N) and graphics into a single image.

When you need words in your art, you can use Paint Shop Pro's text tool (in the Paint toolbox). First, choose a foreground color for the text. Then click the Text tool in the Paint toolbox. The pointer becomes a T.

13

FIGURE **13.8.**

Learning to paint.

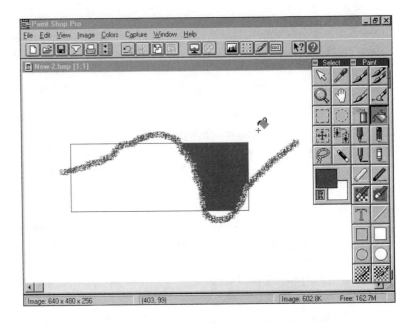

 If you make pictures out of words that matter, be sure to provide the same text elsewhere in non-graphical form (for the graphics-impaired). Use an *alternative representation* (see Hour 14) or repeat the text nearby on the page.

Click the spot in the image where you want the text to appear. The Add Text dialog box appears (see Figure 13.9). In the dialog, you can format the text in familiar ways (font, size, style) and in a few unique ways (adding a shadow or rotating the text 90 degrees).

After choosing any text formatting, type your text (it appears as you type it at the bottom of the Add Text dialog box). When you're finished, click OK. The text appears in the image.

 Although the feature is called "Add Text," and although you deal with the text in Paint Shop Pro like any other text, it's important to understand that the "text" you've added is really just part of the image file that looks like text—it's not really text at all.

That sounds like a semantic distinction, but it's important. In non-graphical browsers (and browsers with image loading disabled), the "text" in an image is not displayed, just like the rest of the image.

FIGURE 13.9.

Adding text.

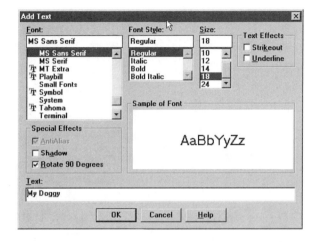

To Do: Saving an image and choosing its file type

When you first save an image in Paint Shop Pro, you choose its file type (GIF or JPEG for our purposes). To save, click the Save button or choose **F**ile, **S**ave. The Save As dialog box appears (see Figure 13.10).

1. In the Save As dialog box, type a name for the image in the File Name box. Do not type a filename extension (such as .jpg); that will be added automatically in step 2.

2. Drop down the List Files of Type list and choose GIF or JPG from the list. Observe that the appropriate filename extension is added automatically to the filename.

3. If necessary, use the Drives and Directories boxes to specify a location in which to save the file.

4. Click OK.

It's smart to store the image files for a page in the same folder in which you will store and edit the page itself (before publishing it on a server). You can save yourself a few steps by simply saving a new image in that folder from the start.

13

FIGURE 13.10.

Saving a file.

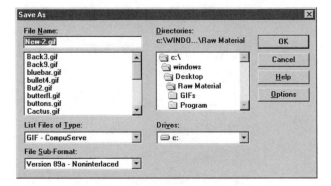

Choosing GIF Interlacing and Transparency Options

When saving a GIF file, you have the option to save it as an interlaced GIF file, and you can set the transparency options. (See "Understanding Interlacing" and "Understanding Transparency" earlier in this hour.) Note that the options below are only available after you have used the List Files of Type list in the Save As dialog box to indicate that the file type is GIF.

To save an interlaced GIF, drop down the File Sub-Format list in the Save As dialog box (refer to Figure 13.10) and choose Version 89a-Interlaced.

The GIF transparency options are available only if the entry in File Sub-Format (in the Save As dialog box) is 89a (either interlaced or non-interlaced). GIF sub-type 87a does not support transparency.

To choose transparency options, click the Options button in the Save As dialog box. The GIF Transparency Options dialog box opens, as shown in Figure 13.11. The options include:

Maintain Original File's Transparency Information—Use this option to preserve the transparency settings in clip art or another image you did not create.

Do Not Save Any Transparency Information—Makes no color in the image transparent; all colors show.

Set the Transparency Value to the Background Color—Automatically determines the current background color and sets the transparency color to match, so that the image background does not show. Use this option to omit backgrounds from images.

If you plan to make the background color transparent, never use that color in the foreground. Areas of the foreground using the same color as the background will be made transparent as well. (Of course, you can choose to make parts of the foreground transparent to achieve a special effect.)

FIGURE 13.11.

Choosing GIF transparency options in Paint Shop Pro.

> **GIF Transparency Options**
>
> ○ Maintain Original File's Transparency Information
> ○ Do Not Save Any Transparency Information
> ⦿ Set the Transparency Value to the Background Color
> ○ Set the Transparency Value to [0]
>
> [OK]
> [Cancel]
> [Help]

Converting Other File Types to GIF or JPEG

Sometimes, you'll have an image file you want to use that does not happen to be in GIF or JPEG format. Fortunately, most image editing software programs (including Paint Shop Pro) can convert many types of image files to GIF or JPEG.

If you choose to convert images, however, keep in mind that images often don't survive the conversion process unscathed. After conversion, they might require a little sizing, cropping, or other cleanup editing, or you might want to adjust GIF transparency or other options before pulling the file into Composer. In such cases, it's best to use your image editing program to convert and edit the image file, and then insert the finished file in Composer.

- To convert a file to GIF or JPEG with Paint Shop Pro, open the file for editing (choose File, Open). Edit the file as desired, then choose File, Save As to open the Save As dialog box. (Don't use the Save button on the toolbar or choose File, Save; doing so simply saves the file in its original file type.) On the Save As dialog, choose the new file type from the List Files of Type list.

- To convert a whole batch of files at once, choose File, Batch Conversion to open the Batch Conversion dialog box (see Figure 13.12). In the dialog box's Input section, you can select a range of files, then you can specify the new file type and other characteristics in the Output section. When you click OK, all of the selected files are converted.

13

FIGURE 13.12.

Converting files.

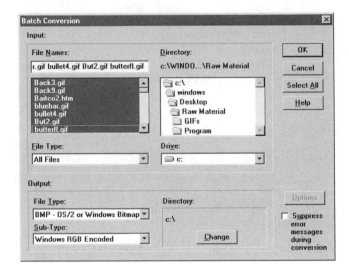

Summary

As you'll see in the next hour, getting your pictures into your pages is pretty simple. Nearly everything that can go wrong with pictures happens because there's something wrong with the file—wrong type, wrong size, and so on. But that won't happen to you now that you know the rules.

Workshop

Quiz

Take the following quiz to see how much you have learned.

Questions

1. Which of the following is best to use inline in your Web page?
   a. A 120KB GIF image
   b. A 15KB JPEG image
   c. A 15KB GIF image
   d. A true-color JPEG image

2. To make your GIF images seem to materialize more quickly, save them in _____ format.

    a. JPEG

    b. hi-color

    c. interfaced

    d. interlaced

3. True or False: Most folks online use browsers that can show both GIF and JPEG images inline.

Answers

1. (c) The other choices can be used inline but are better suited to be used as external media (see Hour 15).

2. (d)

3. True. Most folks use recent versions of Netscape Navigator or Internet Explorer, which both support both GIF and JPEG.

Activity

Start thinking in images. What pictures does your page need? Does it need any? After choosing what the pictures should be, start planning which you can borrow and which you must create.

13

HOUR 14

Adding Pictures and Picture Backgrounds

Pictures are like salt: Add the right amount in the right way, and your Web page becomes tastier—but add too much, and your visitors will wind up logging off the Internet to go get a soda.

In this hour, you'll learn not only how to add pictures (and picture backgrounds) to your pages and how to control the appearance of those pictures, but also how to use pictures wisely, for the best effects. At the end of the hour, you will be able to answer the following questions:

- How do I insert pictures into my Web pages?
- Can I control the alignment, spacing, and even the size of the pictures?
- How do I create "alternatives" to pictures, for those whose browsers can't display pix?
- How do I make a picture into a link?
- How do I add a background picture?
- Can I create fancy bullets for lists and snazzy horizontal lines, like those I saw in the Page Wizard pages (Hour 3, "Wizarding Up an Instant Web Page")?

Inserting a GIF or JPEG Picture in Composer

Before beginning the steps to insert a picture file in a Web page, first prepare your image file or files as discussed in Hour 13, "Getting (or Making) Pictures for Your Page."

Ideally, any image files should be stored in the same folder as the HTML file for the page in which they will appear. If images reside in other folders, disks, or directories, Composer can copy them automatically to the same directory. (See the section titled "Keeping Images and Pages Together" later in this hour.)

> In Web-authoring parlance, "picture," "graphic," and "image" all mean the same thing. Composer uses the term "image" most often, so I'll use that term most of the time, from here on out. But a picture is an image is a graphic is a rose; or rather, a rose is a rose is a rose, unless it's a picture of a rose, in which case it's also an image and a graphic.

To Do: Insert an image

Once your images are ready to go, insert them as follows:

1. Position the edit cursor in your page where you want to insert the image.
2. Click the Insert Image button on the toolbar or choose **I**nsert, **I**mage. The Image tab of the Image Properties dialog box opens, as shown in Figure 14.1.

FIGURE 14.1.

Image properties.

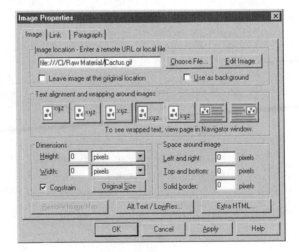

▼

3. In the Image Location box, enter the full path and filename of the image, or click Choose File to browse for it.

4. Click OK. The image appears in the page with no alternative representations, and

▲ with the default settings for Text alignment, Dimensions, and Space around image.

To change the properties for Alignment, Dimensions, and Space around an image, see the section titled "Formatting an Image," next in this hour. To create alternative representations, see the section titled "Creating Alternatives for Images."

Formatting an Image

You can change the way an inline image is displayed and treated in a variety of ways by using the Image tab of the Image Properties dialog box. It's possible to make these changes in the dialog box while inserting the image (see the preceding section), or you can open the Image tab of the Image Properties dialog box to format an image at any time by

- Double-clicking the image.
- Right-clicking the image and choosing Image Properties.

Changing Alignment

On the Image tab of the Image Properties dialog box, the row of buttons under Text Alignment enables you to choose how the image should be positioned relative to the adjacent text. You can position the text in five different ways to the right of the image. You can also wrap paragraphs around the image on either side of it.

To choose Alignment, click any of the seven alignment buttons. The choices (in button order, from left to right) are as follows:

- The first line of text goes to the right of the image, and any remaining text starts beneath the image. The top of the first line of text aligns with the top of the image (see Figure 14.2).

- The first line of text goes to the right of the image, and any remaining text starts beneath the image. The horizontal centerline of the first line of text aligns with the center of the image.

- The first line of text goes to the right of the image, and any remaining text starts beneath the image. The first line of text sits on top of the centerline of the image (see Figure 14.3).

14

FIGURE 14.2.

An image aligned by the first alignment button from the left.

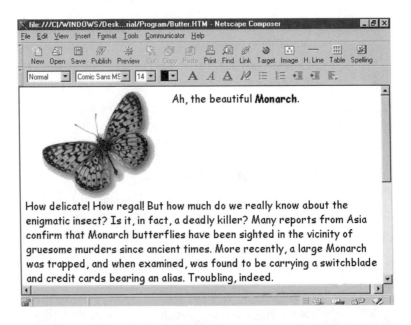

FIGURE 14.3.

An image aligned by the third alignment button from the left.

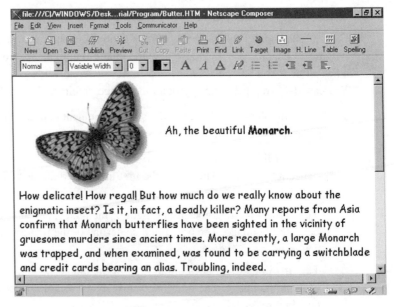

- The first line of text goes to the right of the image, and any remaining text starts beneath the image. The first line of text aligns with the bottom of the image (descenders in the text hang below the line).

- The first line of text goes to the right of the image, and any remaining text starts beneath the image. The first line of text, including descenders, sits above the bottom line of the image.

If you choose either of the two text-wrapping alignment buttons, you must browse the page to see the results. Text wrapping around an image does not display properly in Composer.

- Text wraps around the right side of the image. The first line of text starts directly above the image.
- Text wraps around the left side of the image. The first line of text starts directly above the image (see Figure 14.4).

FIGURE 14.4.

An image aligned by the alignment button farthest to the right.

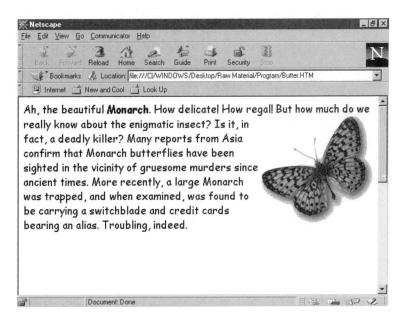

Changing the Dimensions of the Image

As a rule, images should be properly sized before you insert them. For example, you get better results if you size a new image in the application used to create it, or in a good image-editing program, than in Composer; see Hour 13. Scanned images come out best if size is determined in the scanning software before the scan even happens; after that, you're still better off sizing the image in the scanning software than in Composer.

14

Why? First, Composer can't really change the dimensions of an image. Instead, it applies tags to the HTML file that Netscape extension-compatible browsers use to resize the image when displaying it. A browser is not as sophisticated a graphics scaler as a real image-editing program, and the likelihood of unattractive "artifacts" in the scaled image (such as streaks through the image) is high.

However, the most important reason that using the Dimensions box in Image tab of the Image Properties dialog box is inadvisable is because the scaling relies on a Netscape extension. If you use dimensions to scale your image, the image will still appear in its original size in all graphical browsers that don't support Netscape extensions. On the other hand, if you scale the image in an image editor and leave the Dimensions box in Image Properties alone, the image will appear in the proper size in any graphical browser.

If you decide to change dimensions anyway, choose a height and width for the image in the Image Properties dialog box. You can choose the height and width either in pixels or by the percentage of the window size. The default you see when you first open the Image Properties dialog box is the image's original size (in pixels).

You can restore the image's original size at any time by clicking Original Size.

> When you're changing the dimensions, you might accidentally stretch out the image vertically or horizontally by failing to maintain the correct ratio between height and width. To avoid this, check the Constrain check box. Composer will automatically maintain the image's original aspect ratio.

Changing Spacing and Adding Borders

In the Space Around Image section of the Image tab (of the Image Properties dialog, of course), you can add extra space all around the image, just on the sides, or just on the top and bottom. You can also add a black border all around the image, and choose the border's width (in pixels).

Note that there's a reasonable amount of space around the image even when the default choices in these fields—0 pixels for space and 0 for border (no border)—are selected. Take a look back at Figure 14.4. The image in that picture uses the default selections for spacing around and does not butt hard against the text. The following are the spacing and border options:

- To increase the space between the sides of the image and adjacent text, enter the number of pixels in **Left** and **Right**.

- To increase the space between the top and bottom of the image and adjacent text, enter the number of pixels in **T**op and Bottom.
- To add a black border all around the image (see Figure 14.5), enter a number of pixels for the thickness of the border in Solid **B**order.

FIGURE 14.5.

The same page shown in Figure 14.4, but with additional space around the image (30 pixels left and right) and a 4-pixel border indicated.

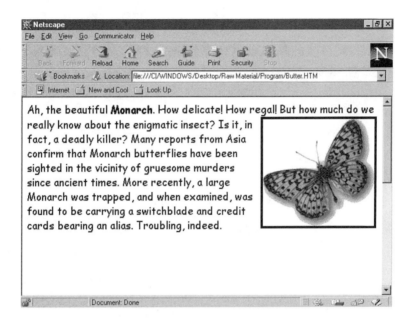

Keeping Images and Pages Together

You can check a check box labeled Keep Images with Page in the Publishing subcategory of the Composer category in Communicator's Preferences dialog box.

If you do so, images you insert in Composer are automatically copied to the same folder that holds the HTML file. The path to the file is automatically rephrased to match the file's new location. When you publish the page, Composer's one-button publishing (see Hour 21, "Publishing Your Page") automatically uploads the image files to the same server directory as the one on which the HTML file is published. It's a handy feature that helps you keep your HTML files and their images together.

If you have checked the Keep Images with Page check box, but do not want a particular image you're inserting to be copied to the HTML file's folder, check the check box next to Leave Image at the Original Location on the Image tab. The image will not be copied.

14

If you want to use the same image multiple times in a page, you don't need multiple copies of the image. With one copy of the file available on the server, you can enter the same image filename in as many Image Properties dialogs as you want.

Creating Alternatives for Images

You can help some browsers cope with your images through two special options: alternative text and low-res versions. You can apply these options by clicking the Alt.Text/LowRes button on the Image tab of the Image Properties dialog box. When you do, the Alternate Image Properties dialog box opens (see Figure 14.6).

To apply either option, fill in the appropriate box (you can use both options together).

If you enter an empty string—two quotation marks together (" ")—as the text alternative, text-only browsers display no text alternative, but they don't display an image placeholder either and will ignore the image entirely.

In the Alternate text box, you can enter the text you want to appear in place of the graphic in browsers that do not support graphics. Try to supply informative text to replace the idea that was originally communicated by the picture. Also, many browsers that support text alternatives will display an image placeholder, something like "*<image>*", if you don't supply a text alternative representation. The text alternative is not only more informative in such browsers, but also better looking.

In the Low resolution image box, enter the path and filename for a low-resolution version of the image. (You can also click Choose File to browse for the low-res version.)

Editing Images

The Edit Image button on the Image tab of the Image Properties dialog box opens the image editor defined in the Composer category of Communicator Preferences (see Figure 14.7).

You can enter the path and filename of any image editor you like. Figure 14.7 shows the path and filename of Paint Shop Pro as installed by the CD-ROM. With this configuration, I can open the Image Properties for an image in a Composer page, click Edit Image, and be transported to Paint Shop Pro to edit the image.

FIGURE 14.6.

The Alternate Image Properties dialog box.

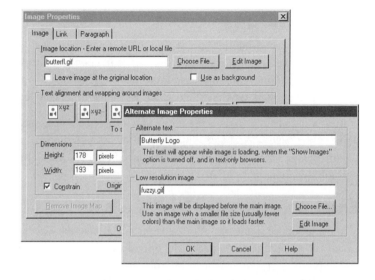

FIGURE 14.7.

Defining an image editor in Communicator Preferences.

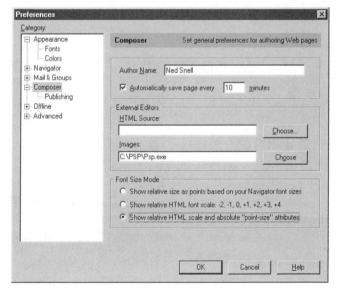

Deleting Images

To delete an image, click it once to highlight it and then press Delete or click the Cut button on the toolbar. Note that deleting an image merely removes it from the Web page—the file itself is not deleted; it remains on your hard disk to be used another time.

14

Moving Images

To move an image from one spot within the text and other page elements to another, you can simply delete it in one spot and re-insert it in another. However, you can also use drag and drop to move an image. Point to the image so that the pointer becomes the "grab" hand pointer, click and hold, drag the image to its new location, and release.

Note that drag and drop does not allow you to precisely drop the image at any precise point on the page; the regular limitations of positioning images still apply. You can move the image, for example, from a position preceding a text block or other image to a position following that page element.

Entering Images in Table Cells

You put an image in a table cell (see Hour 8, "Organizing Text with Tables and Rules") exactly as you put one in a page. The only difference is that you must first click in the cell to position the edit cursor there. You can then click the Insert Image button on the Composition toolbar and use the Image Properties dialog box to select and format a GIF or JPEG image file.

If the image is larger than the cell in which it is inserted, the cell expands (as does its row and column) to accommodate the image. If an image does not fill a cell completely, you can enter some text in the same cell and align it to the image using the options in the Image Properties dialog box.

Making Fancy Bullets and Rules

If you've seen the pages created by the Netscape Page Wizard (see Hour 3, "Wizarding Up an Instant Web Page") or some other highfalutin' pages, you might have seen cool, multicolored graphical bullets and horizontal lines (see Figure 14.8). These are not actual bullets and lines of the kind you create with the Unnumbered List property and Insert Horizontal Line. Instead, they're inline images that *look* like bullets and lines.

Line-type images, sometimes called *bars,* are simply inserted between paragraphs. The bullets are inserted before individual lines of text, using any paragraph style other than List. (If you use List, you get your cool bullets plus the List's bullets or numbers. Icky.) To get the best results when inserting a bullet image next to a line of text, choose the second button from the left under Text alignment in the Image tab of the Image Properties dialog box.

FIGURE 14.8.

Fancy bullets and rules.

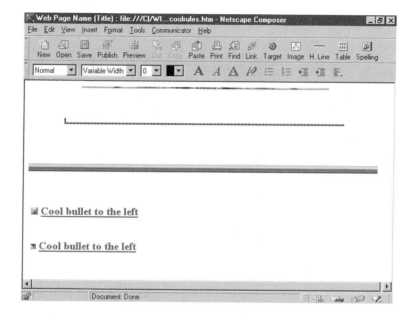

You'll find a great selection of GIF image files for fancy bullets and rules on the CD-ROM at the back of this book. See Appendix D, "What's on the CD-ROM?"

Using an Image as a Link

As you learned in Hour 9, "Understanding Links," every link has two parts: the link source (the thing a visitor sees and clicks) and the URL (or local path and filename) to which Navigator points when the link source is clicked. Making a picture into a link is just a matter of attaching the URL to the picture.

To Do: Make a picture link

When you make an image into a link, all you're really doing is using the image as the link source instead of text. To do that,

1. Insert the image into the page, as described earlier in this hour (in "Inserting a GIF or JPEG Image in Composer"), and format it as desired.

2. Right-click the image and choose Create Link Using Selected from the context menu. (Alternatively, you can double-click the image to open its Image Properties dialog box, and then select that dialog's Link tab. The Link tab of the Image

To Do

14

▼   Properties dialog box opens (see Figure 14.9), showing the image's filename as the
            Link Source.

FIGURE 14.9.

*The Link tab of the
Image Properties dia-
log box, with an image
as the Link Source.*

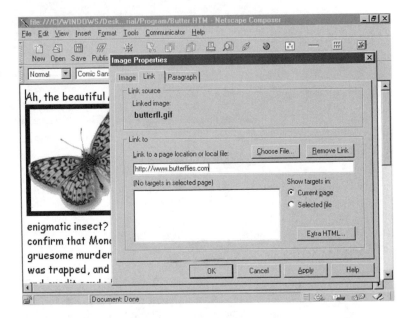

3. Enter a URL, local pathname, or target name in the Link to a Page Location or
▲   Local File text box, as described in Hour 10, "Making Links."

Adding a Picture Background

As an alternative to a background color, you can apply as a background a *tiled image*, an
image file (GIF or JPEG) repeated across the entire background.

When this image has been designed carefully to match up perfectly with its mates at all
four corners, the tiling creates a seamless "texture" effect, as if one enormous image covered the background (see Figure 14.10). Fortunately, the effect is created out of only one
small image; accessing an image file large enough to cover a page would choke most
Internet connections.

You'll find a selection of image files for background textures on the CD-
ROM at the back of this book (see Appendix D).

FIGURE **14.10.**

A tiled background texture.

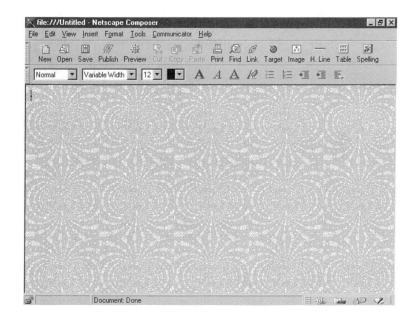

As an alternative to a background texture, you can choose to tile an image that doesn't match up perfectly with its copies at the edges. Using this technique, you can create some fun background effects, as shown in Figure 14.11.

FIGURE **14.11.**

A fun background made of a tiled image.

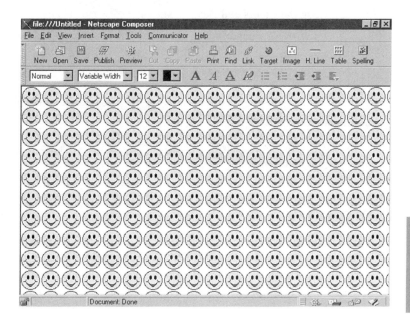

14

Finally, you can use as a background a single, large image file that covers the entire page background (and thus requires no tiling). But doing so is not advisable, since such a large image would take a very long time to download. Many visitors would jump to another page before your background ever showed up.

Be careful with backgrounds. If you don't choose carefully, you can wind up making your text illegible, or at least hard on the eyes.

Use custom text colors (see Hour 5, "Choosing a Title, Colors, and Other Page Properties") to contrast the text with the background. Use light colors to stand out against dark backgrounds, and dark colors to stand out against light backgrounds.

Even with those precautions, a tiled-image background is usually too much when seen behind a page with lots of text on it. A way around this is to use a snazzy tile background behind your logo or brief text on a top page, then switch to a solid color or no background on text-heavy pages to which the top page links.

To Do: Add a picture background

To Do

1. Open the Page Properties dialog box by choosing Format, Page Colors and Properties.

2. Click the Colors and Background tab.

3. Under Background Image, check the check box next to Use Image.

4. Enter the path and filename of the image to tile or click Choose File to browse for it.

Observe that a check box appears for Leave image at original location. This check box has the same effect as the one on the Image tab of the Image Properties dialog box—it prevents Composer from automatically copying the background image to the HTML file's folder if Composer's preferences are configured to keep images and HTML files together.

Summary

In the cookie that is a Web page, images are the chocolate chips. And as we all know, the best cookie strikes just the right chip-to-cookie ratio—too many chips is as bad as none at all. (Replace with your favorite ratio-balancing analogy: pizza crust:cheese, peanut butter:jelly, RAM:processor speed, longevity:fun, and so on.)

The issue is not just whether you use graphics, or how many you use, but *why* you use them. Do the images add something useful to your page—like photos of people the page is by or about, or images of products and places described—or are they mere decoration? An image or two added for the sake of style is worthwhile, but only if the image succeeds in actually enhancing style. If it seems like a generic image dropped there merely for the sake of having an image, dump it. Dress your page with careful text formatting, the natural beauty of solid organization, and strong writing.

Workshop

Q&A

Q You sure are a downer about images. But on the coolest, award-winning pages out there, I see lots of graphics. Aren't you being a little puritanical here?

A Perhaps—and yes, there are some great, highly graphical sites out there. But for every slickly produced, award-winning site, there are a hundred others that overuse pointless graphics or obliterate text with poorly chosen background textures. The award winners use all their graphics smartly, and to a purpose. My point is not to discourage the use of images. I just want you to ask yourself the right questions before dumping any old picture on your page. You can bet the award winners do.

Quiz

Take the following quiz to see how much you have learned.

Questions

1. When you use pictures, how can you make sure that visitors who can't display pictures (and those who have switched graphics off in their browsers) can still understand your page?

   a. You can't. Their tough luck.

   b. Use only JPEG pictures.

   c. Supply descriptive "alternative" text for all pictures you use.

   d. Any of the above.

2. The best place to scale an image (edit its size) is in:

   a. Composer (or another Web page editor)

   b. An image-editing program, such as Paint Shop Pro.

   c. Miami.

   d. The kitchen.

3. True or False: Most browsers can display picture backgrounds, but not all can.

14

Answers

1. (c)
2. (b)
3. True.

Activity

Now that you know how to add pictures, start putting more thought into *what* you want to show. Go through old family photos—any you should scan or have scanned for your personal home page? Look around you—see anything you'd like to photograph for your page?

Hour 15

Snazzing Up with Sound and Video

You might expect sound and video to be among the most challenging aspects of Web authoring. In truth, embedding such multimedia is usually a matter of inserting an ordinary link that points to a multimedia file; if you know how to make a link, you know how to embed multimedia (see Part III, "Linking to Stuff").

Your only responsibility is creating the link and getting your page and the multimedia file properly published on the server. After that, making multimedia work is the visitor's problem. If the file type the link points to can be played or displayed in the visitor's browser or in an associated helper program, the file works. If not, it doesn't. Either way, there's not much you can do about it other than trying to stick with the most widely supported file types.

However, that doesn't mean there's nothing to learn about adding such external media to your Web pages. At the end of this hour, you'll be able to answer the following questions:

- How does "external media" work and what can I do with it?
- What are the most common types of files offered as external media?
- How do I choose media types to serve either the widest possible Web audience or a targeted audience?
- How do I insert links to external media in my Web document?
- How do I present my links to external media in ways visitors will find attractive and functional?

About External Media

External media files do not display or play automatically when a visitor accesses a Web page; rather, they are downloaded to the visitor's PC and displayed or played there only when the visitor executes the link.

 External media. Media files—images, video clips, sound clips, documents, and so on—to which links in a Web page point.

Often, the browser does not play or display the file itself. Instead, a helper application (or, in Navigator's case, a plug-in) opens to do the job. Some browsers have native support for some types of files, but when the file is set up as external media, the effect is the same as if a helper application were used.

For example, Navigator has native support for JPEG image files; it can handle them either as inline or external media. But when a JPEG image is supplied as an external file, it has no home on the page—Navigator doesn't know where to put it. So despite its ability to display a JPEG image inline, Netscape always opens an empty window to show a JPEG image accessed as an external file (see Figure 15.1).

What if the visitor's browser has no native support and no helper application for a particular external media file? When the visitor clicks the link, the browser downloads and saves the file on a disk. That way, the visitor can install an appropriate application later to play the file offline. Because unplayable files are downloaded and saved, text-only browser users can still capture media files from the Web and then play them later in an application or a system that supports them.

Understanding Media Types

(Yes, I know, Dan Rather is a "Media Type"... but you won't learn about him here. Stay with me.)

FIGURE 15.1.

Viewing an external JPEG image through Navigator.

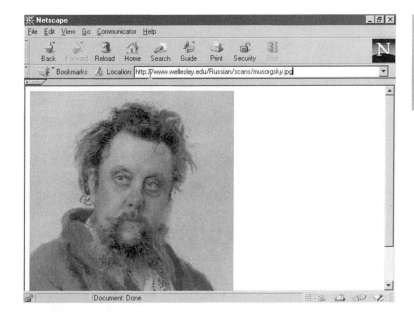

Using techniques for embedding external media, you can build links to any type of file, from video and sound clips to the dynamic link library (.dll) files used by Microsoft Golf.

You can help your visitors deal with whatever media you supply by including links to sites where they can download helper applications to play the files. See the section titled "Tips for Proper Presentation" later in this hour.

Although video and sound clips might be playable by the visitor, the .dll files from Golf are useless (except to Golf). The important question is not "What can I supply as external media?" but "What can the browsers and helper applications out there actually play or display?"

Unfortunately, there's a tendency for external media file types to be system-specific, or at least favored by certain systems. Some types of files will play only in Windows, others only in Macintosh, and so on. More commonly, a type of file will work across multiple systems but is favored by one system.

For example, Video for Windows (.avi) video clips play natively in Windows but require a special player on a Mac. When you're faced with a choice between formats that don't reach everyone, you have three options:

- Use the most widely supported format, even if it is not universally supported.
- Choose the file type most easily supported by your target audience. For example, professional graphic artists tend to use Macs. If your page and its external media files are aimed at that community, choose file types that favor the Mac.
- Offer multiple versions of your media files, each in a different format (see the section titled "Tips for Proper Presentation" later in this hours).

Finally, although inline images are lost on those using text-only browsers, keep in mind that the text-only crowd often can use external media. When a browser doesn't know how to display or play an external file, it simply downloads the file to disk and saves it. That gives the text-only visitor the ability to play or display that file outside the browser in a compatible application, or to copy the file to disk and take it to another computer properly equipped to display or play the file.

In the descriptions of the various types of external media, the standard file extension for each type is shown. These file types are extremely important because they help the browser determine which helper application (or internal program) to open to display or play the file.

If you publish an external media file and violate the extension conventions—for example, using an extension of `.vid` on an AVI video clip—the file will almost certainly fail to appear or play to visitors, although it will still be downloaded to the visitor's computer.

Images

As explained in Hour 13, "Getting (or Making) Pictures for Your Page," the main image file format for inline graphics in Web pages is GIF. Also appearing inline, but much less frequently than GIF, are JPEG graphics, which can look better than GIF images. Although GIF and JPEG images can be used inline, there's no reason why you can't offer them as external media instead; in fact, there are some good reasons to do so.

Suppose you had lots of graphics you wanted to show—for example, pictures of products you sell or head shots of your employees or family. Inserting many such images inline, even in GIF format, will dramatically increase the time required to transmit your full page to a visitor. The longer the page takes to shape up onscreen, the more likely a visitor is to jump elsewhere without fully appreciating your message. In such a case, consider using a minimum of inline images in a page that's compellingly organized and written. Then offer your images as external media, from a menu or from thumbnails (see the section titled "Tips for Proper Presentation" later in this hour).

15

Offering images as external media has other advantages as well. When you're using inline images but want to avoid building a page that takes a week to appear on the visitor's screen, you must compromise the appearance of the images by using few colors and by making the images fairly small (covering a small area).

When images are external, you can publish the highest quality images you want to—even full-screen, photorealistic, 24-bit color JPEG images. (True, when the visitor clicks the link to view such images, the wait for such a picture to appear can be long. But by the time a visitor chooses to see external media, he or she has already been pulled into your document and is much more likely to wait patiently.) Professional artists who publish their portfolios on the Web nearly always offer their work as external JPEGs so they can show the best.

Although GIF and JPEG are the only image formats supported inline, any other image format can be used externally. There is, however, one caveat: GIF and JPEG have been favored for a reason. They are broadly supported across the principal graphical systems—Windows, Macintosh, and X Window. Other image file types tend to be supported by applications on one or two systems but rarely on all three. So although you can offer these alternative image formats, you should convert these and publish them as GIF or JPEG files whenever possible:

Publisher's Paintbrush (PCX) and Windows Bitmap (BMP) (the principle graphics formats used in Windows (3.1, 95, NT, and 98): Graphics created in Windows 95's Paint program can be saved in either format. Any Windows-based graphical browser that uses helper applications can display external PCX and BMP files because Paint can be used as the helper. In the Mac world, there is some application support for PCX files but very little for BMP. As a rule, use PCX or BMP formats only when your intended audience includes only Windows users.

Tagged-Image File Format (TIF or TIFF): TIFF files are a longtime standard for scanned images, and most scanning software saves TIFF files (along with other formats). TIFF files are great for high-resolution images destined for printing but tend to be rather large as external media in comparison to other formats. TIFF files are used on all types of systems but are not widely supported by applications other than desktop publishing programs.

Macintosh Picture (PIC or PICT): A Macintosh picture file. The Mac has native support for PICT, so any Mac visitor to your page can display PICT files. But PICT support is rare beyond the Mac world.

XBM: An X Window bitmap image. X Window systems and most other graphical interfaces to UNIX environments have native support for XBM, so almost any visitor using a UNIX system with a graphical interface can display XBM files. However, XBM support is rare beyond the UNIX world.

Video

Three principal video file formats appear on the Web. Each offers acceptable video quality (by the standards of computer-based viewing), and all three can include audio with the video. MPEG offers the best overall quality, but MPEG files are generally larger than comparable files for similar clips in the other formats.

Video for Windows (AVI, or Audio-Video Interleave): AVI files, which include both picture and sound, are the standard for video clips in Windows 3.1 and Windows 95. Windows 95's Media Player applet has native support for AVI, whereas Windows 3.1 users must install a Video for Windows player to play AVI files. Mac users can install players for AVI as well (or use a browser that supplies native AVI support, such as Internet Explorer), but outside of the Windows world, MPEG and MOV files are supported far better.

Motion-Picture Experts Group (MPG, or MPEG): An independent standard for high-quality audio and video. An MPEG player is required on any system type (although upcoming advancements in Windows 95/NT and the Mac will soon permit MPEG to play natively on most computers). Because MPEG offers such high quality and because there are so many MPEG clips on the Web, most surfers interested in using video have installed an MPEG player.

QuickTime (QT or MOV): QuickTime is the Macintosh video standard, Apple's counterpart to Video for Windows. All Macs have native support for QuickTime, whereas users of other systems must install a player or plug-in (or use a browser that supplies native support). For example, Windows users can install a QuickTime player as a helper program or add an extension to Windows 95's Media Player that enables it to play QuickTime video files.

There is also Shockwave Director. Shockwave is a plug-in (available in versions for Navigator and Internet Explorer) that enables a browser to display multimedia content created with Macromedia's Director program. The Shockwave plug-in is free, so Director-based content is accessible to any Netscape or Internet Explorer user who bothers to download and install it. However, to create the content you must purchase Director, and often modifications must be made to the server on which you will publish.

Creating Director multimedia content for the Shockwave plug-in exceeds the scope of this book. To learn more about it, visit Macromedia's Web site at http://www.macromedia.com.

Audio

Audio is perhaps the most confusing area of Web multimedia. There are many formats now, and a few more emerge each year as developers try to improve the quality or download speed of audio information.

Although some browsers contain native support for some sound formats, the effect is the same as when a helper application is used. A pop-up window opens with controls for the sound, such as Play or Rewind:

Basic audio (AU or SND): The most common sound format, several browsers and most audio player helpers provide native support for Basic audio. Although Basic audio offers only so-so sound, its combination of wide support and relatively small file size make it the recommended media type except when high audio quality is required.

Windows Sound Clip (WAV): The sound clip standard for Windows (3.1, 95, 98, and NT). The audio quality is about the same as Basic audio, but the format is not well supported outside of Windows. WAV is best used for distributing sounds to Windows users.

RealAudio and TrueSpeech: These are two competing standards for realtime audio over the Web. What realtime means in this context is that audio data can play as it arrives at the client; the surfer needn't wait for the whole file to download before hearing it. As a result, much longer sound files can be published in these formats, including whole radio programs and live broadcasts. To supply RealAudio or TrueSpeech as external media on your Web page, you must set up special proprietary software on the Web server. Free players are available for these formats, but you must pay for the server.

To learn more about using RealAudio, TrueSpeech, and Shockwave, visit their home pages. The URLs appear in Appendix C, "Online Resources for Web Authors."

Other File Types

Although the principle use of the techniques described in this hour is to offer links to multimedia files through your Web pages, note that the steps described in the next section can be used to offer any file to your visitors. Again, supplying a file to visitors through an external link is always the same process, regardless of what the file contains. Your task is to determine whether your target audience has the appropriate hardware or software to use what you offer.

Some of the other file types commonly offered through the Web as external media include

Adobe Acrobat (PDF): Adobe Acrobat is an effort to create a cross-platform document format. A PDF file—including its fonts, formatting, and colors—is readable across many different systems, including Windows, Macintosh, and X Window.

Adobe PostScript (PS): Adobe's page description language, PostScript is used primarily for printed documents. Few people have the necessary viewers to read a PostScript file onscreen, but many—especially Mac users—have PostScript printers and can print PostScript files. PostScript is an excellent way to distribute manuals or books intended for printing.

Flat ASCII text (TXT): Not the prettiest way to offer information, but unquestionably the most widely supported. Everybody on the Net can read a text file. The only thing you have to worry about is whether your intended audience reads English.

To Do: Link to external media

To link to external media:

1. Prepare the external media file. Ideally, the file should share the same directory as the document file so that the link to it can be phrased as a relative pathname.

> When naming a file intended for use as external media, you must use the standard filename extension for the file's type. See the section titled "Understanding Media Types" earlier in this hour.

2. Create the link source in either of two ways:

   Compose text for the link source.

   Insert an image for the link source.

3. Select the link source (by highlighting the text or single-clicking the image).

▼ 4. Click the Link button on the Composition toolbar. The Link tab of the Character
Properties dialog box opens (see Figure 15.2). The selected link source is shown in
the upper half of the dialog.

15

FIGURE 15.2.

*Setting up a link to
external media.*

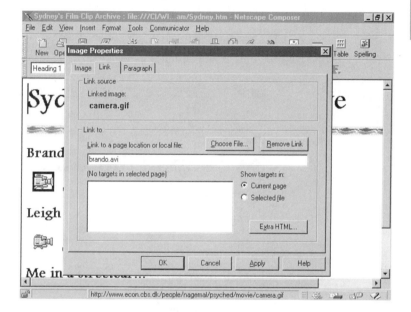

5. In Link to a Page Location or Local File, enter the full filename of the external
media file.

6. Click OK. The link is complete.

7. Click the Preview button on Composer's toolbar to see the document in Navigator.

8. Execute the link to make sure it and the file work properly in your Navigator configuration. That won't tell you whether the media will function properly in a different environment, but it's a start.

▲

Tips for Proper Presentation

As you can see, making the link to external media is simpler than creating or acquiring
the media file in the first place. But the secret to effective use of external media isn't setting up the link and file. The secret is presenting the link to external media in an attractive, inviting, and useful way.

The next few sections offer tips for properly presenting your external media.

Show File Type and Size

Whenever offering external media, always show the file type and its size (see Figure 15.3) as part of the link (or very close to it) so that visitors can make two decisions before clicking a link in your document:

- Do I have the necessary software to play, display, or run a file of this type?
- Do I have the time and/or patience to download a file of this size?

FIGURE 15.3.

File type and size of an image linked to external media.

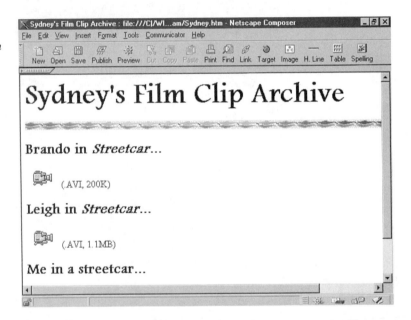

Keep in mind that many Web surfers today are still novices, especially when it comes to dealing with external media types. Configuring helper applications baffles many browser users, so they just don't do it. You can make your document newbie-friendly if, in addition to showing the file size and type, you

- Describe what the file type means and what's required to use the file. Don't just say the file is AVI; say the file is a Video for Windows (AVI) file, which requires Windows 95/98/NT, or a Video for Windows player in Windows 3.1 or Macintosh systems.
- Tell visitors where they can find the helper applications they need to play or display your file. If you know of a good source online, you can even provide a link to that source. That way, a visitor who wants to use your external media file but lacks the right software can jump to the helper application source, get the right helper,

15

and then return to your page. (The visitor can also download and save your external media file, go get the helper, and then play or display the file later, offline.)

• Offer media in multiple formats, as described later in this hour (see "Supply Media in Multiple Formats").

Use Descriptive Images as Link Sources

In addition to labeling a link to external media with its file type, it's a good idea to use an image that represents the file type as the link source. For example, a camera icon makes a great link source for any video clip. A sound-related icon, such as an ear or speaker, visually informs visitors that the link leads to a sound file. Note that using these images is not a replacement for properly labeling the link with text describing the file. For one thing, a little movie projector indicates a video clip but doesn't communicate whether that clip is an AVI, MPEG, or MOV file. Also, text descriptions are essential for the text-only crowd.

Remember: Under certain circumstances, text-only browser users can still use external media. If you use an image as a link source, be sure to provide a text link as well.

Show Inline Thumbnails for Large External Images

As I mentioned earlier in this hour, thumbnails are a great way to create meaningful link sources for external images. A thumbnail is a very small, low-resolution version of a larger image. The thumbnail appears on the page as an inline image and also serves as the link source to the larger, full-resolution image. Thumbnails provide visitors with a general sense of what the full image looks like, so they can decide whether to bother downloading it.

Using an editor or converter, you can create GIF thumbnails of JPEG images and use the GIFs inline as links to their external JPEG versions. This lets you exploit the wide support for inline GIFs when offering high-quality external JPEGs.

As with any link to external media, you must provide the file type and size along with the thumbnail. If a group of thumbnails all link to files of the same type and of about the same size, you can describe the files once for the group, as shown in Figure 15.4.

FIGURE 15.4.

Thumbnails linked to larger JPEG images.

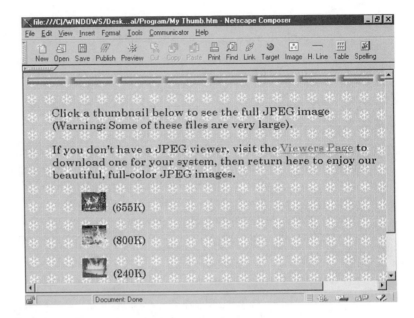

Supply Media in Multiple Formats

You can convert images between different file formats either by using image editing software or graphics converters. You can also convert video and sound file formats, although doing so is tricky and the converted versions are often inferior to the original. Still, to the extent that you can acquire or create multiple versions of an external media file, each in a different format, you expand the visitor's options.

For example, if you offer the same video clip in both MOV and AVI versions, you can rest assured that almost any Windows or Macintosh visitor can play it. If you offer an external image in both JPEG and GIF versions, you provide the higher image quality of JPEG to those who can display JPEG images, while still offering the GIF-only world something to look at. Figure 15.5 shows links to different formats of the same video clips.

Summary

Embedding external media files in Composer is a snap: Make sure the file is in the right place, build a link, and you're done. The only way you can blow it after that is if you forget to copy the media file to the server when you publish your page—and Composer can even make sure you get that right (see Hour 21, "Publishing Your Page").

Figure 15.5.

*Links to the same
video clip in differing
file formats.*

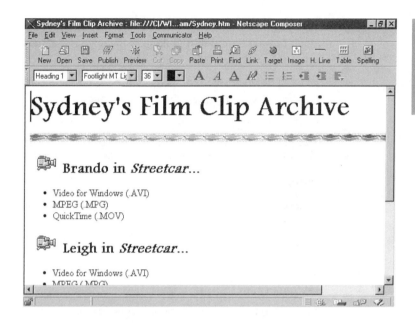

15

The tricky part is creating or choosing the right type of file to reach either the broadest possible audience or the specific audience you most want to reach. PCs are more common in homes than Macs, so if you're trying to reach homes, it helps to slant your file choices to whatever makes Windows happy. Many corporate users, especially those in engineering and technical departments, are on UNIX systems with X Window interfaces. Web authors often overlook the UNIX crowd when choosing media types. If your message is aimed at that crowd, try to aim your media files that way, too.

Workshop

Q&A

Q If a video clip or other file I like is already available through a link on another Web page, can I simply link to it instead of supplying my own file?

A Sure you can, and doing so is quite common. There are, however, a couple of rules:

First, as always, email the Webmaster of the site to which you will link and ask permission to link to the site and file.

Second, avoid linking directly to the file. Instead, link to the page on which the link appears. After all, the site providing the file is doing you a favor—the least you can do is give visitors a glimpse of the site's message before retrieving the link. Also, if the site is using the file in violation of a copyright (something that's difficult for you to find out), linking to the page rather than the file better insulates you from sharing the blame for the violation.

When you do create the link, you can use Composer's support for drag and drop or cut and paste to easily insert the link into your document.

Quiz

Take the following quiz to see how much you have learned.

Questions

1. Which of the following should always be offered as external media?

    a. JPEG images

    b. GIF images

    c. Video files

    d. Audio clips

2. Which of the following helps your visitors make the most of the external media you offer in your Web page?

    a. Thumbnails for large image files

    b. Links to player programs (helpers and plug-ins)

    c. Link source text telling the file size and type

    d. All of the above

3. True or False: Most people who surf the Web—no matter what type of computer they use—are equipped to play the most popular sound and video file formats.

Answers

1. (c) All other choices (even d) may sometimes be offered inline.

2. (d)

3. True

Activity

Review the media files and Web pages (including pictures) you're considering. Pick out the ones that can only be offered as external media. From the remaining files (those that can be offered either as inline or external media), are there some that would be best offered as external media?

Hour 16

Animating Pictures

Ever visit a Web page where you see a spinning logo, steam rising from a picture of a coffee cup, or graphical rules that flash, strobe, and dance? You may not have known it, but you were experiencing *animated GIFs*, a special kind of inline GIF image file that moves when viewed through a Web browser.

You're about to learn how easy it is to create these puppies all by yourself. At the end of this hour, you will be able to answer the following questions:

- What's an animated GIF?
- How do I create the various frames that serve as each step of the animation?
- How do I combine the frames into a single, animated file?
- How do I customize aspects of the way the animation plays, such as how quickly the animation flips through the frames?
- How do I insert an animated GIF into a page?

Animating Pages with Animated GIFs

Animated GIFs are exactly what they sound like: GIF images that move. Unlike other types of multimedia files discussed in this chapter, you can incorporate an animated GIF into the layout of a Web page and control its alignment, borders, and other formatting just like any other inline image (see Hour 14, "Adding Pictures and Picture Backgrounds").

But unlike a regular GIF file, an animated GIF can *move*—well, a little. An animated GIF is not a suitable vehicle for a Disney film. Rather, animated GIFs provide very short, simple animations that add a little zip to a page without slowing its download to a crawl. A candle flickers. A cartoon bomb explodes. A horizontal line flashes and undulates. This is the kind of stuff animated GIFs do best.

The hands in Figure 16.1 are an animated GIF; they clap. (I can't prove it on paper, but it's true.)

FIGURE **16.1.**

These hands clap (honest!).

To learn the addresses of some good clip art sites for animated GIFs, see Appendix C, "Online Resources for Web Authors."

To learn how to copy an image—even an animated GIF—from the Web to your PC, see Hour 13, "Getting (or Making) Pictures for Your Page."

The best way for beginning authors to get animated GIFs is to pick them up as clip art. Dozens of clip sites on the Web feature animated GIFs (see Figure 16.2); in fact, if you use the Netscape Page Wizard (see Hour 3, "Wizarding Up an Instant Web Page"), you can pick up some animated GIF bullets or rules as part of the page you create.

Composer features full WYSIWYG support for animated GIFs. They animate normally when viewed in the Composer window, so there's no need to browse the file to see the animation.

FIGURE 16.2.

Animated GIFs are easy to find online.

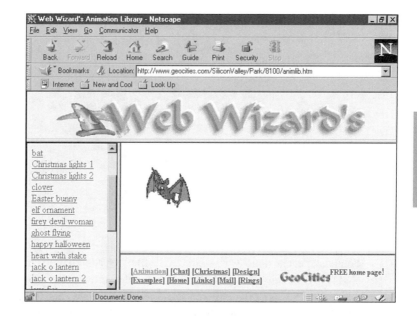

Inserting Animated GIFs Into Pages

Once you have an animated GIF file that you want to use, insert it in your Composer document just like any other inline image by using the Insert Image button or choosing Insert, Image.

After inserting the images, you treat animated GIFs like any other inline GIF image. Using the exact same techniques used for ordinary GIFs, you can:

- Position the GIF on the page
- Wrap text around the GIF
- Scale the GIF
- Add a border to the GIF

You make all of these changes using the Image Properties dialog box, which opens when you double-click the animated GIF image in your page. To learn more, review Hour 14.

Creating Animated GIFs

If you want to create your own animated GIFs, you have two major steps to perform. Although an animated GIF is a single file, it is made up of multiple *frames*, just like a piece of movie film.

Each frame is slightly different from the others (see Figure 16.3); when the frames appear in rapid sequence, the illusion of a single image in motion is created. (Most animated GIFs are made up of a dozen frames or fewer.)

FIGURE 16.3.

Like all animation, animated GIFs start out as a series of separate images, or frames.

The two steps in creating an animated GIF are

1. Creating the separate frames.
2. Combining the frames into one file.

You create each frame as a separate GIF file. For example, using Paint Shop Pro, you could create a single, static GIF image of a closed blossom. After saving that image, you could edit it to show the blossom opening slightly, then choose **F**ile, Save **A**s to save the edited version as a new file. You could continually edit and save new versions of the file to create a series of separate images that, viewed in sequence, would show the flower bloom.

An easy but effective technique is to use an animated GIF to make text appear little by little. For a company logo, for example, you can add a new letter of the company name with each frame or two. Now animated, the company name appears to write itself onscreen, one letter at a time.

To Do: Create a series of images for an animation

If you want a quick way to practice animation, create a series of images as described below, then combine those images into an animation as described later in this hour.

1. Open Paint Shop Pro (included on the CD).
2. Start a new image (choose File, New).
3. In the New Image dialog, enter `100` for Width and `100` for Height, to create a new image 100 pixels wide by 100 pixels high.
4. Choose File, Save As and save the blank image as `Name1.gif`. (This creates one blank frame to start off the animation, so the rest can pop into view.)
5. Click the Text tool in the Paint toolbar.
6. Click in the empty image area. The Add Text dialog opens, as shown in Figure 16.4.

7. Choose a fun font and a large size (18 points or larger).

8. In the box at the bottom of the dialog, type just the first letter of your name, and then click OK.

9. Click near the left edge of the image to insert the letter there.

10. Choose File, Save As and save the file as Name2.gif.

11. Repeat steps 6–10 for each letter of your name, each time adding the new letter to the right of the previous letter and saving the file with a higher number: Name3.gif, Name4.gif, and so on. When finished, you will have created a series of images like the one in Figure 16.5.

16

FIGURE 16.4.

Using Paint Shop Pro's Add Text dialog to build practice frames.

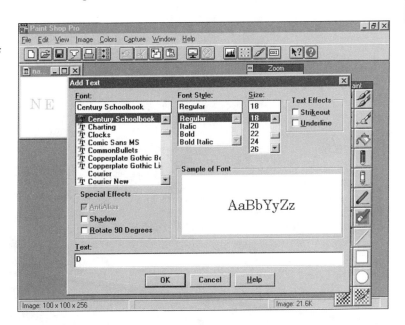

Turning Images into Animations

Once you've created the series of frames, you must combine them into a single type-89a GIF file. Doing so requires a special utility program.

One such program, GIF Construction Set 32, can be found at http://www.mindwork-shop.com/alchemy/alchemy.html. You can often acquire other such utilities from links on clip art sites that offer animated GIFs.

When you finish combining your GIF images with a utility program, you will have a single GIF 89a file that contains all of the frames within it. You can insert that file as an inline image in Composer, just as you would any other file (see Figure 16.6).

Figure 16.5.

A series of images like this one makes a great practice case for animating GIFs.

Figure 16.6.

Using GIF Construction Set to bundle multiple GIF images into one animated GIF file.

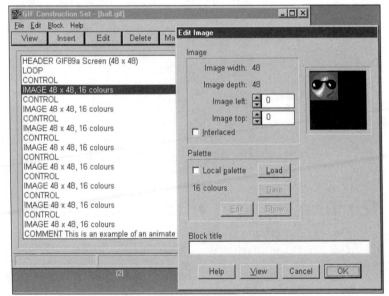

To Do: Combine GIF pictures into an animation

To Do

GIF Construction Set 32 includes a wizard which leads you through choosing the image files to use (and their order in the animation sequence), and other options for animated GIFs, such as whether the animation should play once and stop or play over and over again ("loop").

1. Begin by creating your series of frame images, as described earlier.

2. Open GIF Construction Set 32 (Programs, GIF Construction Set 32, GIF Construction Set 32), and choose File, Animation Wizard. The wizard opens and shows a Welcome screen.

3. Click Next. The wizard asks whether you want the animation for use on a Web page. Make sure the Yes option is selected, then click Next.

4. The wizard asks whether you want the animation to "loop" (play continuously, over and over, as long as the visitor views the page) or play once and stop. Make your choice, then click Next.

5. The next screen prompts for the type of GIF images you are using. Since you created them in a drawing program, choose Drawn and click Next.

6. The next screen (see Figure 16.7) prompts for the "delay" between frames. The higher the number you select, the more slowly the animation will move from frame to frame.

   To achieve the smoothest animation, you'll want a high number of frames (10 or so) and a short delay (1 hundredth of a second). When you have only a few frames, a short delay may make the animation whiz by too fast to see. As a good middle-ground for practice, choose 50 hundredths of a second (each frame displays for a half second before the next replaces it).

16

FIGURE 16.7.

GIF Construction Set's wizard lets you choose the speed of the animation.

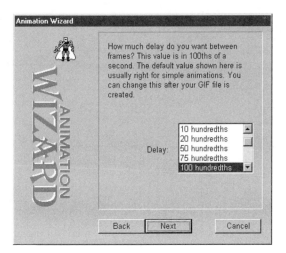

7. The next screen prompts you to select the frame files. Click the Select button and browse to the folder where the GIF files you create are stored. Select all of the frame files and click Next.

8. The wizard reports that it is ready to create the animation. Click Done.

9. The code for the animation you have just created appears in GIF Construction Set (see Figure 16.8). Choose File, Save to save your new animation.

10. Click the View button to watch your animation play.

> GIF Construction Set can do more than stitch your GIFs together. Using it, you can create animated banners from scratch, edit your animations, turn video clips into animated GIFs, and much more. Explore the program's menus and manual (Programs, GIF Construction Set 32, Documentation) to learn more.

FIGURE 16.8.

You can change your finished animation from within GIF Construction Set.

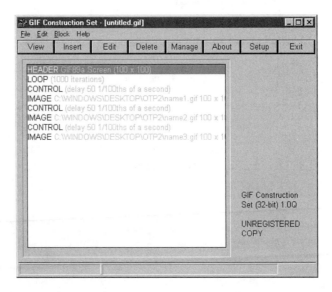

Summary

If you can make pictures, you can make an animated GIF. All it takes is creating a series of images, then binding them together. It's a fast, easy way to build action into a page.

Workshop

Q&A

Q **Do animated GIFs affect the download speed of a Web page?**

A An animated GIF is an image file, and because it contains multiple frames, it is a larger file than a similar non-animated GIF. As with any image, you must consider whether the effect of an animated GIF is worth the wait it can cause.

The major factors affecting the size (and thus the download time) of an animated GIF file are the number of frames it contains and the area it occupies (height pixels×width pixels). Try to limit area and frames while still creating an effective animation.

In addition to the extra download time, note that the animation can increase the memory demand and processor load in your visitor's browser. The impact is generally slight, but a visitor with an overburdened machine—for example, someone running Communicator on a 486 PC with only 8MB of memory—might see a significant performance degradation when viewing animated GIFs.

16

Quiz

Take the following quiz to see how much you have learned.

Questions

1. True or False: A finished, ready-to-use animated GIF is a collection of files.

2. Creating an animated GIF typically requires which two programs?

    a. One to create each frame as a separate image, and another to combine the frames into an animated GIF file.

    b. One to create each animation as a separate file, and another to combine the animations into an animated GIF file.

    c. One to create the animation, and another to destroy it.

    d. It's a trick question—you do it all in Composer.

Answers

1. False. An animated GIF is a single GIF file, although you do need multiple image files to create one.

2. (b)

Activity

Experiment with animation. Because animation is one of the trickier tasks for a new Web author, don't wait until you really need one to begin experimenting with them. Play around now, and when you really need one, you'll be ready.

PART V
Fine-Tuning Your Page

Hour

Hour 17

Editing HTML

The easiest way to create a Web page is to use a WYSIWYG editor—that's why I gave you Composer on the CD-ROM with this book, and that's why you've spent 16 hours with it. But no matter what editor Web authors use, they eventually reach a point where they want to do something the editor isn't equipped to do. To create forms and imagemaps and do several other advanced things in your Web page, you must move beyond Composer into the realm of the HTML source file itself.

This hour introduces you to HTML source files and how new tags and attributes are applied. Armed with that knowledge, you're ready to take on the three remaining hours in Part V, "Fine-Tuning Your Page," each of which shows another cool way to fine-tune your Web pages. At the end of the hour, you'll be able to answer the following questions:

- How can I read and understand an HTML source file?
- How do I insert HTML codes from within Composer?
- What other programs can I use to edit HTML source code?
- Can I configure Composer to automatically jump to my HTML editing tool when I need to edit the code directly?

How to Read an HTML File

Recall from Hour 1, "Understanding Web Authoring," that an HTML source file consists of four basic elements:

- The text to be displayed on the page
- The filenames of inline images
- The URLs or filenames for links (and the text or image filenames for the link source)
- HTML tags and attributes, which tell browsers which lines are images, links, headings, normal paragraphs, and so on

The best way to learn about HTML is to study HTML files and compare them with the output in a browser. Figure 17.1 shows a basic Web page displayed in Navigator, and Figure 17.2 shows the HTML source file for the page.

FIGURE 17.1.

A basic Web page, as interpreted by a browser.

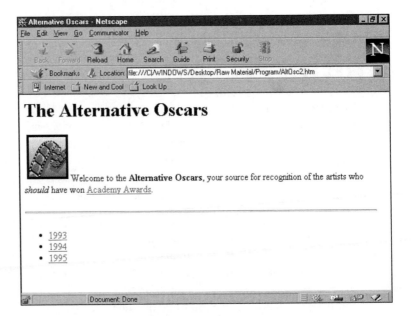

In Figure 17.2, notice that HTML tags are always enclosed within angle brackets (< >) and that each content element of the page—a paragraph or image filename—is surrounded by a pair of tags. Compare Figures 17.1 and 17.2 carefully, and you'll quickly see how HTML tags tell a browser what to do with the text and files that make up a Web page.

Most Web pages contain more elaborate coding than what you see in the example illustrated by Figures 17.1 and 17.2. However, this example contains all the basics and shows how HTML tags are applied. When you understand this example, you know enough to apply virtually any other HTML tag.

You can find a directory of HTML tags and attributes in Appendix B, "HTML Reference."

FIGURE 17.2.

The HTML source code for the Web page shown in Figure 17.1.

```
<HTML>
<HEAD>
    <META HTTP-EQUIV="Content-Type" CONTENT="text/html; charset=iso-8859-1">
    <META NAME="Author" CONTENT="Ned Snell">
    <META NAME="GENERATOR" CONTENT="Mozilla/4.0 [en] (Win95; I) [Netscape]">
    <TITLE>Alternative Oscars</TITLE>
</HEAD>
<BODY>

<H1>
The Alternative Oscars</H1>
<IMG SRC="movies.gif" HSPACE=4 VSPACE=4 BORDER=4 HEIGHT=66 WIDTH=64>Welcome
to the <B>Alternative Oscars</B>, your source for recognition of the artists
who <I>should</I> have won <A HREF="alum.gif">Academy Awards</A>.

<P>
<HR>
<UL>
<LI>
<A HREF="Awards93.HTM">1993</A></LI>

<LI>
<A HREF="Awards94.HTM">1994</A></LI>

<LI>
<A HREF="Awards95.HTM">1995</A></LI>
</UL>
```

While examining Figure 17.2, observe that you typically (but not always) need two HTML tags to identify a page element: one tag that has no slash (/) inside the first angle bracket and another that has a slash there. The no-slash version is used to mark the beginning of a page element, and the slash version (sometimes called the *close* tag) marks the end. For example, the tag <HTML> at the top of the file marks the very beginning of the entire HTML document, and the close tag </HTML> marks the end.

If you're wondering why you see some tags in uppercase letters and some in lowercase letters, see the "Q&A" section at the end of this hour.

Now take a look at how the tags, text, and filenames work together to build a page. Every HTML document begins with the following command:

`<HTML>`

This tells the browser that it's reading an HTML document and should interpret it as such. Typically (but not always), the next tag is the following:

`<HEAD>`

This informs the browser that what follows `<HEAD>` is header information. Information entered in the header does not display as part of the page but is important because it describes your document to the browser and to Web search engines and directories. The header portion of an HTML file created in Composer contains all the information you entered in Composer's Page Properties dialog. This includes not only such standard elements as the document title, but also header elements created by Netscape extensions. These are indicated with either of two tags, both of which contain text you entered on the General and Advanced tabs of the Document Properties dialog:

```
<META NAME=...>
<HTTP-EQUIV>
```

The next two tags, `<TITLE>` and `</TITLE>`, surround the text of the title. After the title and any other header lines, the `</HEAD>` tag informs the browser that the header is over. Next comes the body of the page, kicked off by the `<BODY>` tag. The body contains everything that displays on the page itself.

The first element of the body in Figure 17.2 is a heading. The heading tags are easy to remember: `<H1>` is a level 1 heading, `<H2>` is a level 2 heading, and so on. The first heading in the example is a level 1 heading:

`<H1>The Alternative Oscars</H1>`

Notice that the end of the heading is marked with `</H1>`.

The inline image (GIF file `movies.gif`) is indicated with the `<IMG SRC...>` tag, like this:

`<IMG SRC="movies.gif"...>`

Note that the image filename must be enclosed in quotes. In Figure 17.2, optional attributes for spacing, image dimensions, and a border around the image appear between the beginning of the `<IMG SRC...>` tag and the close angle bracket (>) that ends it. Attributes are always optional and go inside the tag itself (between the angle brackets).

Observe that the <IMG SRC...> tag requires no close tag.

Immediately following the end of the <IMG SRC...> tag comes a normal text paragraph (beginning with Welcome). Note that no tag is required to identify it; any text in an HTML document is assumed to be a normal paragraph unless tags indicate otherwise. However, keep in mind that while entering normal text, you cannot simply type a carriage return to start a new paragraph. To break a paragraph and begin a new one, you must enter the new paragraph tag (<P>). It's proper to end a paragraph with a close paragraph tag (</P>), but doing so is not required.

Embedded within the normal paragraph, you can see a few more tags:

- The set <B> and </B> surrounding Alternative Oscars applies bold character formatting.
- The set <I> and </I> surrounding should applies italic character formatting.
- The tag beginning with <A HREF... creates a link to another page, using the text Academy Awards as the link source. In the link, the <A HREF= portion indicates that, when activated by a reader, the link should open the file or URL named in quotes. The text between the close angle bracket following the filename and the close tag </A> is the text that is displayed in the page as the link source.

Following the normal paragraph is a new paragraph tag that inserts a blank line before the horizontal line (<HR>) that follows. All by itself, the tag <HR> inserts a line; the width=100% is an attribute, one of Netscape's line properties extensions (see Hour 7, "Formatting Text").

The <UL> tag starts an unnumbered list. (Look for the </UL> tag that closes the list.) Each list item is surrounded by <LI> and </LI> and contains a link (<A HREF) to another page in the document.

At the bottom of the file, the </BODY> tag closes off the body, and the </HTML> tag indicates the end of the HTML document.

That's it. To learn more about the HTML source code of pages you've created in Composer or any page you see on the Web, follow the steps in the next section.

Hours 18–20 describe tags you might want to add with Insert, HTML Tag or with an HTML editor. In addition, Appendix B, "HTML Reference," describes all the tags and attributes you can apply.

17

Viewing the HTML Source Code of a Document

A great way to learn more about HTML is to study the source code for Web documents. You can study the source code for pages you view on the Web or look at the underlying source code for documents you create in Composer. You can even view the source code for a document you're editing, make a small change in Composer, and then view the source code again to see how the source file has been changed.

To view the HTML source for the current document from within either Navigator or Composer, choose View, Page Source.

Using Composer to Insert an HTML Tag

When you've built a document in Composer but need to add a tag here or there for which Composer offers no button or menu, Composer's Insert Tag function allows you to do so conveniently, without having to exit Composer and edit the document in another program.

In Composer, Insert, HTML Tag can be used to insert any HTML tag—even those that Composer inserts automatically when you apply properties to text or an image. However, it's wise to use Insert, HTML Tag only for tags not supported by another menu item or button in Composer.

The reason isn't just convenience. When you use Insert, HTML Tag, the results are displayed as a tag icon in the document instead of displaying in the Composer window as they would through a browser; you do not get WYSIWYG results with Insert, HTML Tag, even when the tag you insert applies formatting that Composer can display.

For example, if you click the Insert Horiz. Line button, a line is displayed in the document in the Composer window (just as it would display in the browser), and an <HR> tag is added to the HTML source file. But if you use Insert, HTML Tag to insert the <HR> tag, a tag icon is displayed in the Composer window, not a line, even though the same <HR> tag has been added to the HTML source. To see the line you've created (instead of the tag icon), you must switch to the browser.

In the example that follows, you insert the horizontal line tag (<HR>), which is supported by Composer's buttons and menus. The <HR> tag is used in the example only to provide an easy-to-follow test case without introducing a tag not yet covered in this book.

To Do: Insert a tag

To insert an HTML tag with Composer, follow these steps:

1. Position the edit cursor in the document at the spot where you want the tag to go.
2. Choose **I**nsert, **H**TML Tag. The HTML Tag dialog opens (see Figure 17.3).

> To edit a tag, double-click the tag icon. The HTML Tag dialog opens so you can edit the tag and verify your changes. To delete a tag, click it and press Delete.

FIGURE 17.3.

Inserting an HTML tag.

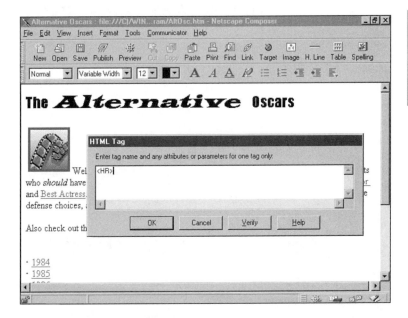

17

> The HTML Tag dialog supports long entries (by including scrollbars) not so you can enter multiple tags, but so you can enter a very long tag (one with many attributes or long text strings or paths inside it) if the need arises.

3. Type the complete text of your tag entry. Note that you can enter only a single tag this way (one set of angle brackets at the beginning and end).
4. Click **V**erify so Composer can check your tag for proper phrasing. If you've phrased the page correctly, nothing happens and you can continue. If you've made

▼   an error (for example, leaving the close angle bracket off the tag), an error message
    is displayed describing your mistake.

5. Click OK. A tag icon is displayed in the document at the spot where you positioned the edit cursor (see Figure 17.4). To see the effects of the tag, click the View
   in Browser button.

FIGURE 17.4.

The tag icon in
Composer.

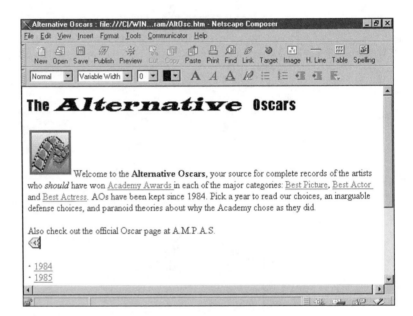

▲

Using Composer's Extra HTML Button
to Edit a Tag

When inserting or formatting an image, horizontal rule, or table, you'll see the Extra
HTML button (see Figure 17.5) in some of the dialogs you use in those tasks. The Extra
HTML button enables you to code attributes or other options manually into the HTML
tag controlled by the dialog.

However, the Extra HTML button has little immediate value when you're writing
HTML. For the most part, all optional attributes you might want to use are already available on the dialog. Also, the Extra HTML button enables you to insert any attributes or
other code between the tag and its close tag—for example, anywhere between <TABLE>
and </TABLE> when you click the Extra HTML button on the Insert Table dialog.
However, this method does not give you control of the position of the added attributes
among other attributes within the tags, and position is sometimes important.

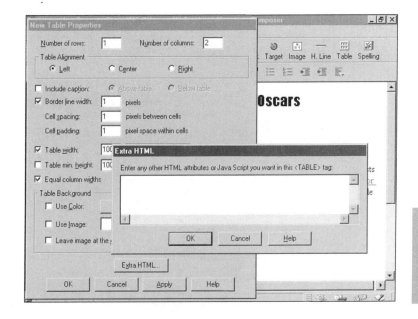

FIGURE 17.5.

Adding extra HTML.

Using an HTML Editor

Composer's Insert HTML Tag function is terrific for inserting a tag or two in a file, but for more serious work, you'll find it easier to open your HTML file in an HTML editor, perform any major work there, and return to Composer to finish up and fine-tune.

> Tags entered with another HTML editor are displayed in Composer in full WYSIWYG fashion unless they're tags Composer doesn't support. Unsupported tags show up in Composer as tag icons; their actions show up properly in the browser.

In principle, for your HTML editor you can use any program capable of saving flat ASCII text files. On a PC, Windows' Notepad program is ideal because it edits and saves *only* flat text files and it's small; it opens and closes quickly so you can get in, make your edits, and get out. Windows WordPad (see Figure 17.6) also works well for editing HTML, although when saving the file, you must be sure to choose Text document from the Save as **T**ype list on the Save dialog (and use the extension .htm or .html).

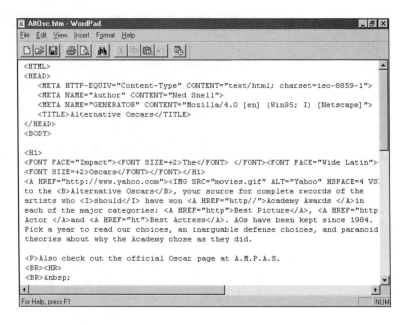

FIGURE 17.6.

*An HTML file in
WordPad.*

Although any text editor—including Simple Text for the Macintosh or Windows
Notepad—can be used to edit HTML, a text editor knows nothing about HTML, so it
can't give you any help. That's what makes actual non-WYSIWYG HTML source editors handy accessories to Netscape Communicator.

Although an HTML editor produces and edits simple text files like Notepad can, it also
offers menus and toolbar buttons to make entering tags more convenient and accurate.
For example, in a typical HTML editor, you might apply the tags for bold character formatting simply by highlighting text and then clicking a B button on the toolbar. Instead
of seeing the text turn bold (as you would in Composer), you'll see the bold tags (<B>,
</B>) display around the text.

There are many HTML editing utilities for Windows, including commercial, shareware,
and freeware examples you can find on the Web. (See Hour 24, "Developing Your
Authoring Skills.")

About HTML Assistant

The general-purpose HTML editor on the CD-ROM, HTML Assistant (see Figure 17.7),
is a shareware application that makes an excellent companion to Communicator because
it's good at doing things Composer won't, especially forms (see Hour 19, "Designing
Interactive Forms"). In HTML Assistant, you can define Navigator as the "test program"
for the files you edit (choose File, Set Test Program Name); after you do so, clicking

HTML Assistant's Test button opens Navigator to display the file you're editing as it would display in a browser compatible with Netscape extensions.

Although HTML Assistant gives you direct editing access to the HTML code, it's not a WYSIWYG environment like Composer. Still, HTML Assistant is more than just a text editor. As Figure 17.7 shows, HTML Assistant is well equipped with buttons and menu items for quickly applying tags to text.

Typically, you compose in HTML Assistant by typing only the text you want to display (or entering filenames for images or URLs for links), highlighting the text with your mouse, and then clicking a toolbar button to apply a set of tags to the selected text. The tags are displayed instantly in the document. For example, you could type a line of text, and then click a number (1–6) under Heading in the top toolbar to assign heading tags to the text.

Observe in Figure 17.7 that a Title button is displayed, so you can create the title from selected text. Note too that you needn't manually code such structure tags as <HTML>, <HEAD>, or <BODY>; HTML Assistant adds these automatically when you save the file.

> In Hour 24, you'll learn about other Web authoring environments, such as FrontPage, that you can add to your arsenal as your skills advance.

As a Communicator user, you'll typically create documents in Composer (to take advantage of Communicator's WYSIWYG capability as you work), switch to HTML Assistant to create forms or compose other code that's too complicated for Composer's simple Insert HTML dialog, and then you'll switch back to Composer to fine-tune. (You can make switching easy by defining HTML Assistant as your default HTML editor, as described in the next section titled "Setting Up an HTML Editor in Composer.")

Setting Up an HTML Editor in Composer

To make editing HTML source code convenient, configure an HTML source editor in the Composer category of Communicator's Preferences dialog (see Figure 17.8). The program you define opens automatically when you choose Edit, HTML Source in Composer.

FIGURE **17.7.**

*Raw HTML code edit-
ed in HTML Assistant.*

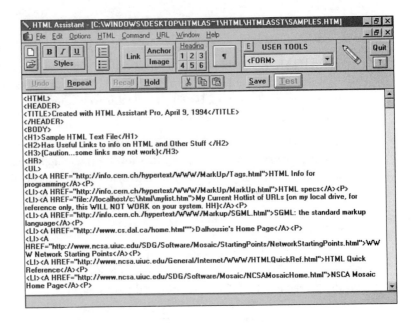

If you have not yet defined an HTML editor in the Preferences dialog when
you use **Edit, HTML Source**, an Open File dialog opens so you can browse for
and select a program file to use.

FIGURE **17.8.**

*Configuring an HTML
source editor in the
Composer category of
the Communicator
Preferences dialog.*

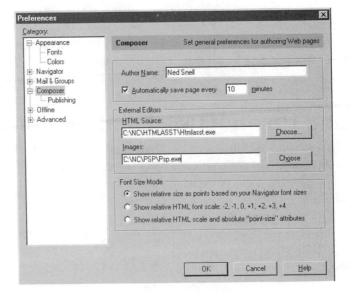

If you are in Composer when you open the Preferences dialog, it opens in the Composer category automatically.

1. Open the Preferences dialog by choosing **E**dit, **P**references; then click the Composer category.

2. Under External Editors, in the box for **HTML** source, enter the path and filename for your editing application (or click Choose File to browse for one). You can use any program you like: HTML Assistant, WordPad, another HTML editor, and so on.

3. Click OK.

Summary

Coding HTML is no great challenge. In fact, the beauty of HTML is that coding simple stuff—such as text paragraphs, links, and inline images—is actually simple, and coding more complex elements builds naturally on the skills required for the easy stuff.

As a Composer author, you won't spend much time coding the simple stuff because Composer offers buttons and menus for all of it. Instead, you'll lay out most of your document in Composer, and then use **I**nsert Tag or an HTML editor to code the rest.

Workshop

Q&A

Q I noticed in the HTML source code example (refer to Figure 17.2) that the lines of code in the header were indented. What does indenting do?

A Nothing. The indenting of blocks of HTML code has no effect on the display of the page. Authors (and Composer) indent portions of code to make the structure of the file easier to identify when a person reads it. Browsers don't care; they pay no attention to indents in HTML source code. So do whatever works best for you.

Q I've also noticed that tags are sometimes typed in uppercase letters (`<TITLE>`) and other times lowercase (`<title>`). Does it matter which I use?

A As a rule, type your tags in uppercase letters. You are not required to do so; browsers will correctly interpret the tags if they appear in lowercase. As you can see, if you use **V**iew, Page So**u**rce to see your own HTML code in Composer, Composer itself does not bother to use uppercase tags.

Uppercase is the accepted convention, and using uppercase tags can help you easily distinguish tags from content text in your document (unless, of course, your page content is in uppercase, too). If you add your own uppercase tags in a document otherwise created by Composer, you can also easily distinguish your own coding from Composer's, which could be helpful to you when trying to locate the source of a problem.

Q I've looked at the source for some pages on the Web, and I've seen lines of text preceded by a <!- tag. The text doesn't seem to be part of the header, but it is displayed nowhere in the browser view of the page. *Que pasa, mi amigo*?

A Any text preceded by <!- is a comment, a note inserted in the file to explain something to anyone who might read the HTML source code. Comments are inserted in all types of program code, including HTML, by programmers to help others (or the programmer himself) understand the code when reading it. Comments have no effect on the display or actions of the document, and the text within comments is hidden when the browser displays the document. (To add comments to your HTML source file, use Insert Tag or an HTML editor. Precede your comment with <!-, type anything you want, and then wrap up with a </!-.)

The HTML source example in this hour, shown in Figure 17.2, contains no comments because it was created by Composer, which does not automatically insert any comments. But you will see comments in other HTML source files you view. When you use Composer to view a file containing comments, those comments display as tag icons. When you view the file in the browser, the comments simply don't show.

Quiz

Take the following quiz to see how much you have learned.

Questions

1. If a section begins with the tag <BODY>, what tag marks its end?

    a. <BODY>

    b. <END>

    c. <FINITO>

    d. </BODY>

2. True or False: All tags require a companion close tag.

Answers

1. (d)

2. False. The <HR> tag, for example, inserts a rule and requires no close tag.

Activity

Examine the HTML source code of pages you've created in Composer. Read the tags and try to connect the menu and toolbar choices you've made to the HTML tags you were really creating.

17

HOUR **18**

Dividing a Page into Frames

Frames are simultaneously the best and worst thing to happen to the Web lately. If you've hit a frame-based document in your browsing, you know that they're cool. They make your display look like the control panel of a jet fighter—so many different, independent chunks of information stimulating your brain at once. It's like picture-in-picture on a new television for people with eyes so info-hungry that just one program—or one page—at a time provides inadequate sensory input. Of course, frames also greatly expand the author's ability to offer a variety of document navigation scenarios to visitors.

For all that excitement, frames make us pay. Frames generally slow down initial access to a page (because the browser must download multiple files), and when poorly designed, frames force visitors to do a lot of scrolling simply to read the contents of a single page.

The moral? Before cramming your document into frames, ask yourself three questions: "Are frames appropriate for the content I'm presenting?" "Can each portion of my content be effectively presented within the frame size I'm planning?" and "Do the advantages of frames presentation justify leaving behind the many Web surfers who can't see frames?" If the answer to all three questions is Yes, push ahead with frames. You'll find making them fun.

At the end of the hour, you'll be able to answer the following questions:

- How do I create the frame definition document, an HTML file that creates frames?
- Do I have to do anything special with each frame's contents?
- How do I create a complete frame-based Web page?
- How can I help visitors whose browsers cannot display frame-based documents?

What Does It Take to Make a Frame Document?

In a frame-based document, the content of each frame is contained in a separate HTML document (see Figure 18.1). The multiple documents are tied together by yet another HTML file, the *frame definition document*.

NEW TERM **Frame definition document.** A special HTML file that creates and controls a frame-based Web page. The file contains the filename of the HTML file that's to be displayed in each frame, plus tags dictating the number and size of the frames.

FIGURE 18.1.

A frame-based document.

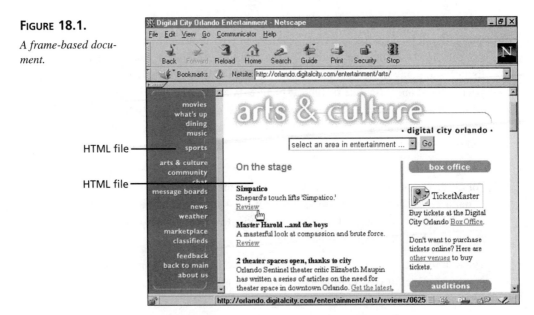

When publishing and publicizing your frame-based document, take care to direct visitors to the frame definition document, not to one of the files that is displayed within a frame (see Hour 21, "Publishing Your Page").

The Frame Definition Document

The frame definition document supplies no content to the page; it merely specifies how the page is to be split up and which HTML document is to be displayed in each frame. In Figure 18.1, the URL shown in the Location box is that of the frame definition document; that's the URL a visitor accesses to open the document. The frame definition document then takes care of accessing the page within each frame.

Creating a frame-based document requires creating the various HTML documents that will be displayed within the frames; composing the frame definition document to define the number, size, and other aspects of the frames; and tying a specific file to each frame.

In the frame definition document, you can insert a message to be displayed only to visitors who can't see links. (See the section titled "Accommodating the Frame-Intolerant," later in this hour.)

18

Rows and Columns

Within the frame definition document, you can break up the page into frames by applying either of two attributes (or both together):

- The ROWS attribute splits the page into horizontal rows
- The COLS attribute splits the page into vertical columns
- Used together (see the section titled "Building a Complex Frame Document," later in this hour), ROWS and COLS split the page into any combination of rows and columns

The ROWS or COLS attribute is always followed by an equals sign (=) and a measurement in quotes. The measurement determines the relative size and number of frames on the page and is expressed in one of three ways:

- A number value: Creates a row (or column) the given number of pixels high (or wide)
- A percentage: Creates a row (or column) the given percentage of the total height (or width) of the browser window

- An asterisk: Creates a row (or column) whose size is determined automatically by the space left over after other frames are created

Avoid using a number of pixels as a measurement because the number of pixels available in a window varies with the browser platform.

The number of measurement entries between the quotes determines the number of frames on the page, such as in the following examples:

`<FRAMESET ROWS="40%,60%">` creates two rows: the first (top row) is 40 percent of the height of the window and the second (bottom) is 60 percent of the height of the window.

`<FRAMESET COLS="200,*">` creates two columns: the first (left) column is 200 pixels wide and the second (right) column takes up the rest of the window.

`<FRAMESET COLS="*,20%,50%">` creates three columns: the first (left) column fills the space left by the other columns, the second (middle) column is 20 percent of the width of the window, and the third (right) column is 50 percent of the window.

`<FRAMESET ROWS="*,*,*,*">` creates four rows of equal size. (When multiple asterisks are used, each is given the same value.)

The Frame Content

A separate HTML file, which you compose like any other Web document, supplies the content of each frame. However, when composing files that will be displayed in frames, you must try to account for the size and shape of the frame in which the file will be displayed.

Browsers help adjust content for frames: They automatically wrap text to fit within a frame and shorten horizontal lines. Alignment properties are also preserved in a frame; for example, if your text is centered in the page when you compose it, the browser centers it within the frame when displaying it. However, browsers cannot adjust the positions or spacing of images (or images used as rules or bullets); images often make framing difficult.

Frames are not created in Composer, so although you can create your content files in Composer, you must use an HTML source editor to compose the frame definition document. After composing all your files, you'll want to browse the frame definition document and adjust it and/or the formatting of the content files to make the frames fit nicely.

Browsers automatically add scrollbars to a frame when the contents exceed the frame size. But a frame document showing a collection of fragmentary files and scrollbars is unappealing, and visitors tire quickly of excessive scrolling—especially horizontal scrolling to read wide text. Whenever practical, make the content fit the frame—or vice versa.

To Do: Build a simple, two-frame document

1. Using the medium of your choice (such as Composer), compose the content documents that will be displayed in the frames. Be sure to organize and format them, if possible, in a way that will minimize the need for visitors to scroll them in their frames.

> If you're unfamiliar with HTML source files and editors, see Hour 17, "Editing HTML."

2. In an HTML source editor, create a new HTML file, including the required structure tags and the title for your frames document, as shown here:

```
<HTML>
<HEAD>
<TITLE>Frames Demo</TITLE>
</HEAD>
   <BODY>
   </BODY>
</HTML>
```

3. Replace the <BODY> tags with <FRAMESET> tags, as shown in the following code. (Note that in a frame definition document, the <FRAMESET> block replaces the <BODY> block, and you cannot include a <BODY> block elsewhere in the file.)

```
<HTML>
<HEAD>
<TITLE>Frames Demo</TITLE>
</HEAD>
   <FRAMESET>
   </FRAMESET>
</HTML>
```

The <FRAMESET> tags enclose the entire definition. All further coding is inserted between these tags.

4. My frame document will be split into two columns without any rows. Therefore, in the <FRAMESET> tag, I add the COLS attribute. I want the first column to be narrow

18

▼   (30 percent of the window), and the second column to take up the remainder of the
window:

```
<FRAMESET COLS="30%,*">
</FRAMESET>
```

In the `<FRAMESET>` tag in the example, `COLS="*,70%"` or `COLS="30%,70%"`
would have the same effect as the entry shown.

5. Having defined the frames, I define their content by adding the `<FRAME SRC>` tag
and the filenames of the content files (in quotes). In the columns on the page, the
files will be displayed in the same order (left to right) in which they appear in the
`<FRAMESET>` block (top to bottom). In the following example, `MULTI.HTM` will be
displayed in the first (left) column:

```
<FRAMESET COLS="30%,*">
    <FRAME SRC="MULTI.HTM">
    <FRAME SRC="DESCRIP.HTM">
</FRAMESET>
```

6. The finished frame document is displayed in Figure 18.2. Here's the complete code
of the frame definition document:

```
<HTML>
<HEAD>
    <TITLE>Frames Demo</TITLE>
</HEAD>
    <FRAMESET COLS="30%,*">
        <FRAME SRC="MULTI.HTM">
        <FRAME SRC="DESCRIP.HTM">
    </FRAMESET>
</HTML>
```

Note that each document in a frame can have its own unique background
image or color, defined in the content file.

Observe that a single change to the attributes in the `<FRAMESET>` block dramatically alters
the resulting page. Suppose, for example, I wanted rows instead of columns. Besides
reformatting my source documents so that they conformed better to wide rows than to
narrow columns, I'd need to do nothing to the frame definition document but change the
`COLS` attribute to `ROWS`, as shown in the following:

```
<FRAMESET ROWS="30%,*">
<FRAME SRC="MULTI.HTM">
<FRAME SRC="DESCRIP.HTM">
</FRAMESET>
```

FIGURE 18.2.

The finished frame page.

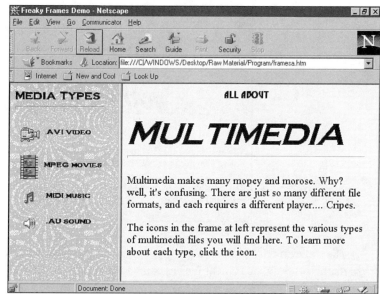

The files referenced in the `<FRAME SRC>` tags will be displayed in rows from top to bottom, in the order listed. In other words, `MULTI.HTM` is displayed in the top row because it is in the first `<FRAME SRC>` tag, and `DESCRIP.HTM` is displayed in the second (bottom) row.

The result of the `ROWS` variation is displayed in Figure 18.3.

Building a Complex Frame Document

Although the examples shown in Figures 18.2 and 18.3 are legitimate frame documents, they have certain limitations:

- They involve only rows or columns, not both within the same page.

- If you execute a link in either frame, the file the link points to replaces the file in the frame containing the link. Often in frame documents, you want visitors to click a link in one frame to open a file in another frame.

18

FIGURE **18.3.**

A ROWS *variation of the page shown in Figure 18.2.*

The following two sections show you how to modify your frame definition document and the links within the content files to build a leading-edge frame document.

To Use Both Rows and Columns

Creating a document like the one in Figure 18.4, which has both rows and columns, requires nesting multiple framesets, each with its own ROWS and COLS attributes.

To begin, you must first determine which frameset—one for ROWS or one for COLS—comes first, or which frameset is the parent frameset within which the next frameset is nested. You decide this on the basis of the configuration of the page you want to create:

- If any row in the page will extend all the way across the window (without being broken up into columns), the parent frameset defines the rows (ROWS).

- If any column in the page in the page will extend the entire window height, top to bottom (without being broken up into rows), the parent frameset defines the columns (COLS).

- If all rows are broken into columns and all columns are broken into rows, the parent frameset defines columns (COLS).

FIGURE 18.4.

A frame document with both rows and columns.

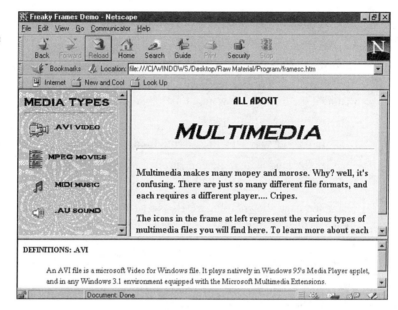

For example, in the page shown in Figure 18.4, the bottom row stretches across the entire window. Therefore, the parent frameset will define the rows of the page. The page has two rows (the bottom row and the top row, which is broken into columns), at a 75/25 split. So here's the parent frameset:

```
<FRAMESET ROWS="75%,*">
</FRAMESET>
```

Next, you must break that top row into two columns (at a 30/70 ratio). To do this, insert a new frameset within the parent frameset, as shown:

```
<FRAMESET ROWS="75%,*">
<FRAMESET COLS"30%,*")
</FRAMESET>
</FRAMESET>
```

Finally, add the <FRAME SRC> tags to each frameset to call document files into the three frames:

```
<FRAMESET ROWS="75%,*")
<FRAMESET COLS"30%,*")
<FRAME SRC="MULTI.HTM">
<FRAME SRC="DESCRIP.HTM">
</FRAMESET>
<FRAME SRC="DEFINI.HTM">
</FRAMESET>
```

18

To Specify the Frame in Which a Linked Document Opens

If you code your frame definition documents as shown up to this point in the hour, a link displaying in any of the documents will open its corresponding file in the same frame that held the link. If you want a link in one frame to open a new document in another frame, you must do two things:

- In the `<FRAME SRC>` lines of the frameset, you must give each frame a name.
- In the links within the content files, you must reference the name of the frame in which the linked file will open.

Using the page shown in Figure 18.4 as a starting point, we'll name the frames. Add the `NAME=` attribute to the `<FRAME SRC>` tag after the filename (and a blank space), as shown in the following code:

```
<FRAMESET ROWS="75%,*")
<FRAMESET COLS"30%,*")
<FRAME SRC="MULTI.HTM" NAME="Icons">
<FRAME SRC="DESCRIP.HTM" NAME="Text">
</FRAMESET>
<FRAME SRC="DEFINI.HTM" NAME="Definitions">
</FRAMESET>
```

It doesn't matter what you call the frames, as long as you give each a unique name. The frame names do not display on the page, just in the source code.

Within the content files, edit the links to add the name of the frame in which the linked files should open. This is done by adding the attribute `TARGET=` and the frame name (in quotes) to the link, following the filename, as in the following example:

```
<A HREF="avidef.htm" TARGET="Definitions"></a>
```

Although adding the `TARGET` attribute is easy enough in an HTML source editor, you can also add `TARGET` attributes in the Netscape Editor.

When entering the filename in the Link tab of the Image Properties dialog (see Figure 18.5), place a double quote mark (") following the filename and leave off the closing quote mark following the frame name after `TARGET`. The Editor automatically places quotes around the entire string you enter in this field. If you quote it as shown, your entry comes out correctly in the HTML source with quotes around the filename and the frame name.

FIGURE 18.5.

Adding a TARGET
attribute to a link in
Composer.

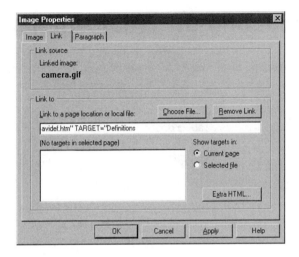

If you omit the TARGET attribute from any link, that link will open its file in the same frame that contains the link.

18

When the link shown in Figure 18.5 is executed, the file AVIDEF.HTM opens in the frame named Definitions (the bottom frame), replacing DEFINI.HTM.

Now suppose you wanted every link in the MULTI.HTM file to open its file in the Text frame. When all links are to open in the same frame, you can save time by using the <BASE TARGET> tag in the content file's header. All links in a file containing a <BASE TARGET> tag open their files in the frame named by <BASE TARGET>; you do not need to add any TARGET attributes to the link tags, as in the following example:

```
<HTML>
<HEAD>
<TITLE>
<BASE TARGET="Text">
</HEAD>
<BODY>
page definition goes here
</BODY>
</HTML>
```

All links in the sample content file will open their files in the Text frame.

Accommodating the Frame-Intolerant

As mentioned earlier in this hour (twice, in fact, so you wouldn't miss it), frame-based documents cannot be displayed by browsers that don't support Netscape's frames extensions.

In most other cases, extensions don't prevent whole pages from displaying—at worst, a portion of a page (such as a table) doesn't show up, or the page layout or character formatting reverts to the browser's defaults. But frames are evil—they render the whole page *terra incognita* to frame-intolerant browsers, which show nothing of a frame document but a sad, empty page (sniff!).

What can you do about it, short of denying yourself frames as an authoring tool? In your frame definition document, you can add the <NOFRAME>...</NOFRAME> tag to display a message or a link to the no-frames world. In the following example, I've added a <NOFRAME> message containing a link that leads to a no-frames version of my document:

```
<FRAMESET ROWS="75%,*")
<FRAMESET COLS"30%,*")
<FRAME SRC="MULTI.HTM">
<FRAME SRC="DESCRIP.HTM">
</FRAMESET>
<FRAME SRC="DEFINI.HTM">
<NOFRAME>This document uses frames. If your browser does not support
frames, please view our <A HREF="framefree.HTM">no frames
version.</A></NOFRAME>
</FRAMESET>
</FRAMESET>
```

When a visitor browses the frame definition document, the content within <NOFRAME> does not display in frame-supporting browsers—even you won't see it in Navigator. Only when the browser does not support frames does the <NOFRAME> content display.

Here's one instance in which Composer's lack of frames support is handy: Because Composer lacks WYSIWYG support for frames, it displays the <NOFRAME> message when you open a frameset document that uses NOFRAMES (see Figure 18.6). Therefore, you can use Composer itself as a test browser to see how the file looks to the frames impaired, while using Navigator to see how the document looks to the frames capable.

All too frequently, Web authors use <NOFRAME> to inform frame-impaired visitors that they're out of luck. Messages like "Sorry, this document must be viewed with Netscape Navigator 2.0 (or 3.0, or Communicator)" almost always mean frames lie ahead. This approach needlessly abandons millions of Web denizens—a shrinking minority, true, but millions is still millions. Besides, do you want to be the type who only cares about the majority?

FIGURE 18.6.

The <NOFRAME> *message as seen through Composer, which acts like a browser that can't display frames.*

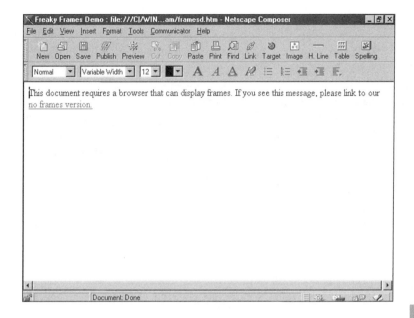

Alternatively, you can supply a link to a no-frames version of your document, as I do in the example. Creating the no-frames version is a no-brainer: Just copy and rename the content files and adapt their formatting and links so that they look and act properly as a multipage, nonframe document. In the <NOFRAME> block of the frame definition document, supply a link to the top page of your frame-free version.

Instead of supplying a no-frames version (or in addition to it), you can apply for Netscape Now!, a program in which Netscape Communications Corp. grants you the right to put the Netscape Now! button on your page. The Netscape Now! button is the link source for a link to a page at Netscape Communications. This page leads visitors through a series of forms and selections to download a version of Netscape for their system. (They'll need version 2.0 or higher to see frames.)

Through the program, you can add the Netscape Now! button to your <NOFRAME> block, so visitors who find themselves locked out of your frame-based document can hop over to Netscape, pick up a copy of Communicator, and return to see your page.

Pages created with the Page Wizard (see Hour 3, "Wizarding Up an Instant Web Page") or with Netscape's templates automatically include the Netscape Now! button and link.

Should you use the button? On the one hand, you help your visitors acquire the software they need to use your page. On the other hand, you're spending your time and server dollars to supply free advertising to a multimillion-dollar company. It's up to you.

About FrameGang

The CD-ROM that accompanies this book includes a program called FrameGang, which makes creating frame definition documents a snap. The program requires that you understand the basics of coding frames yourself, but it still makes framing simpler by automatically supplying some of the code and adjusting the measurements in the <FRAMESET> lines when you drag frame borders on the screen.

Summary

Frames are an exercise in careful choices and organization. Most important among the choices is deciding whether to use frames at all. When you're committed to using frames, always try to supply a useful <NOFRAME> message and an alternative for the frameless.

Workshop

Q&A

Q Sometimes, Navigator adds scrollbars to my frames when they're not really necessary. What can I do about that?

A By default, browsers add scrollbars whenever a file's contents seem to exceed the frame. You might be able to eliminate the problem by adjusting the formatting of the content file or the size of the frame in which it is displayed so that the contents sits comfortably in the frame.

Keep in mind, however, that just because everything fits in your display does not mean it will always do so in every visitor's browser. Variations in font size, display resolution, and other display factors can cause material that fits in a frame on your computer to exceed the frame on someone else's. Leaving scrollbars enabled helps ensure that all frames-capable visitors will be able to navigate your page.

If you're confident that scrollbars are unnecessary, but they still show up, you can prevent them from displaying by adding the attribute SCROLLING="NO" to the <FRAME SRC> line for the frame, like this:

```
<FRAME SRC="sample.htm" SCROLLING="NO">
```

By the way, you can force browsers to display scrollbars on a frame, even when the browser considers them unnecessary, by adding SCROLLING="YES" to the <FRAME SRC> line.

Q Can a link that is displayed within a frame open a new file not in a single frame, but filling the entire window (replacing all the frames)?

A Yes. Instead of a frame name, use "TOP" as the value for the TARGET attribute in the link. (See the section titled "To Specify the Frame in Which a Linked Document Opens.") When the link is executed, the file it opens fills the browser window, replacing the frame definition document. Clicking the Back button restores the frame document.

Quiz

Take the following quiz to see how much you have learned.

Questions

1. True or False: All browsers can display frames.
2. Which of the following is true about frame-based Web pages?
    a. They can be kinda cool
    b. They're pretty easy to create
    c. Some visitors have trouble navigating them properly
    d. All of the above.

Answers

1. False.
2. (d)

Activity

Look over any pages you're working on and consider their content. Are any of your pages reasonable candidates for frames?

18

HOUR **19**

Designing Interactive Forms

In one sense, any old HTML document is *interactive,* in that it lets you jump around to other URLs and anchors. You click, it responds. That's interactivity.

But there's another level of interactivity possible, one that is not directly supported within the confines of HTML code. A *script* is a program that accepts input of some kind from the visitor to a page, does something with that input, and spits back a result. The interaction can be as simple as collecting a user's name and address and adding them to a mailing list, or it can be as elaborate as showing the visitor a monthly mortgage payment calculated from a home price and interest rate the visitor enters.

HTML cannot support such functions on its own. To provide interactive functions to visitors, your page usually must call a script program residing on the client or server. HTML is smart enough to collect input from the visitor and pass it on to the script program, and HTML can display what the script produces, provided the script formats its output with HTML codes.

But the actual processing of the visitor's input is the exclusive province of script programs. In this hour, you'll learn about one of the most important applications of scripting: *forms*. (In Hour 20, "Putting Multiple Links in One Picture," you'll discover the other: *imagemaps*.) At the end of the hour, you'll be able to answer the following questions:

- Get a general introduction to the concepts of scripting
- Learn how to create and format interactive *forms*, which collect information from visitors to your page
- Discover how a program on the CD-ROM makes using forms more convenient

About CGI Scripting

A book this size devoted entirely to CGI scripting would be too short. And at that, reading such a book might not be the most effective use of your time. The need to know CGI scripting is evaporating, as JavaScript, Java, and other approaches to scripting gain popularity.

 CGI. Short for Common Gateway Interface. A language for scripts that are run on the Web server when a Web page invokes them.

 Java, JavaScript. Two separate and largely unrelated languages. JavaScript is a language for scripts that run not on the server but in the browser, and it does many of the same things that CGI does. Java is a general-purpose programming language sometimes used to add advanced capabilities to Web pages.

For now, though, CGI scripts are the best way to enable forms and imagemaps in your document. But before you can consider scripting, you must know a few things about CGI.

CGI programs run, not in the browser, but on the server. The rules and preferred programming languages for scripting vary with the server type and platform. Most Web servers today are UNIX-based and work best with scripts written in either of the well-known, popular UNIX shell languages: Bourne shell or Perl shell. Windows-based servers, on the other hand, are configured for Visual Basic scripts. As a result, it's impossible for this book to offer sample script code that will work on any server. The HTML code shown here that defines the way a form or imagemap is displayed in the document will work fine in Communicator, but the scripts shown are for Bourne and Perl, which your server might or might not support.

Even if your server does support scripting, there's no guarantee that your server supplier will permit you to use scripts. The increased interaction between visitors and the server that scripts enable is a potential security risk for the server. Before building a document that uses CGI scripts, talk to your server supplier or system administrator to find out whether, and how, you are permitted to use scripts. Then work closely with the system administrator on the testing and implementation of any script you write.

Personally, I think the best solution to scripting is this: You worry about what appears onscreen and let someone else (usually whoever controls the Web server where you will publish) worry about the scripting. For a form, you define the form's onscreen appearance in HTML. Then you take that file to someone else (a programmer, or even your Internet supplier), explain how you want the form data handled, and let the pros take it from there.

To learn about CGI scripting in detail, see either of the following Sams titles (choose depending on whether you have two weeks to spare or three):

Sams Teach Yourself Web Publishing with HTML in 14 Days (by Laura Lemay)

Sams Teach Yourself CGI Scripting with Perl 5 in 21 Days (by Eric Herrman)

Creating Interactive Forms

As a surfer, you've seen forms. For example, when you enter a search term for a search engine (such as Yahoo), you're using a form. Search forms like Yahoo's work like this:

1. Following instructions embedded in the HTML file, the browser takes the search term that you've entered and passes it to Yahoo's server, along with the filename and location of a script for processing that input.

2. The server starts the designated script program and provides your search term as an *input* variable to the program.

3. When the script program finishes, it produces *output*—a listing of hits on your search—plus instructions on how to display the output in an HTML document.

4. The server sends the output back to the browser to be displayed.

How Forms Are Made

There are two parts to making an interactive form:

1. Using special HTML tags, create the visible form that is displayed in your Web page. The form definition includes names for each separate piece of information (input) that the form collects and a pointer to the CGI script that will process that input.

19

2. Write a CGI script that accepts the form input, submits it to the server, processes it, and returns it in a particular format.

> Because of the problems associated with server variability and the complexity of writing CGI scripts, this hour focuses primarily on step 1, creating the onscreen form.

About GET and POST

When you build a form, you must specify one of two values in the METHOD attribute of the FORM tag: GET or POST. Both of these values indicate that the entries visitors make in the form should be submitted as input to a specified script; but how they present that input differs.

For most forms, POST is the preferred value because it directs the server to pass the input directly to the script as standard input. GET, on the other hand, is put into a special environment variable and then submitted to the script. Using an environment variable allows programmers to define more specifically how the input is to be treated by the script, which opens up a range of advanced processing capabilities. But for ordinary forms processing, POST is simpler and better.

About Submit Buttons

One of the HTML tags used for forms, when used with the SUBMIT attribute, creates an onscreen button labeled "Submit." (Look ahead to Figure 19.2.) For example, the following line creates a Submit button:

```
<INPUT TYPE="Submit">
```

> The Submit button is optional if your form is designed to send only one input value to the server; pressing Enter automatically submits the form. However, it's good practice to add a Submit button for every form.

The Submit button is what your visitors must click to confirm that they have finished making entries in a form. When a visitor clicks the button, the browser sends all input in the form to the designated script for processing.

By default, the label text on the button reads "Submit." By adding the VALUE attribute to the tag, you can label the button anything you want. (It still does the job of a Submit button.) For example, this line creates a Submit button labeled "Send Answers":

```
<INPUT TYPE="Submit" VALUE="Send Answers">
```

Forms coding requires multiple lines of HTML code, and Composer's Insert HTML Tag function inserts only one line at a time—which makes it a labor-intensive choice for building forms. Also, Composer cannot display forms in WYSIWYG form; you must view your document in the Netscape Browser to see your forms.

The best approach for coding forms is to write them in an HTML source editor and to check your work by viewing them in the Netscape browser. For maximum convenience, compose and format the rest of your page in the Netscape editor first, leaving out the forms. Then choose View | Edit Document Source to open the page file in an HTML editor and insert your form's code.

Scripting a Form

To begin, compose your document and leave out the form. For the following example, I've created a page for collecting visitors' email addresses (see Figure 19.1). Here's the source code:

```
<HTML>
<HEAD>
<TITLE>Address Form</TITLE>
</HEAD>
<BODY>
<H2>Tell Us Your Address</H2>
</BODY>
</HTML>
```

FIGURE 19.1.

The sample document, sans form.

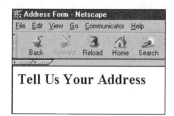

19

To Build the Form Definition

The form definition goes in the body of the document, surrounded by the tags `<FORM>` and `</FORM>`. The form definition includes not only the tags that create form fields, but also any text associated with those fields.

In the `<FORM>` tag, you enter an attribute for input METHOD (GET or POST), plus the ACTION attribute. The ACTION attribute points to the filename (in quotes) or the script program used to process the form input.

My form definition uses POST as the input METHOD, and my input is to be processed by a script I'll call MAILPOST.CGI. Also, my server requires that all CGI scripts be stored in the CGI-BIN directory.

 Observe that to point properly to the CGI-BIN directory, I must use a double period (..) to move upward in the hierarchy on my server.

Here's the form definition so far:

```
<FORM METHOD="POST" ACTION="../CGI-BIN /MAILPOST.CGI">
</FORM>
```

 There are several values for the TYPE attribute of `<INPUT>` and two alternatives to `<INPUT>`, each of which creates a different type of input field: a text box, a radio button, and so on. See the section titled "Form Input Types and Formatting" later in this hour.

Having defined the input method and the name of the script file, all I need to do now is create the onscreen input field and give it a name so that the script will know what the value refers to. Input fields are created with the `<INPUT>` tag and two attributes: TYPE and NAME. TYPE identifies (in quotes) the type of input field to use; for example, TEXT is used in the following code to create a one-line text field. The value entered in quotes following NAME= is the name you assign to the value the visitor enters.

```
<FORM METHOD="POST" ACTION="../CGI-BIN /MAILPOST.CGI">
<INPUT TYPE="TEXT" NAME="VisitorAddress" SIZE="40">
</FORM>
```

Now I want to label the form field to tell the visitor what to enter. I can enter text adjacent to the input field and assign it paragraph or character properties, just as I would anywhere in the HTML body, as in the following code:

```
<FORM METHOD="POST" ACTION="../CGI-BIN /MAILPOST.CGI">
Tell us your <b>E-mail Address</b><INPUT TYPE="TEXT"
NAME="VisitorAddress">
</FORM>
```

Following the "TEXT" value for the TYPE attribute, I could have added the SIZE attribute and a value (for example, SIZE="20") to set the length (in characters) of the text field.

Finally, I'll add a Submit button inside the </FORM> tag. Note that I've also added a <P> tag before the button to create a little extra space.

Here's the complete document file, including the Submit button. The final onscreen form is displayed in Figure 19.2.

```
<HTML>
<HEAD>
<TITLE>Address Form</TITLE>
</HEAD>
<BODY>
<H2>Tell Us Your Address</H2>
<FORM METHOD="POST" ACTION="../CGI-BIN /MAILPOST.CGI">
Tell us your <b>E-mail Address</b><INPUT TYPE="TEXT"
_NAME="VisitorAddress">
<P>
<INPUT TYPE="Submit Query">
</P>
</FORM>
</BODY>
</HTML>
```

To Write the Script

To acquaint you with a CGI script, here's the simple MAILPOST.CGI script. The following is what happens in this script: First, note that lines beginning with echo are meant to send information back to the browser. The first line describes the type of data (according to the MIME specification) that's being sent to the browser, so the browser knows how to treat it (in this case, as an HTML file).

As you can see, subsequent lines define an entire HTML file to be displayed in the browser. Within the body of that file, notice the two lines beginning with echo. The first displays the line Thanks! You told us your address is, and the second displays the VisitorAddress value, which is the value the visitor entered in the form. Near the end of the file, a link back to the original form page is displayed, so after viewing the script output, visitors can return.

19

FIGURE **19.2.**

The final form.

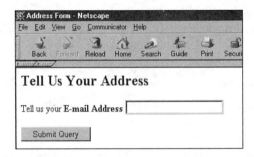

The EOF at the end of the file stands for End of File. Figure 19.3 shows the output from a visitor's queries.

```
echo Content-type: text/html
echo
cat << EOF
<HTML>
<HEAD>
<TITLE>Your Address</TITLE>
</HEAD>
<BODY>
EOF
echo "Thanks! You told us your address is "
echo $WWW_VisitorAddress
fi
cat << EOF
</P>
<P><A HREF="../www/Address.html">Return to previous page</A><P>
</BODY>
</HTML>
EOF
```

FIGURE **19.3.**

The output from a visitor's queries.

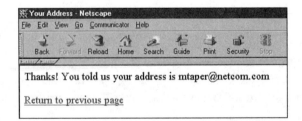

Form Input Types and Formatting

The example shown earlier uses a text input field (TYPE="TEXT"), which creates an onscreen box into which the visitor types an entry.

However, there are two other values you can enter in TYPE: RADIO and CHECKBOX. Each creates a different type of form field. These values are useful when there are only a few possible entries for a form, making a text box unnecessary.

Radio Buttons (<INPUT TYPE=RADIO>)

The RADIO type is used to create a list of items from which a visitor chooses only one by clicking its radio button. When the Submit button is pressed, a predetermined value for the selected radio button is sent as input to the script. Observe in the following example that the lines are formatted as an ordered list (<OL>).

Each item in a list of radio buttons is created by a separate <INPUT> line. All of the radio buttons in the list use the same name but have different values, as in the following example:

```
<OL>
<LI><INPUT TYPE="RADIO" NAME="Character" VALUE="Vito">Vito
<LI><INPUT TYPE="RADIO" NAME="Character" VALUE="Michael">Michael
<LI><INPUT TYPE="RADIO" NAME="Character" VALUE="Fredo">Fredo
</OL>
```

Observe that the lines are identical, except for the VALUE value and the text at the end of the line (outside the tag), which provides the onscreen label. This form definition is displayed in the page shown in Figure 19.4. When a visitor clicks a radio button and then the Submit button, the VALUE of the radio button selected is sent to the server as the input for Character.

FIGURE 19.4.

Radio buttons.

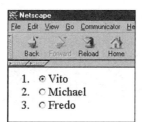

19

Check Boxes (<INPUT TYPE=CHECKBOX>)

The CHECKBOX type is similar to RADIO, except that it allows the visitor to make more than one selection from the list. Each selection is submitted as input for a different NAME (see Figure 19.5), as in the following example:

```
<LI><INPUT TYPE="CHECKBOX" NAME="Vito">Vito
<LI><INPUT TYPE="CHECKBOX" NAME="Michael">Michael
<LI><INPUT TYPE="CHECKBOX" NAME="Fredo">Fredo
</UL>
```

FIGURE 19.5.

Check boxes.

When a visitor clicks a check box and then the Submit button, the value of the check box selected is sent to the server as the input for `Character`.

Selections and Text Areas

Instead of using an `INPUT TYPE` attribute to determine your formatting, you can use either of two optional alternatives to the `INPUT` tag: `SELECT` or `TEXTAREA`.

The `SELECT` and `TEXTAREA` tags replace `<INPUT>`; in other words, you can use them just as you would the `<INPUT>` tag, including the `NAME` and `VALUE` attributes. But they each create a different type of form.

`<SELECT>` creates a drop-down list of choices. You code each choice with an `<OPTION>` tag within a `SELECT` block, as in the following code:

```
<SELECT NAME="TVshow">
<OPTION>Friends
<OPTION>Seinfeld
<OPTION SELECT>Hee-Haw
<OPTION>The Simpsons
<OPTION>NBC Nightly News
</SELECT>
```

Note that one `<OPTION>` tag includes the `SELECT` attribute. This is the choice that will be preselected as the default when the visitor first sees the form. When the user makes a selection from the form described by the example, the selection option will be submitted to the script as a value for `TVShow`.

The form is shown in Figure 19.6.

FIGURE 19.6.

A SELECT list.

<TEXTAREA> also replaces <INPUT> and produces a text box in which a visitor can make a long text entry. <TEXTAREA> is especially useful for collecting comments from visitors to your page.

The size and behavior of the text box is determined by a long list of attributes. These include the following:

- ROWS="*value*"   The number of rows in the text box
- COLS="*value*"   The number of columns in the text box
- WRAP="OFF"   Shuts off automatic text wrapping in the box.

The following code is an example:

```
<TEXTAREA NAME="Comments" ROWS="10" COLS="50">
</TEXTAREA>
```

This produces a text box like the one shown in Figure 19.7. When the visitor types an entry and clicks the Submit button, the entry will be submitted to the script as a value for Comments.

FIGURE 19.7.

A TEXTAREA *box.*

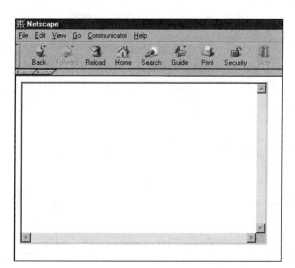

Building a Form in HTML Assistant

If you want a form, but the HTML coding seems daunting to you, note that there are a number of utilities that can help, including one on the CD-ROM with this book, HTML Assistant. (Note that HTML Assistant, like virtually all forms tools, produces the onscreen form only; you still must code the script to process the form separately.)

HTML Assistant includes an easy-to-use drop-down list of "user tools." You can customize the list, but by default, the list contains many of the tags you'll use when coding forms (see Figure 19.8).

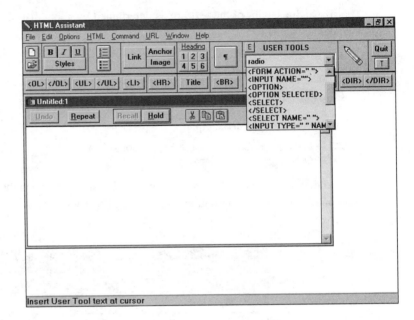

FIGURE **19.8.**

*Creating forms in
HTML Assistant.*

Summary

If you're willing (and able!) to face the world of CGI, you can do a lot with forms. Other authoring techniques are flashier, but none is more powerful.

Workshop

Q&A

Q In a frames document, can I create a form in one frame whose output is displayed in another?

A Sure—in fact, the Netscape Page Wizard is just such a document (see Hour 3, "Wizarding Up an Instant Web Page"). Every time a user submits a form in the bottom frame (which offers forms for creating parts of a page), a script processes the input, and the preview page in the upper-right frame reflects the change.

To specify the frame in which the output from a form script should be displayed, include the TARGET attribute and the name of the desired frame in the <FORM> tag following the script filename, as shown:

```
<FORM METHOD="POST" ACTION="../CGI-BIN/SAMPLE.CGI TARGET="TopFrame">
```

Of course, for this to work, you must have named your frames. For more about frames, see Hour 18, "Dividing a Page into Frames."

Quiz

Take the following quiz to see how much you have learned.

Questions

1. Which of the following is used for scripting in Web pages?

    a. Java

    b. CGI

    c. JavaScript

    d. All of the above.

2. True or False: You create a working form entirely in HTML.

Answers

1. (d)

2. False. Only the appearance of the form, and some aspects of how the form collects data, are specified in HTML. For the form to actually collect and process data, a script of some kind is required in addition to the HTML.

Activity

Call your Internet supplier (or visit its Web site) and find out what scripting services the company offers.

19

HOUR **20**

Putting Multiple Links in One Picture

You've seen 'em—those cool-looking pictures and button bars in Web pages that contain multiple links. Click one button or one part of the picture, and you go one place; click another part, you go somewhere else. It's a pro touch.

But it's not out of your league, now that you have 19 hours of Web authoring training already under your belt. In this hour, you learn how to apply some of the HTML skills from Hour 17, "Editing HTML," and scripting skills from Hour 19, "Designing Interactive Forms," to make these multi-link pictures happen. At the end of the hour, you'll be able to answer the following questions:

- How do I create an inline image that contains multiple links?
- Is there anything on the CD-ROM that can help me do it more easily?

About Imagemap

You know that an image file can serve as a link source; clicking the image activates the link. By creating an *imagemap* script, you can make different areas within one image activate different links. Figure 20.1 shows an imagemap.

NEW TERM **Imagemap.** An inline image containing multiple links, each of which is activated when the visitor clicks a different area of the image.

Imagemaps are used for fancy jobs, such as maps; click a country, and a link opens a document about it. But they have more mundane uses, as well; for example, the button bars that are at the top and bottom of every page on Netscape's Web site are imagemaps. The whole bar is one big GIF file, but the imagemap assigns a separate URL to each button.

FIGURE 20.1.

Clicking on different parts of this image map activates different links.

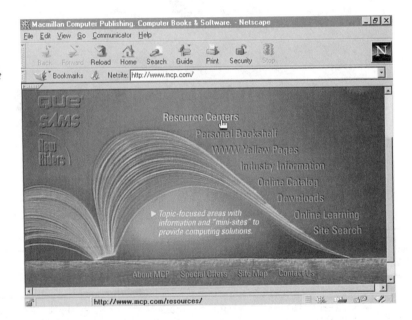

Server-Side Versus Client-Side

An imagemap can be written to reside on the server and be processed by a server-based, imagemapping CGI program, or it can be coded into the HTML file itself to be run by the browser, or *client*.

From an authoring standpoint, client-side imagemaps have great advantages: You needn't store an extra map file on the server, and you needn't deal with the fact that server-side imagemaps are CGI scripts and must therefore accommodate the CGI peculiarities of the server. Unfortunately, client-side imagemaps work only if the browser understands the relatively recent Netscape extensions for client-side maps. Right now, that's just Navigator and Internet Explorer 4.

Eventually, though, client-side imagemaps will probably become the norm because they're simpler to use and will be standardized across all browsers (when browser support catches up).

Choosing an Image and Regions

Regardless of which type of imagemap you choose to use, the essential steps in imagemapping are as follows:

- Select an appropriate image.
- Decide in what way the image will be divided up into different regions for different URLs.
- Determine the coordinates of each region.

> You can use any GIF image for an imagemap, but geometrical images work best. You can use photos or other images that aren't characterized by clearly defined shapes, by arbitrarily defining regions within them; but visitors might find using such imagemaps confusing.

For example, consider the Windmill image (W6.GIF) shown in Figure 20.2. This image is a good choice for mapping because it is divided naturally into identifiable shapes that visitors will naturally assume contain different links.

I want this imagemap to call four different URLs. I'll use the top two blades of the windmill (both rectangles) as two regions. For my other two regions, I'll use the circle that forms the hub of the windmill and the polygon making up the windmill house.

> The image editor Paint Shop Pro is included on the CD-ROM that accompanies this book.

Having selected my regions, I need to find out what their coordinates are within the graphic. If I open the image within an editor like Paint Shop Pro, as shown in Figure

20

20.3, and move the mouse to any spot within the graphic, I can see the exact x,y coordinate of that point in the center of the status bar. Using this technique, I can discover the exact coordinates for each corner in each region. The corners define the region.

FIGURE 20.2.

A GIF image for an imagemap.

FIGURE 20.3.

Determining region coordinates in PaintShop Pro.

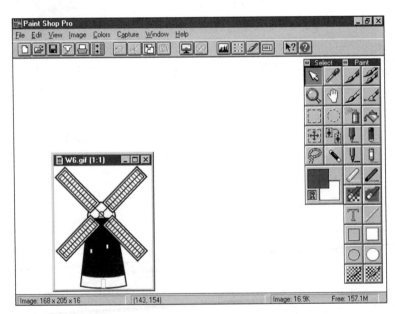

 You needn't be pixel-perfect when noting the coordinates of your regions. Getting in the ballpark—within two or three pixels of a precise corner, for example—is usually good enough, unless the region is so small that precision is critical.

For example, the regions in the image shown in Figure 20.3 can be described as follows. Note that, for rectangles, you typically need to enter only two corners: the upper-left and lower-right. (Because it's a rectangle, the other two points are easily calculated by the mapping program.) However, because these rectangles are at an angle, I might get inaccurate results unless I enter every corner. For a circle, I list the coordinates of the center point and the length of the radius (in pixels). For the polygon, I must note every corner. I used the following coordinates:

Left blade: 3,19 18,5 78,64 60,76

Right blade: 139,4 158,17 99,75 84,58

Circle hub: 80,80 24

Polygon house: 56,87 104,87 124,197 44,198

These shape names, coordinates, and the URLs to which I want each region to point are all I need to know to create my imagemap.

To Do: Create a client-side imagemap

To Do

1. Start with the <MAP> tag, which informs browsers that what follows is an imagemap. The <MAP> tag contains a NAME attribute and a name you assign to your imagemap (any name you like), like this:

```
<MAP NAME="MyMap">
```

 As long as you put it in the body of the HTML file, it doesn't matter where you insert your imagemap definition or where it is in relation to the <IMG SRC> line that embeds the image.

2. Next, define each region and its associated URL with the AREA tag. The AREA tag contains a SHAPE attribute in which you enter a value for the type of shape (CIRCLE, RECT, POLY), followed by a COORDS attribute in which you enter the coordinates (in quotes), followed by the link (<HREF> tag). Each set of coordinates is separated by a space. Here are the <AREA> lines for my imagemap, plus the <MAP> tag and closing </MAP> tag. The following is the entire map definition for MyMap:

```
<AREA SHAPE="RECT" COORDS="3,19 18,5 78,64 60,76"
HREF="leftblade.htm">
<AREA SHAPE="RECT" COORDS="139,4 158,17 99,75 84,58
HREF="rightblade.htm">
<AREA SHAPE="CIRCLE" COORDS="80,80 24 HREF="hub.htm">
<AREA SHAPE="POLY" COORDS="56,87 104,87 124,197 44,198
HREF="house.htm">
```

20

▼   3. The `<IMG SRC>` tag that embeds the inline image does not display within the map definition. It is displayed in the body of the HTML file wherever you want it to be (or rather, wherever you want the image to display on the page), just as if it were not an imagemap, but a regular inline image. To connect the image to its imagemap, you add the `USEMAP` attribute, using as a value the `NAME` you gave the imagemap in the `<MAP>` tag:

▲

```
<IMG SRC="W6.GIF" USEMAP="MyMap">
```

Creating a Server-Side Imagemap

The concepts behind server-side imagemaps are analogous to those used in client-side maps, but the execution is different. Most importantly, the imagemap file defining the regions of the image is contained, not in the HTML file, but in a separate map file you must upload to the server.

Your first step in creating a server-side imagemap is to find out which of the popular CGI imagemap programs is running on your server and where the program is located in the directory structure. Most servers use one of two CGI imagemap programs:

- Imagemap, used on NCSA HTTPd servers
- HTImage, used on w3c httpd servers

Each of these programs requires slightly different coding in the map file and in your HTML document.

To create the map file, you list each region one line at a time, including in the line for each region the name of the shape, the coordinates, and the URL to which the region will point.

For Imagemap, you list the shape, the URL, and then the coordinates, as shown:

```
rectangle /leftblade.htm 3,19 18,5 78,64 60,76
rectangle /rightblade.htm 139,4 158,17 99,75 84,58
circle /hub.htm 80,80 24
polygon /house.htm 56,87 104,87 124,197 44,198
```

For HTImage, you list the shape, the coordinates, and then the URL. Each set of coordinates must be placed in parentheses (observe that the circle radius does not go in parentheses):

```
rectangle (3,19) (18,5) (78,64) (60,76) /leftblade.htm
rectangle (139,4) (158,17) (99,75) (84,58) /rightblade.htm
circle (80,80) 24 /hub.htm
polygon (56,87) (104,87) 124,197 44,198 /house.htm
```

Save your file with the extension .MAP and upload it to the server. Your system administrator must tell you which directory to use.

In your HTML document, you build a link that uses the image as a link source and also identifies the server program and the map file. Also, in the IMG SRC tag that identifies the image file, add the attribute ISMAP to indicate that this is the image to use for the imagemap.

For example, for the Imagemap program, use the following code:

```
<A HREF="../cgi-bin/htimage/maps/MyMap.map">
<IMG SRC="W6.GIF" ISMAP>
</A>
```

And for HTImage, use this code:

```
<A HREF="../cgi-bin/imagemap/maps/MyMap.map">
<IMG SRC="W6.GIF" ISMAP>
</A>
```

In the examples shown, the paths assume the imagemap program is stored in the directory CGI-BIN, and the imagemap file is stored in a MAPS directory within CGI-BIN.

Using the CD-ROM for Imagemaps

One program provided on the CD-ROM that accompanies this book can help you generate server-side map files for Imagemap or HTImage servers: MapEdit.

In this program, you can open the GIF file you will use for your imagemap, and then select regions with a mouse and enter the URL for each region. The program automatically generates a map file, coordinates and all, for the specified server type. This capability is no substitute for knowing how to code imagemaps, but it's a great time saver (see Figure 20.4).

20

FIGURE 20.4.

MapEdit.

Summary

Imagemaps are pretty cool, and not too hard to make. Just be sure you choose an image in which the regions to which you'll attach links are easy for the visitor to recognize.

Workshop

Q&A

Q **Can a link in an imagemap in one frame open a file in another?**

A Sure—the steps are much the same as for a form in a frame that opens a file in another. In the AREA tag, follow the URL with the TARGET attribute and frame name, as in the following:

```
<AREA SHAPE="CIRCLE" COORDS="35,10" 20 HREF="topframe.htm"
TARGET="TopFrame">
```

Quiz

Take the following quiz to see how much you have learned.

Questions

1. Which of the following would make a good picture for an imagemap?

    a. A yellow smiley face.

    b. A picture of the ocean.

    c. A map of Central America.

    d. A blue ball.

2. If you expect your whole target audience to be using leading browsers, it's best to use which type if imagemap?

    a. Client-side

    b. Server-side

    c. Patri-cide

    d. Apple-cide

3. On most servers, CGI scripts are stored in a special directory called:

    a. SCRIPTS

    b. SPECIAL

    c. CGI-COMPARTMENT

    d. CGI-BIN

Answers

1. (c) Only (c) is clearly divided into easily distinguishable regions.

2. (a)

3. (d)

Activity

20

In pages you're creating, look at any that contain more than one link. Can you think of a picture that could serve logically as an imagemap for all links now on the page? Is that picture one you might find in a clip art library, or do you need to create it?

PART VI

Getting It Online

Hour

Hour **21**

Publishing Your Page

You didn't become a Web author just to share your accomplishments with your canary. Of course, you want to get your work onto a Web server so it can be visited, loved, and lauded by those burgeoning Web masses.

Composer is a big help with publishing. By setting up a few defaults and properly organizing your files, you'll wind up with the ability to publish your pages (and then update them later) with a few quick clicks.

At the end of this hour, you'll be able to answer the following questions:

- Where do I publish?
- What should I do before publishing to make sure everything's ready?
- How can I configure Composer to make publishing easy?
- How do I use Composer's "one-button" publishing to publish my page?

About Web Servers

At this point in the workshop, you probably already know where you intend to publish your page. But in case you haven't decided, here are your options for finding a Web server on which to publish your pages:

At work or school. Your employer or school might have a Web server on which you are permitted store your page. Certainly, if your page is strictly work-related (or school-related), you're most likely to gain permission to publish it on the server for free.

However, note that free access to corporate and university servers is diminishing rapidly as demand grows and as organizations look for ways to earn money from their Internet connections. Also, many university systems, as well as some corporate systems, are overtaxed and might have outdated server hardware or inadequate connection speeds. Using a slow or unreliable system provides poor service to your visitors; forking over a few dollars a month for space on a fast commercial server might be a better choice in the long run than using free space on a poor server.

From commercial Internet service providers or their online service counterparts. Currently, these providers offer the best balance of service and cost for most new Web publishers. Many commercial providers include a modest amount of server space free with each Internet account and also might offer a wide range of space and pricing options. Although it might be convenient and cost-effective to lease Web space from the same company that provides your Internet account, there's no reason not to lease your space elsewhere. A good account provider might be a lousy Web space provider, offering high prices and/or poor service. In other words, shop around.

Before choosing a provider for Web space, visit that company's Web page a few times at different hours. If the server slowly sends pages at certain hours or seems to be unavailable from time to time, look for a better-equipped provider.

Build your own. If your Web page requires extra-tight security (for online sales) or makes extensive use of CGI scripts (especially for forms), an in-house Web server is your answer. Building your own Web server is a more practical solution (even for relatively small companies) than ever before thanks to lower-priced server computers (especially Pentium-based PCs), cheaper, simpler server software (primarily from Netscape and Microsoft), and the wide availability of high-speed data lines (such as ISDN or T1).

A Web server is not cheap. The hardware and software for a decent server might easily cost $4,000 (and up), but the 24-hour, high-speed dedicated Internet connection that a Web server demands might cost four times that much—every month.

More important, while effectively administering a Web server is getting easier all the time, the job essentially demands a full-time expert. All of these requirements are well within the means of most companies with over 100 employees, or smaller companies whose line of business makes Web service a high priority. For other small companies, however, leasing space is a far more sensible option.

Preparing to Publish

Publishing a page is a lot like painting a house: Doing the job is easy, but doing it right requires careful preparation. Before publishing, you need to take some time to prepare Composer's publishing features and your page files properly. Doing this first can prevent problems later (and make publishing a breeze).

Communicating with Your Server Supplier

The most important prelude to publishing is finding out about the requirements and limitations of the server to which you'll publish. Specifically, you'll need to know the following:

- *The communications protocol required for uploading your files*—Many servers allow you to use the Web protocol (HTTP) for uploading files, whereas some require that files be uploaded via FTP. (Composer supports both methods.)

If you're comfortable using an Internet FTP client, you may prefer to use it to upload your files to the server via FTP. If you will post your page on your ISP's server, your ISP will supply you with instructions (usually on the ISP's Web site) for publishing pages to the server via FTP.

While you needn't use One-Button Publishing, doing so has several advantages over using FTP. One-Button Publishing helps you make sure you post all the necessary files, and when it comes time to update a page you've previously published, One-Button Publishing makes updating much easier than using FTP.

21

- *The complete address and path where your files will be stored*—You'll need to know the complete URL of the directory in which your files will be stored, including the server name, path to your directory, and the name of your directory. Ideally, you'll have your own separate directory for all your files. Having your own directory prevents conflicts that might arise if any other file on the system (a page, image, or other file) uses the same filename as one of your files.

- *The rules or restrictions for filenames on the server*—Different server platforms have different rules for filenames. For example, DOS-based servers and some UNIX servers do not permit filenames longer than eight characters or file extensions of more than three characters. Ideally, you'll find out such restrictions before you create and name your files. But, if you composed your page without first finding out about the server, you should check for naming restrictions and change any filenames as needed.

Unless you have your own server directory, do not name any page `index.htm(1)`. Although this name is often used for the top page in a multi-page Web page, if the directory already contains a file called `index.htm`, the server will reject yours—or overwrite the other!

If you alter any filenames or directory locations before publishing, be sure to check and adjust any links or other internal references (`<FRAME SRC>`, `<IMG SRC>`, and so on) to the files, as well.

- *The amount of disk space you're allowed*—If you're publishing your page on a corporate or university computer system, you might be required to keep the total disk space occupied by all of your files (including HTML files, images, external media, and scripts) below a certain minimum. If you're leasing space from a commercial Internet provider, your monthly fee is typically determined by the amount of space your files occupy. Therefore, it's important to know the size of your entire fileset.

An easy way to find out the size of your fileset is to open Windows Explorer or the Macintosh's file system, highlight all of the files in your page, and then read the total size of the selected files in the status bar at the bottom of the Explorer window (see Figure 21.1). Note that this works only if all your files are in the same directory; if some files, such as your image files or scripts, reside in separate directories, you'll need to find the number of bytes taken up in each directory used by your page, and then add the directory totals together in order to find your page total.

FIGURE 21.1.

Determining the total size of your page, shown at the bottom of the Explorer window.

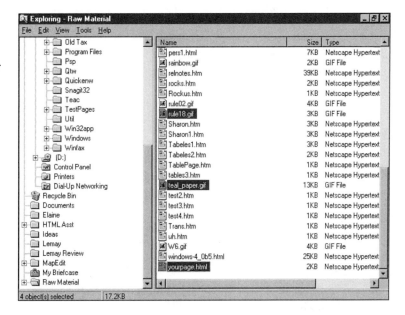

- *Where you store your scripts*—If you use CGI scripts (see Hours 19 and 20), you must first make sure your server supplier supports the type of script you have written. Then you must find out the specific procedures for uploading your scripts, which might be different from uploading the rest of your page. For example, CGI scripts are usually stored in a directory called `cgi.bin`; uploading files to `cgi.bin` might require a special password or other security procedure.

- *Your unique username and password for gaining upload access to the server* — Your server supplier should give you a username and password for uploading your files. If your supplier does not require a password, find another supplier; your pages will not be secure on a server that is not password protected.

Files Checklist

Once you know everything you need to know about the server, check (and recheck) your files and all links between the files. Make sure that the links have been adjusted for any files you might have moved or renamed in the course of composing your page or preparing it for publishing.

21

As mentioned throughout this book, it's wise whenever possible to copy all files that make up a page—including any inline images *and* external media—into a shared folder. When you use One-Button Publishing, you'll discover that it's nearly impossible to upload all of the files in a complex page at once unless they share a folder, both on your PC and on the Web server.

Remember that the "links" you must check include not only the links that bind your pages together, but also the paths and filenames for the following items:

- Inline image files
- Links to external media
- <FRAME SRC> tags, which indicate the names and locations of the content files that fill in framesets
- Links to external script files

Also, make absolutely sure that the filenames of all external media use the appropriate filename extension for the media type (see Hour 15). The filename extensions are used by browsers to determine which helper application or plug-in to use to play or display the file. (If you find that you have to correct a filename extension, don't forget to go back and change the link so that it matches the new filename!)

Setting Your Publishing Preferences

By setting up the Publishing part of the Communicator Preferences dialog box, you achieve two terrific things:

- You configure Composer for One-Button Publishing, which not only makes publishing more convenient, but also makes updating your page easier (later on).
- Using check boxes, you set two options that help keep your files together and links accurate to prevent the most common foul-ups that occur when copying pages to or from a server.

To Do: Set your publishing preferences

1. From within any Communicator component, open the Preferences dialog box and choose **Edit**, Preferences.
2. In the list of Categories, click the + sign next to Composer to reveal the Publishing subcategory beneath it.
3. Click the Publishing subcategory. The Publishing preferences appear, as shown in Figure 21.2.

FIGURE 21.2.

Setting Composer's Publishing preferences.

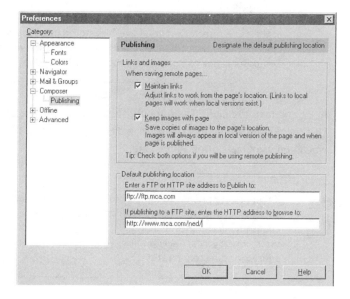

The check marks in the Publishing preferences work in two directions: They keep your files together and your links accurate when you upload to the server, and they do the same with pages, such as templates, that you download from the Web.

4. In the section labeled Links and images, make sure both check boxes are checked. The first check box instructs Composer to automatically make all links among files in the same directory relative rather than absolute pathnames. This ensures that the links will still work on the server, as long as you've uploaded all of the files and they still share the same directory.

   The second check box automatically copies any inline image files of a page along with the page whenever an HTML file is uploaded to the server (with One-Button Publishing) or downloaded from the Web.

Regardless of the settings in the Publishing Preferences dialog box, it's a good practice to set up all links in your page, except those to remote resources (other URLs), as relative pathnames. The Publishing settings might bail you out if you goof in this respect, but that doesn't mean that you shouldn't take care with pathnames.

21

▼

> Also, note that the check marks in the Publishing subcategory only work for image files stored in the same directory as the HTML file or as links to files in the same directory. If you have files stored in a separate location and the links or image tags are invalidated when the page is moved to the server, Composer is not going to save you. Therefore, check your links carefully.

5. In the top text box under Default publishing location, enter the exact location—a URL beginning with either `http://` or `ftp://`—to which files will be uploaded when you use One-Button Publishing.

> If you plan to publish to more than one server or directory, don't worry about what you put in the Default publishing location portion of the Publishing Preferences dialog box. Just enter the address you'll use most often; when you actually publish, you'll have a chance to enter a different address or directory location.

If the URL you enter in the top box is a Web (`http://`) address, Navigator will use that information for browsing your page as well as posting it. However, if the address is an FTP server, you must also fill in the bottom box under Default publishing location with the Web address of the page—the URL through which visitors will access your uploaded pages.

▲   6. Click OK.

Using Composer's "One-Button" Publishing

If you have set up your publishing preferences and prepared your files, publishing your page is a snap. No, it's not really One-Button Publishing; that's the kind of thing software marketing people like to call a *feature*, whereas others just call it a *lie*. Nevertheless, publishing through Composer is quite painless.

> Composer's One-Button Publishing feature can upload to only one server directory at a time. If you intend to publish in multiple directories or subdirectories, you must run through the entire publishing procedure separately for each directory.

To Do: Publish a page

1. In Composer, open the page or any page of the page (for multipage pages).

2. Click the Publish button on the Composition toolbar or choose **F**ile, **Pu**blish. A dialog box similar to the one shown in Figure 21.3 appears.

FIGURE 21.3.

*One-Button
Publishing.*

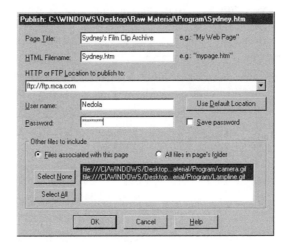

3. Verify that the information in Page Title and HTML Filename (both of which describe the open file in Composer) indeed match the page you intend to publish (or one page within a multipage page). If they don't, click Cancel and open the proper file in Composer.

> Observe that the box is a drop-down list; any address you've previously entered in that field is available from the list.

4. The default HTTP or FTP location to publish to, as shown in the Publish dialog box, is the one you entered as your publishing preference. If that location is not where you want to publish this particular page, you may enter a different URL in the box labeled HTTP or FTP Location to publish to.

> The Publish dialog box will remember the username for each server you publish to and supply it automatically the next time you publish. For security, passwords are not remembered automatically, but you may check the Save password box to save a server password so that you don't need to type it the next time you publish.

21

▼   5. Enter the username and password for the FTP or HTTP server to which you will
          publish. Be careful to capitalize both exactly as you have been instructed by the
          server administrator; some types of Web servers are finicky about capitalization.

       6. In the box under Other files to include, you can select the complete fileset—multi-
          ple HTML files, image files, scripts, and so on—that you want uploaded to the
          specified server directory. To begin, you must specify which files should be dis-
          played in the file list:

> Because the Publish dialog box will not list externally linked files when you
> choose the option labeled Files associated with this page, it's important to
> store all page files in a multipage page—as well as all external media files—
> in the same folder with the HTML file. That way, you can choose the option
> labeled All files in page's folder, and then select all of your files in one oper-
> ation.

          • *Files associated with this page*—The box under Other files to include will
            list all *inline* files—including images and scripts—that are referenced within
            the HTML file. Note that files attached to the page through external links
            (see Hour 10, "Making Links") are not included.

          • *All files in page's folder*—The box under Other files to include will list all
            files (of all types) sharing the folder with the HTML file. If you have been
            careful to copy all inline and externally linked files to the same directory as
            the HTML file, they'll all be made available through this option.

          After choosing which list to display, select the files to upload. By default, all files
          in the list are selected. You may deselect (or reselect) any file by clicking it.

       7. When all files you want to upload appear highlighted in the list, click OK.
          Communicator connects to the Internet or your intranet (if it is not already con-
          nected), connects to the server, and submits your username and password. If the
          server accepts your username and password, Communicator uploads the files to the
          directory you specified in the Publish dialog box.

> If you use One-Button Publishing to upload to an FTP address,
> Communicator automatically transfers all the files in FTP's binary transfer
> mode. The HTML files, which are text files, could be transferred via FTP's
> ASCII mode, but image files and many types of external media files might be
> corrupted by ASCII transfers. Binary mode transfers ensure that all files—text
> and otherwise—show up at the server ready to use.

▲

Summary

Publishing is a simple activity (and relatively foolproof) as long as you've taken care in the preparation of your page. Simple mistakes, like putting files for the same page in different directories, are the kinds of things that most often cause publishing problems. If you are careful with your filenames and locations, obey your server's rules, and configure Composer correctly, you'll find publishing one of the more satisfying aspects of authoring—the reward for a job well done.

Workshop

Q&A

Q What if the HTML standard changes? Will my page suddenly not work in browsers that conform to a new standard or support new extensions?

A Updates to HTML are backward-compatible; in other words, when HTML changes, new tags and attributes are added, as are new ways to do old things. But older approaches and tags still work, indefinitely.

In Hour 23, "Testing and Maintaining Your Page Online," you'll learn about testing your page's HTML online.

Q How do I update my page when it changes?

A That, too, is coming in Hour 23. But first you need to learn how to announce your newly published page to the world; see Hour 22, "Announcing Your Web Presence."

Quiz

Take the following quiz to see how much you have learned.

Questions

1. If you have a Web page file named `index.htm`, you should change that file to a different name unless:

   a. you don't feel like it.

   b. you have your very own directory on the server, containing no files other than yours.

   c. you have a letter of permission from the server's Webmaster.

   d. you like to live dangerously.

21

2. True or False: On most servers, you can publish your page by using an FTP client to upload the page files to the server.

Answers

1. (b)

2. True.

Activity

Did you actually upload some files into your Web space or just read through this hour? No points for you—you have to take the plunge sometime. Go back and publish.

HOUR 22

Announcing Your Web Presence

After your page is on the server, it doesn't do you much good if nobody knows it's there. You need to get the word out, so anyone who might have an interest in your page knows it's there and can find it easily.

In this hour, you learn how to announce your page to the world. At the end of the hour, you'll be able to answer the following questions:

- Where are the major Web directories on which my page should be listed?
- How do I get listed on the directories?
- In what other ways can I publicize my page?
- How do I broadcast an email announcement to my friends, family, or clients?

Listing Your Page in Web Directories

There are two kinds of people who you may want to know about your Web page: the people you know and the people you don't know.

You will inform the people you know directly, as you learn to do later in this hour. But the most efficient way to inform the people you don't know is to get your page listed on the major Internet search services, including the following:

- Yahoo (see Figure 22.1):

  `www.yahoo.com`

- Excite:

  `www.excite.com`

- Lycos:

  `www.lycos.com`

- Alta Vista:

  `www.altavista.digital.com`

- InfoSeek:

  `www.infoseek.com`

- WebCrawler:

  `www.webcrawler.com`

FIGURE 22.1.

Yahoo is one of the Web directories to which you'll want to add your page.

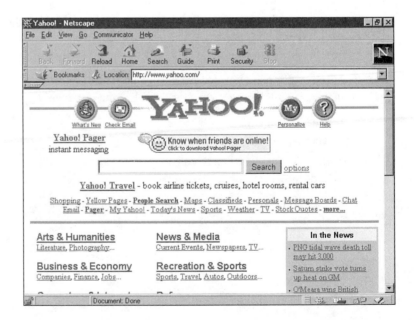

22

> If your page covers a particular subject, it's a good idea to use the directories to find other pages about the same subject and explore them.
>
> Many such pages offer a list of links to related pages; when you find such a page, you can email its Webmaster to ask that a link to your page be added to the list. (An email link to the Webmaster usually appears on the same page as the links.) You can also add to your Web site your own list of links to related pages, thus returning the favor.

When your page is properly listed by these services, folks will find your page whenever they search for something related to your page's subject, title, or keywords (see Hour 5, "Choosing a Title, Colors, and Other Page Properties").

Actually, some search pages will find your page all by themselves. Services such as Excite and Alta Vista use programs, sometimes called spiders or crawlers, to methodically search the Web and add new pages to their directories.

But by adding your pages to these and other directories manually, you get them listed more quickly, and you improve the chances that they'll be categorized properly—which improves the chances that your page will be found by people who will actually want to see it.

Each directory has different rules for adding new pages. You always begin by navigating to the directory's top page. From there, by hunting around, you can usually find instructions, a button, or some other indication of how to add a site.

> When adding the URL of a business site to directories, do searches to find out how your competitors are listed. Then, be sure your document is associated with the same categories or keywords. If anyone finds your competitors, they find you, too.

To Do: Add your site to Yahoo

▼ **To Do**

1. Go to Yahoo at

    www.yahoo.com

2. Explore Yahoo's categories and choose the precise category in which your page belongs.

3. Return to Yahoo's top page and choose How To Suggest Your Site near the top of the page. A list of instructions appears, as shown in Figure 22.2.

▼

FIGURE 22.2.

Adding your site to the Yahoo directory.

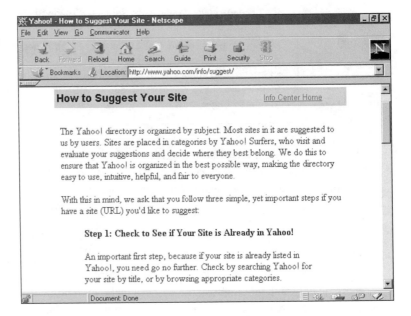

4. Following the instructions, browse to the category in which you want your site listed.

5. Scroll to the bottom of the directory listing for your selected category and choose the link Suggest a Site. A page opens, showing important notes about suggesting a site.

6. Scroll to the bottom and click the button labeled Proceed to Step One. A form opens, as shown in Figure 22.3.

7. In the form, enter your page's title, its URL, and any additional categories in which you want it listed.

When you add a site to many directories, including Yahoo and Excite, the URL does not show up in the directory immediately. You may have to wait as long as two weeks before your addition becomes official.

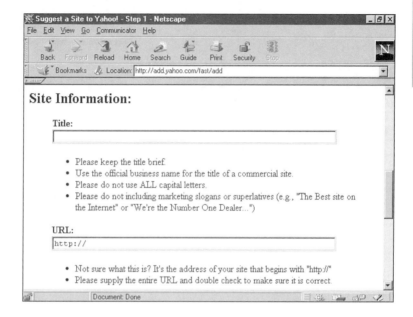

FIGURE 22.3.

Adding information about your site to the Yahoo directory.

To Do: Add your site to Excite

Like all spider-based search tools, Excite crawls around the Web cataloging its contents and will eventually catalog your site. But by suggesting your site, you'll get it listed more quickly.

1. Go to Excite at

   www.excite.com

2. Scroll to the bottom of the page and choose the link Add URL near the bottom. A form opens, as shown in Figure 22.4.

3. Complete the form.

> To make sure your page is located and properly cataloged by Web spiders, be sure to carefully and thoughtfully phrase the page's title, description, and keywords in the Page Properties dialog box. Refer to Hour 5 for help.

Getting In Multiple Directories at Once

Recently, some commercial services have emerged that offer (most for a fee) to list your site with many of the most popular directories and spiders, all in one quick step.

FIGURE 22.4.

Suggesting your site to Excite.

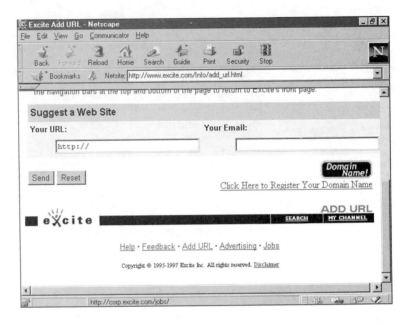

Such services charge from as little as $10 (Site See) to over $100. Note that these services submit not only to the major search engines, but also to hundreds of topic-specific directories.

Check out:

- Site See (see Figure 22.5) at
  www.site-see.com
- Submit It (see Figure 22.6) at
  www.submit-it.com/
- WebWeaver (see Figure 22.7) at
  http://www.websitepromote.com/dls/index.html

Publicizing Your Page off the Web

Don't forget that not all ways to publicize you Web page are on the Web (or even online). Be sure to list your Web site address:

- In your email signature
- On your business cards
- On personal or company stationery
- In company advertising and marketing collateral

FIGURE 22.5.

Site See.

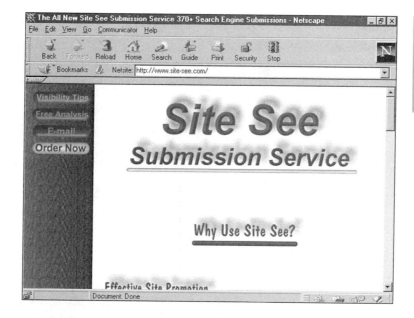

22

FIGURE 22.6.

Submit It.

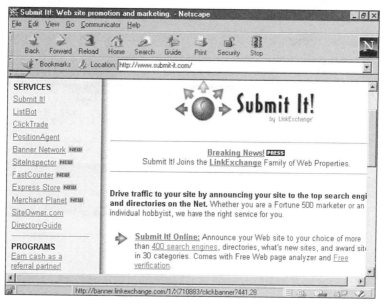

Remember: In theory (and in reality, too!), everyone among your acquaintances who will visit your Web page has Internet access, and therefore he or she probably has an email address, too. So a great way to make a targeted announcement to people you know is to broadcast an email message announcing your page's URL.

FIGURE 22.7.

WebWeaver.

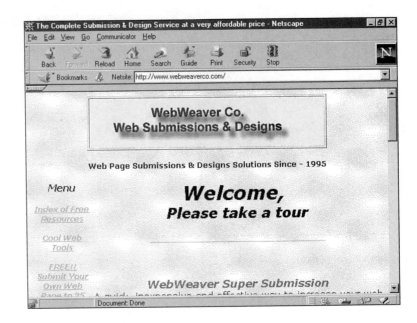

To broadcast an email message, compose the message and include in the To portion of the message header the email address of everyone you want to receive the message (see Figure 22.8). In most email programs, you separate the addresses with semicolons.

FIGURE 22.8.

Broadcasting an email message to announce your page.

Summary

If a page falls on the Web, and there's no one around to hear it, does it make a sound? I dunno. I shouldn't ask dumb questions I can't answer. The point is that after you create and publish a Web page, your job isn't done. It pays to advertise.

Workshop

Q&A

Q Do I have to check or update my listings on the directories?

A Well, after adding your page to the directories (and after the addition has been made formal on directories that make you wait a few days), you should always find your listing and test it to make sure it works as advertised.

After that, you can pretty much forget about it, unless you change your Web page's address or filename. Anytime you make such a change, you must change your listings in the directories to match.

Quiz

Take the following quiz to see how much you have learned.

Questions

1. True or False: There is no reason to add your page to directories maintained by crawlers; they do everything for you.

2. If you don't let people know about your page, they
   a. Won't know.
   b. Will psychically discover it.
   c. Won't love you anymore.
   d. All of the above.

Answers

1. False. Adding your page to such directors manually gets them there quicker and improves the accuracy with which they're categorized.

2. (a)

Activity

Search the directories for pages similar to yours, covering the same type of subject matter. Study the pages that impress you: Do they give you any ideas for changes to your page?

HOUR 23

Testing and Maintaining Your Page Online

You haven't simply published a Web page. You've established a Web presence—hopefully one that will expand and evolve with time (most do). After your page is online, it's important to know how to update it so you can improve and enlarge it over time, and how to test it so you can keep it performing reliably for your visitors.

At the end of this hour, you'll be able to answer the following questions:

- How do I rigorously test my page's programming?
- How do I ensure that my page looks good, no matter what browser the visitor is using?
- How do I keep my links working smoothly?
- How do I evaluate my page's ease-of-use for visitors?
- How do I update my page whenever I need to (or when I just plain feel like it)?

Testing Your Pages

Okay, you know your page operates in Navigator without a hitch. So that means the underlying HTML code is all kosher, right?

Not necessarily. Browsers differ in the extent to which they ignore or forgive minor errors in HTML coding. If you make a small mistake in syntax, the page might look fine in one browser, show minor problems in another, and show still bigger problems in a third.

More importantly, HTML files can sometimes get slightly scrambled when moving from a PC to a server. That's because different computing platforms recognize text characters in the same way, but may have slightly different ways of representing blank spaces or carriage returns. The whole reason browsers ignore carriage returns and blank spaces in your HTML files is so that changes to carriage returns and spaces caused by transferring a file between different computer systems won't cause problems.

Still, the small changes that an intersystem transfer causes might create problems—problems you won't be aware of until the page is online and thoroughly tested.

The next few sections show you how to thoroughly test your page after it's online so that you can make sure your visitors have precisely the experience you want them to have.

Validating Your HTML Code

A good safeguard against minor HTML infractions is to check your page with an HTML validator. An HTML validator checks to see if your page follows the precise rules of HTML.

A good choice for validating your HTML is the WebTechs Software HTML Validation Service, which you can explore by completing the following To Do.

If you use the WebTechs service to evaluate your page's viability in older browsers, you'll also want to view your page in such browsers, paying special attention to the aspects of the page WebTechs identifies as trouble spots.

To Do: Test your page in an HTML validator

1. Browse to the WebTechs service at

   valsvc.webtechs.com/

2. Choose Submit by URL. A questionnaire appears, as shown in Figures 23.1 and 23.2.

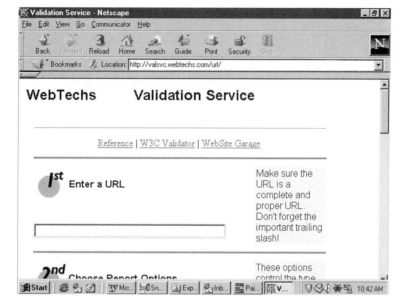

FIGURE 23.1.

The start of WebTechs' software validation questionnaire.

3. In part 1 of the questionnaire, type the complete URL (including the `http://` part) of your page.

4. In part 2 of the questionnaire (see Figure 23.2), choose the aspects of HTML code checking that you want included in WebTechs' report.

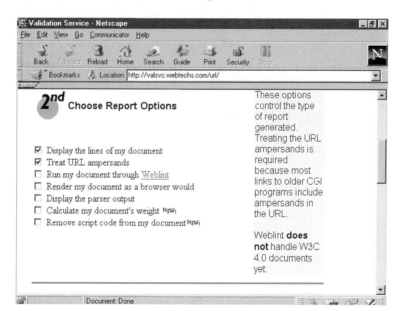

FIGURE 23.2.

Choosing the HTML options.

▼   5. In part 3, choose the specific "flavor" of HTML used in your page. (If you created
       your page in Composer, choose W3C 3.2. Doing so instructs the checker to con-
       sider HTML Level 3 tags and Netscape extensions acceptable.)

> Which level should you test at? If you've used Composer to create your
> page, you've almost certainly used Netscape extensions, since many of the
> best formatting capabilities in Composer employ extensions. Choosing
> Mozilla will restrict the service's complaints to mistakes and prevent it from
> calling your extension-based formatting an error.
>
> On the other hand, if you're concerned about your page's viability among
> browsers outside the Netscape fold, testing at Level 2 or Level 3 will provide
> you with a report of potential trouble spots for users of HTML 2 or non-
> extension-supporting browsers.

   6. In part 4, click the Check URL button to generate the report (see Figure 23.3). The
      service produces a report showing any errors it encounters. You can then decide
      whether and how to edit your HTML code to resolve any errors you consider sig-
      nificant.

FIGURE 23.3.

*WebTechs reports any
HTML problems.*

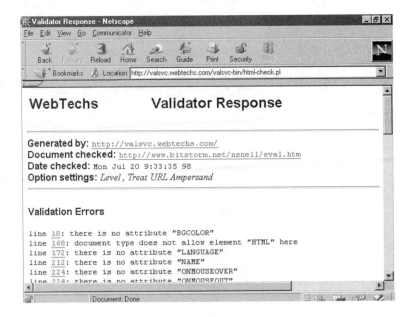

▲

Testing Browser Variability

While working on your page in Composer, you've been periodically previewing it in Navigator to test what it will look like online. But what about the rest of the Web population—those using earlier versions of Netscape, Internet Explorer, and any of a dozen other browsers? How will your page look to them?

After checking out your code validity and making any corrections, you'll want to view your page (online, if possible) through a variety of browsers, just to see if any serious problems arise when using browsers other than Navigator. Figures 23.4 through 23.6 illustrate how the same page can appear dramatically different through different browsers.

If you discover any problems in a particular browser environment, you must decide whether to adjust your page to eliminate the problem (which may involve compromising some of your formatting or other fancy features), or to sacrifice the performance of your page for one segment of the audience in order to preserve its performance for another.

FIGURE 23.4.

A page in Navigator 4 (the Communicator version).

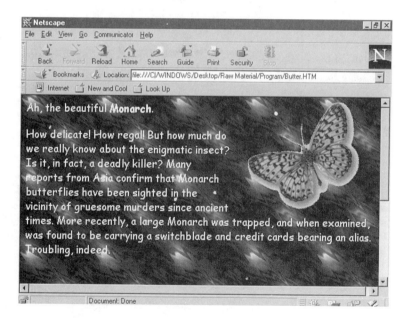

It's a good idea to keep some other browsers around to see how the other half sees you. NCSA's Mosaic and Microsoft's Internet Explorer, for example, can both be downloaded from the Web for free. (If you have Windows 98, you already have Internet Explorer built-in.) You can open your new page in either (check their help files to learn how to open an HTML file on disk) and see how it looks outside Navigator.

FIGURE 23.5.

The same page shown in Figure 23.4 as seen through Cello.

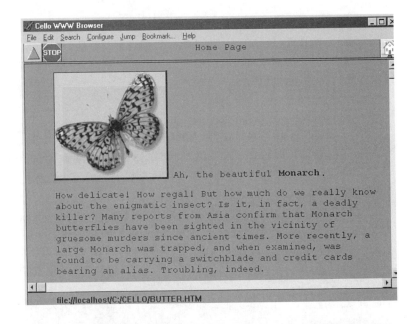

FIGURE 23.6.

The same page shown in Figure 23.4 as seen through DOSLynx.

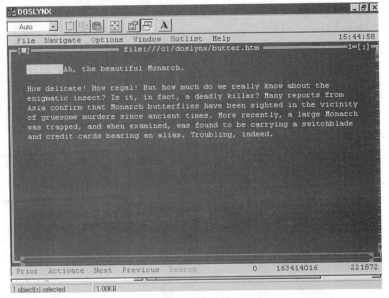

You can find the download addresses for various shareware and freeware browsers in Appendix C, "Online Resources for Web Authors."

Although these two browsers are good choices because they're popular, they're both graphical browsers—similar to Netscape Navigator in most respects—and support many of the same extensions. Therefore, your page is likely to look very similar in Navigator, Mosaic, and Internet Explorer. Given that, try to get your hands on a worst-case scenario browser, one that does not support Netscape extensions—preferably a text-only browser, such as DOSLynx (refer to Figure 23.6). Viewing your pages through this browser will help you determine how your cool page really looks—with its fancy formatting down around its ankles.

Which browsers you test in depends largely on how much of the Web universe you want to appeal to. Nobody knows for sure how many people on the Web use a particular browser. At this writing, however, estimates say that at least 80 percent (some estimates say 90 percent) of Web denizens use some form of Netscape Navigator and/or Internet Explorer. So if your page looks OK in Navigator, you can rest assured that it probably looks OK to most folks on the Web—but not necessarily all.

And even among users of Internet Explorer and Navigator, many still use older versions of these browsers, and they may not have upgraded to the latest versions, or even the version before the latest version. Between Navigator release 1.2 (which is about three years old) and Communicator, differences include support for frames, JavaScript, animated GIFs, tables, and many other refinements.

Once you've tested for the Netscape/Microsoft world, there remains only 10 to 20 percent of Web users whose view of your page you don't know. Of those, many probably use one of the many flavors of NCSA Mosaic. Unfortunately, Mosaic is available in a staggering array of versions from different sources, and each version is different. But, if you view your page through the current version of NCSA Mosaic, you'll know how your page appears to a significant chunk of the non-Netscape world—probably at least half of it.

Finally, there are two more browser types to test in:

- Older, graphical browsers that don't support Netscape extensions, such as Cello (see Figure 23.5).
- Text-only browsers, such as DOSLynx (refer to Figure 23.6).

While such browsers are on their way out, you'll need to test in them and adjust your page as needed if you really want it to behave properly in any environment. However, you must accept that doing so inevitably forces you to restrict your page to the most minimal formatting.

If you're really concerned about reaching everyone, supply your page in two versions: a fancy, extension-rich version and a very plain HTML 2–based version—and offer either from a universally visible top page (no frames, please!).

Testing Link Validity

Finally, it's important to test (and retest) all of the links in your page. Once you've verified the links among your own files—between your pages and to images and external media—you needn't recheck them unless you change a file.

But if your page contains links to remote resources—other people's Web pages or any file other than those you control on the server—you'll need to check these links often because the files they point to might have moved or their names might have changed.

Evaluating Your Page's Ergonomics

The preceding sections in this hour have explained only how to check your page's technical integrity. But what about its fuzzy qualities—its look, its feel, its *mise en scène*? And what about its interaction with visitors? Can they find what they came for? Do they see the parts of your message you want them to see? Do they naturally follow paths through your page to certain items, or are they frustrated by a lot of blind alleys and backtracking?

The best way to answer these questions would be to gather some friends (ideally friends who don't already know too much about your page or its subject) and/or cooperative strangers and watch them browse your page (no coaching!). Watch what they choose to click and what they skip. Note any time they move down a path and fail to find what they expected or hoped to find. And, of course, listen to their comments.

Another way to evaluate usability is to consult the server logs. Server logs keep track of how many people visit your page, which of your files people visit most, and the order in which people tend to view your files. To learn more about analyzing the server logs, talk to your server administrator.

Finally, remember always to use a signature with your email address. That way, people can send you comments and constructive criticisms.

Updating Your Page

Updating your page is publishing *redux*:

- Publish your files exactly as described in Hour 21, "Publishing Your Page." The new files automatically overwrite the old.

- Test, test, and test some more. (When finished, test again.)

23

When selecting files in the Publish dialog box, you need only select the files you have changed since the last time you published.

If your page is complex, however, and if you have changed many files, you might find it's just as easy to republish the entire page, just to be sure you haven't overlooked a file that has changed. For example, people often remember to upload new pages that have been added to a page, but forget to upload new versions of old pages that now contain links to the new page.

When adding new pages to an existing page, carefully reevaluate the structure and usability of the page. Over time, as pages and links are added, a previously well-structured page can begin to lose its structural integrity, branching off in illogical, patched-together ways.

Any time you add a page, reevaluate the entire page's structure from the top. You might find a structurally consistent way to integrate new material. But eventually, after a number of changes and additions, it becomes time to start over from the top and reorganize all of the content back into a cohesive whole.

Summary

Done.

Workshop

Q&A

Q **The material in this chapter seems a little technical. Do I really need to do an HTML check?**

A Well, the most important things are checking your links and testing in a couple of browsers. If your page passes those tests, it's probably fine.

But since I'm about to lose you as a student, I want to send you off with all the tools you might need. As you grow and make your pages more complex, the importance of HTML checking grows. So for now, don't worry about it. But be glad you know it's there for future reference.

Quiz

Take the following quiz to see how much you have learned.

Questions

1. True or False: Checking your code's compliance with HTML Level 2 and fixing any deviations from that level ensures the broadest possible compatibility with browsers.

2. Suppose your page looks great when viewed through an old version of Navigator (such as 1.2). Of the following browsers, which one may not display your page well:

   a. Navigator 4 (Communicator).

   b. Lynx.

   c. Internet Explorer 3.

   d. All of the above.

Answers

1. True.

2. (b) If the page looks fine in an older browser, it will also look fine in later browsers (a and c). But Navigator 1.2 is a graphical browser, and Lynx is text only—so you can't be sure what you'll see in Lynx 'til you test there.

Activity

Consult Appendix C for addresses to download browsers from and get as many as you can. Then test everything you've created so far in all of these browsers. You may be surprised by what you see.

HOUR 24

Developing Your Authoring Skills

This is it—*la chapitre finale*. And guess what? I tell you nothing here that immediately adds to your authoring skill set. (I know…it's a cheap trick. It's like when they forced you to show up for the last day of high school and then let you goof off all day anyway.)

What you do get in this hour is a graduation speech, or rather, a send-off with a purpose. If you've hit most or all of this tutorial, you've built a pretty solid foundation as an author. But there's always more to learn, always that one new trick that can make a good Web page into a great one. You now possess all the prerequisites needed to understand more advanced authoring information that you may find in other books or on the Web. So in this last hurrah, you'll find tips for developing your new skills.

At the end of this hour, you'll be able to answer the following questions:

- When I outgrow Composer, what's next?
- What practices can help me grow as a Web author, no matter what tools I use?

• What can I read now to take me to the next level?

Advancing to New Authoring Tools

Sculptors start with Play-Doh and work their way up to marble. And like a sculptor, if you continue authoring, your needs will one day advance beyond Composer's capabilities.

The next few pages describe some of the leading Web authoring environments and related tools. Any of them would make a fitting next step for an experienced Composer author.

Microsoft FrontPage Express

A few years back, Netscape upped the browser-war ante by adding Web authoring to Navigator (with a program that would become Composer a year later). Not to be outdone, Microsoft volleyed back in 1997 by adding a Web authoring program, FrontPage Express (see Figure 24.1), to Internet Explorer 4. If you have the full release of Internet Explorer 4, or if you have Windows 98 (which includes Internet Explorer 4), you have FrontPage Express. If not, you can download it free from Microsoft (see Appendix C).

A scaled-down version of Microsoft's pro-level FrontPage (described next in this hour), FrontPage Express is remarkably similar to Composer. In it, you can do most of the same things you can do with Composer, often using nearly the same buttons and menu items. As a Composer user, if you choose FrontPage Express as your next program, you will find learning it quick and easy.

FrontPage Express does a few handy things Composer does not; for example, it includes a forms toolbar and a step-by-step forms wizard for easily adding forms to your pages without writing any HTML code.

FrontPage Express's forms tools don't create the script for processing the form data, but they can optionally create forms that do their own data processing without a script, as long as the server on which the page is published has installed on it special software called "FrontPage extensions." (Ask your server supplier whether these extensions are installed on the server.) FrontPage Express also lets you easily add an inline background sound to your page that plays automatically whenever the visitor arrives.

FrontPage Express also has a few quirks. It does not play inline animations (you have to preview the page in a browser to see your animations properly), and it does not have a convenient preview button or menu item for jumping straight to a browser to preview your page. Still, it's a worthy next program for a Composer user, or a handy complement to Composer. And, of course, it's free.

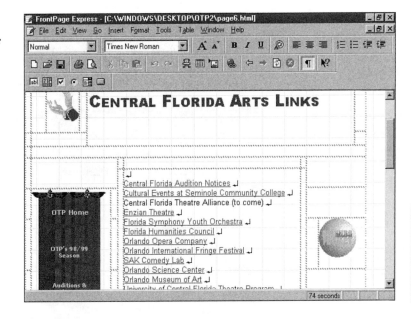

FIGURE 24.1.

Microsoft's FrontPage Express, the Gates answer to Composer.

Microsoft FrontPage

Like Composer, Microsoft's FrontPage is a full-featured, WYSIWYG Web authoring environment for Windows 95/98/NT. Using the FrontPage Editor (FrontPage's authoring component), you can compose HTML files quickly and easily by typing text and using toolbar buttons and menu items to format that text and add images and links. Better still, FrontPage includes a whole family of easy-to-use, step-by-step wizards for quickly building tables, frames, forms, and more.

From an authoring standpoint, FrontPage does everything Composer does, and much more. It's a professional-level Web authoring tool, but it's easy enough for any Composer user to learn.

However, FrontPage is more than a page composer. Through a facility called FrontPage Explorer, shown in Figure 24.2, you can easily manage an entire Web site and all the pages and other files in it. FrontPage also includes Web server software, called Personal Web Server, that turns any PC into a Web server for one or more Web sites. Accompanied by a complete set of administration and security tools, the Personal Web Server, FrontPage Explorer, and FrontPage Editor together supply a complete, single-product solution for creating and maintaining Web sites.

Unlike Composer, FrontPage includes a built-in HTML tag editor to complement its WYSIWYG editor, so there's no need to switch to an external editor such as Notepad or HTML Assistant for HTML jobs.

FIGURE 24.2.

FrontPage Explorer, the Web site management facility included in FrontPage.

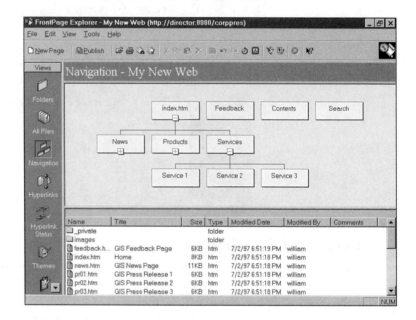

Liquid Motion Pro

Symantec's Liquid Motion Pro is designed to do for Java animation what Composer does for HTML. It enables non-programmers to create and publish Java-based animations without learning Java.

As when creating an animated GIF, you begin by creating the separate image files that when played in sequence will create the animation. You then feed them to Liquid Motion Pro and choose from among a variety of options how the animation will play, such as the speed of playback or the conditions under which the animation should start or stop. When you're done, the program cranks out finished Java code, ready for publishing.

Microsoft Office and Its Internet Assistants

The leading programs in Microsoft's Office suite can, to varying degrees, be used to produce Web page content. Word, Excel, PowerPoint, and Access can all put their data in HTML format for publishing on the Web or, more commonly, for fine-tuning in an editor before publishing—although only Word and PowerPoint really create full Web pages.

The Office 97 versions of these programs—Word 97, Excel 97, and so on—whether acquired individually or in the Office 97 package, each include this functionality (although you must specifically choose to install and enable Web page authoring when installing the program). The 95 versions can be retrofitted for Web page authoring with the addition of a family of Microsoft programs called *Internet Assistants*. Each Internet Assistant is a program that adds Web page authoring to an Office 95 program. There is a separate Internet Assistant for each of the four programs, available in versions for Windows and the Macintosh.

The Internet Assistants—required for enabling Office 95 programs with Web authoring capabilities—are included on the CD-ROM at the back of this book.

24

Of the Office programs, only Word truly functions as a real authoring environment. In fact, if you open an HTML file in Word, Word's menus and toolbars shift to a Web authoring mode and feature only the tools required for Web authoring, such as a drop-down list for applying paragraph formats. Word 97 also features a Web Page Wizard (see Figure 24.3) that leads you through creating a simple home page (including a background pattern and graphical bullets) and several page templates specifically designed for Web page authoring.

FIGURE 24.3.

Word 97's Web Page Wizard.

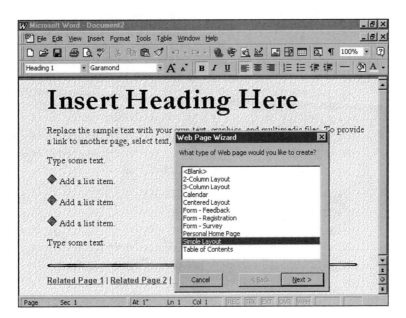

Although Word does the job, it's not a superior authoring environment to Composer or another real Web tool. Its real value to the Composer author is as a conversion tool.

Word enables you to open any Word page (or to open pages in other file formats, converting them to Word) and then save that file as an HTML file. When you do, Word not only converts the page formatting to its nearest HTML equivalent, but also converts all images in the page to GIF format, regardless of their original file type. You can then fine-tune the file in Composer and publish it. That's a very easy way to take existing material you may already have lying around in Word files—resumes, reports, and so on—and get it online in a flash.

For its part, PowerPoint converts any slide presentation into two versions for the Web: an all-graphics version (with added buttons so visitors can move from slide to slide) and an all-text version for the text-only browser crowd.

> The Web site you wind up with out of PowerPoint works, but it would be a nightmare to edit. If I had PowerPoint slides I wanted to put online, I would use Office 97's tools to convert the PowerPoint show to Word format, and then I would use Word to convert to HTML.

Excel and Access can each save files or selected data in HTML format, so you can easily incorporate that data into your own Web projects.

Microsoft Publisher 98

The latest version of Microsoft's easy-to-use desktop publishing program, Publisher 98 (see Figure 24.4), can optionally crank out Web pages in addition to the ads, brochures, and newsletters that are its usual gig.

It's a terrific Web page editor for a very specific type of user—someone who knows little about Web page creation, but has lots of nicely formatted Publisher projects he or she wants to turn conveniently into Web pages. Someone who already knows how to create a page from scratch (like you) would find Publisher 98 a little frustrating.

That said, the results can be pretty nice, and Publisher helps the user along with a collection of Web site templates and other handy tools, such as a forms toolbar (which can hook into the FrontPage extensions, just like FrontPage and FrontPage Express. On the downside, fancy pages from Publisher typically rely on table formatting (see Hour 8, "Organizing Text with Tables and Rules") to position objects, so the page may not look so great in older browsers that do not support tables.

FIGURE 24.4.

Publisher 98, a port-in-a-storm Web page editor.

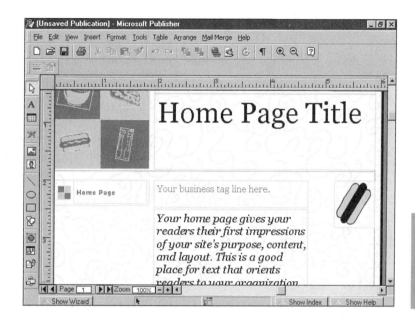

How to Grow as a Web Author

What can you do next? How will you advance to the next level? And more important, how can you keep a keen edge on the skills you've already mastered? Here are a few important habits you can adopt to prosper and grow.

Observe

When on the Web, don't just browse. Think about the pages you visit. Study them carefully, not at a technical level, but at an aesthetic one. If a page impresses you, ask yourself why. Is it the images, the layout, the writing, the colors, or some combination of these factors? Bookmark sites that impress you and visit them often. Make a mental catalog of what grabs your interest (or loses it) as a browser. Odds are, many other people respond the same way.

Dissect

When a page really impresses you, save it in the Editor (click the Edit button while browsing the page) and then study it there. Consider such questions as the following:

- What types of image files were used and what properties are applied to them?
- What is the flow of text elements and properties on the page?

- What special techniques show up in the HTML code if you view the source file (View, Page Source) when browsing the page?
- In a multipage Web site, how much information is on a page?
- How many pages are there and in what ways are they interlinked?

Stay Current

Stay up on new developments, particularly in the areas of evolving HTML standards and Java. One good way to do this is to visit Netscape's home page regularly and read any announcements posted there. You'll also want to check out many of the other Web authoring Web sites described in Appendix C.

For Further Reading

Here are some Sams titles that make excellent advanced reading following this workshop:

Sams Teach Yourself FrontPage 98 in 24 Hours (by Andy Shafran)

Laura Lemay's Web Workshop: FrontPage (by Laura Lemay and Denise Tyler)

Laura Lemay's Web Workshop: Graphics and Web Page Design (by Laura Lemay, Jon M. Duff, and James L. Mohler)

Sams Teach Yourself Web Publishing with HTML in 14 Days, Professional Reference Edition (by Laura Lemay)

The Bridges of Madison County (by Robert James Waller—just to get your mind off Web authoring)

Summary

You've picked up a great start, and now you know as much about Web authoring as you may ever need to. But there's always more to learn, always room to grow.

In the meantime, thanks for the 24 hours. And please come back to this book for a refresher anytime. We're always open.

Workshop

Quiz

Take the following quiz to see how much you have learned.

Questions

1. Which came first, the chicken or the egg?

2. Of the programs discussed in this hour (there are, of course, others), which of the following is probably the best next step up for an experienced Composer author?

    a. Raw HTML, and nothing but.

    b. PowerPoint 97

    c. FrontPage Express

    d. FrontPage

Answers

1. Egg. Just wanted to put that one to rest for you.

2. (d)

24

Activity

Hit your favorite bookstore and browse the bargain bin. In it, you can often find perfectly good Web authoring books for a few bucks that were priced at $30 or $40 less than a year ago when they came out. These books might even contain software on CD. The books are not out of date, really, and they're not broken. They're just yesterday's donuts, and a way for you to expand your Web authoring library for the price of a dozen glazed.

Appendix A

Installing Netscape Communicator

This appendix describes how to install Netscape Communicator from the CD-ROM included with this book. It also shows you how to acquire new versions of Communicator as they materialize from Netscape.

 Before installing the fully licensed version of Communicator included on the CD-ROM, copy the Communicator archive file from the CD-ROM to your hard disk, as explained in the instructions accompanying the disc.

Installing Communicator on Windows 95/98/NT

Whether you download Communicator (see the section titled "Downloading New Versions") or copy it from the CD-ROM, you start out with the

Communicator archive, a single, very large `.exe` file. This file is a self-extracting archive. (No unzip software is required.)

To install Communicator from its archive, follow these steps:

1. Double-click the archive's file icon. After a few moments and a brief display of the Communicator logo, a message is displayed informing you that you're about to install Communicator and asking whether you want to continue.

2. Click Yes. A status message is displayed while the Install Wizard sets up. After a few moments, a wizard like the one in Figure A.1 opens.

FIGURE A.1.

Starting the Install Wizard.

 As in any wizard, you use the Next button to advance to the next wizard page. If you wish to go back to a previous page to change a choice you made earlier, you can click the wizard's Back button.

3. Click Next. The Netscape license agreement appears. Read the license, and then click Yes to continue.

4. Click Next. The screen shown in Figure A.2 is displayed asking whether you want to perform the Typical installation or a Custom one:

   • The Typical installation installs only the most commonly used options. New users should start with the Typical installation and add other optional components later, as necessary.

   • The Custom installation leads you through a few extra Wizard pages on which you select the exact options you want installed. Choose Custom to install only selected options or to install all options.

If you enter a new Destination directory and that directory does not already exist, the wizard creates it for you.

Choose an installation option and check whether the Destination Directory listed at the bottom of the dialog is where you want Communicator installed. If not, enter a new directory or Browse for one. When done, click Next.

If you chose Typical installation in step 4, skip ahead to step 7. If you chose Custom, proceed to step 5.

FIGURE A.2.

Choosing an installation type and confirming the Destination directory.

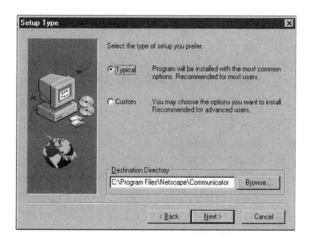

A

5. The first Custom installation dialog is displayed in Figure A.3 with all component options checked. To install all Communicator components, leave the check boxes alone. To choose not to install a component, clear its check box. When finished choosing component options, click Next.

6. The second Custom installation dialog is displayed in Figure A.4 with all extension options checked. For each extension you enable, your copy of Windows will be configured to use Communicator as the default application for the selected file type. For example, if you leave the JPEG Image check box selected, Communicator becomes your default viewer for JPEG images. Any time you open a JPEG file from a Windows folder or from Explorer, Communicator opens to show it to you.

When finished choosing extension options, click Next.

FIGURE A.3.

*Choosing components
in Custom installation.*

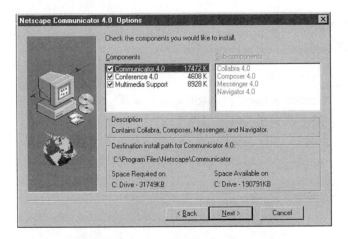

FIGURE A.4.

*Choosing extensions to
enable in Custom
installation.*

7. A dialog opens in which you can choose where in your Start menu Communicator is displayed. By default, the wizard adds a Netscape Communicator item to your Windows Programs menu. Choose Programs, Netscape Communicator from the Start menu; a submenu opens from which you can open any Communicator component. If you want the Communicator submenu set up in a folder other than Programs, choose it from the list of Existing Folders.

8. Click Next. A dialog is displayed, summarizing the choices you have made in the wizard. If the summary matches what you want to install, click Install to complete the installation. If not, click Back to go back to previous dialogs and change your choices.

9. After you confirm the install summary, the wizard decompresses the files and stores them in the chosen directory. A progress display appears while the files are being decompressed.

> To read the README file at any time after installation, open the file README.TXT in the folder Program Files/Netscape/Communicator.

10. After all the files have been decompressed, the Wizard displays a prompt, asking whether you'd like to view the README file. The README file contains important notes and information relating to the specific Communicator release you just installed. You can click Yes to read the file in Notepad now or No to read it later.

11. After you finish reading the README file and close Notepad (or after you click No in step 10), a message is displayed informing you that installation is complete. Click OK.

12. A message appears informing you that you should restart Windows before using Communicator. Click OK to restart Windows.

After Windows restarts, installation is technically complete. However, you still have a few more tasks to perform.

First, you must configure Communicator's communications and other preferences so that it can communicate with your Internet supplier (or local network proxy), mail server, and news server. If you're upgrading from Netscape Navigator version 3.0 or higher, your existing communications settings are used automatically by Communicator.

If you are not upgrading, the first time you open Communicator, a Setup New Profile wizard opens automatically to collect communications information from you. Later, you can manually edit your communications by editing Communicator's Preferences settings (choose Edit, Preferences).

> When you complete the Setup New Profile wizard, you will have created a Communicator *profile*, a set of communications settings for a single user. If you are the only person who will use Communicator on your computer, you don't have to think about profiles once yours is set up. However, you should be aware that multiple profiles can be created so that different users (with different user IDs, email addresses, and other settings) can share Communicator on one computer.

A

> To set up more profiles, choose Programs, Netscape Communicator, Setup
> New User Profile. When a copy of Communicator has two or more profiles
> configured, a dialog opens automatically when Communicator opens,
> prompting the user to select his or her profile from the list that appears in
> the dialog.

After configuring Communicator's communications and learning the basics of browsing
the Web with Navigator, you should register your copy of Communicator with Netscape.
As a registered user, you'll receive news about product updates, new plug-ins, and other
information via email from Netscape. To register, open Communicator's Navigator component and connect to the Internet; then choose **H**elp, Register Now. You'll be connected
to a page at Netscape where you can fill in a simple form to complete your registration.

Installing Communicator on a Macintosh

The Macintosh versions (PPC and 68k) of Netscape Communicator are distributed as
StuffIt Self Extracting archives. Before you begin, make sure you select the appropriate
version of Communicator. Use the PPC version if your Macintosh uses a PowerPC
processor (Apple Power Macintoshes, PowerPC Performas [5x00s and 6x00s], or any
Macintosh clone), or the 68k version if you are using an older Macintosh.

> Communicator recommends that you restart your computer after installa-
> tion, so before you go any further, you should quit and save anything else
> that you are currently working on.

To install Communicator for the Macintosh, follow these steps:

1. Double-click the archive to open it. This will create an installation folder.
2. Open the installation folder.
3. Within the installation folder are several supplementary folders and files. The only
   file you need to be concerned about is the Communicator Installer application.
   Double-click it to begin your installation.
4. You are then presented with a standard installation dialog box. By default, the
   Netscape Installer is set up to perform an Easy Install. This will install everything
   you need to get the most out of Communicator.

You can select Custom Install from the drop-down menu if you wish to install only specific Communicator components. The Installation dialog also gives you the option of selecting which folder you wish Communicator to be installed in. By default this will be your main hard drive. When you are finished selecting your installation options, click Install.

5. When you click install, another dialog box appears to remind you that Netscape Communicator recommends that you restart your computer after installation. Click Continue to go on or Cancel to cancel this installation. If you click Continue, your hard disk will begin to twirl around, and a nice progress bar will be displayed to show you your installation progress. Upon completion, another dialog box will be displayed, giving you the option to restart or quit. It is strongly recommended that you restart here; if you just quit and then try to run Communicator without restarting, certain features might not work correctly.

6. After you restart your computer, open the newly installed `Netscape Communicator Folder` (it will be wherever you told the installer to put it) and double-click the Netscape Communicator icon to start Communicator.

If you are upgrading from Netscape Navigator 3.0 or higher, Communicator will use your existing preferences for its default User Profile. Otherwise, a dialog box will prompt you to create a new user profile. Simply fill in the blanks with your profile name and your account information, and you'll be on your way.

Downloading New Versions

From time to time, new versions of Communicator will emerge, including not only major releases every year or so, but less heralded, little updates to fix bugs or add minor functionality.

You can access software updates in several different ways. One good way to start is to open Navigator and choose **H**elp, **S**oftware Updates. Navigator connects to a page at Netscape that offers one-stop access to links leading to software updates, plug-ins, and more.

It's also a good idea to visit Netscape's home page (`http://home.netscape.com`) regularly. On its home page, Netscape publishes announcements regarding new versions, beta versions, patches, plug-ins, and many other related issues. It's important that you see and read any announcements regarding new Communicator stuff before downloading it.

APPENDIX B

HTML Reference

- HTML Tags
- Images
- Forms
- Tables (HTML 3.0)
- Frame Tags
- Programming Tags
- Colors by Name and HEX Value

This appendix is a reference to the HTML tags (and color values) you can use in your documents, according to the HTML 2.0 specification. In addition, tags defined in both the HTML 3.0 and Netscape Navigator 2.0/3.0 specifications are listed. Tags supported by HTML 3.0 and Navigator 2.0/3.0 are listed as (HTML 3.0), whereas tags that are currently only available in Navigator 2.0/3.0 are listed as (NHTML). There are also a couple of tags listed that Navigator 2.0/3.0 does not yet support; these are listed as (HTML 3.0 only).

HTML Tags

This section lists and explains all of the HTML tags that you may want to use in documents you create with Gold or in an external HTML editor.

To learn the general methods for adding these tags to a document, see Hour 17, "Editing HTML."

Comments

`<!--......-->`

Any text enclosed within a comment tag is completely ignored by the Web browser. This includes tags, elements, and entities.

`<!DOCTYPE HTML PUBLIC "-//Netscape Comm. Corp.//DTD HTML//EN">`

Used with HTML document validation systems, such as Halsoft at `http://www.halsoft.com/html-val-svc/`, to indicate the level of HTML support included in a document. If included in a document, this tag must be placed on the very first line, before the `<HTML>` tag.

`<!DOCTYPE HTML PUBLIC "-//Netscape Comm. Corp. Strict//DTD HTML//EN">`

Used to indicate a more strict set of compliance tests for validation systems such as Halsoft. For more information, visit the Halsoft site listed previously. This site contains both the document validation system and a range of files covering *document type definitions* (DTD) and HTML standards.

Structure Tags

`<HTML>...</HTML>`

Encloses the entire HTML document.

Can Include: `<HEAD>` `<BODY>` `<FRAMESET>`

`<HEAD>...</HEAD>`

Encloses the head of the HTML document.

Can Include: `<TITLE>` `<ISINDEX>` `<BASE>` `<NEXTID>` `<LINK>` `<META>` `<SCRIPT>`

Allowed Inside: `<HTML>`

`<BODY>...</BODY>`

Encloses the body (text and tags) of the HTML document.

Attributes:

BACKGROUND="..."	(HTML 3.0) The name or URL for an image to tile on the page background.
BGCOLOR="..."	(NHTML) The color of the page background.
TEXT="..."	(NHTML) The color of the page's text.
LINK="..."	(NHTML) The color of unfollowed links.
ALINK="..."	(NHTML) The color of activated links.
VLINK="..."	(NHTML) The color of followed links.

Can Include: <H1> <H2> <H3> <H4> <H5> <H6> <P> <OL> <DIR> <MENU> <DL> <PRE> <BLOCKQUOTE> <FORM> <ISINDEX> <HR> <ADDRESS> <TABLE> <SCRIPT> <APPLET> <EMBED>

Allowed Inside: <HTML>

Tags That Can Be Included Inside the <HEAD> Block

`<TITLE>...</TITLE>`

Indicates the title of the document.

Allowed Inside: <HEAD>

`<BASE>`

Defines base values for the current document.

Attributes:

HREF="..."	Overrides the base URL of the current document.
TARGET="..."	Defines a default target window for all links in the current document.

Allowed Inside: <HEAD>

B

`<ISINDEX>`

Indicates that the document is a gateway script that allows searches.

Attributes:

`PROMPT="..."`   (HTML 3.0) The prompt for the search field.

Allowed Inside: `<BLOCKQUOTE> <BODY> <DD> <FORM> <HEAD> <LI> <TABLE>`

`<LINK>`

Indicates the relationship between the document and some other document. Generally used only by HTML-generating tools.

Attributes:

`HREF="..."`	The URL of the referenced HTML document.
`REL="..."`	The forward relationship.
`REV="..."`	A reverse relationship, usually the mailto address of the document's author.
`URN="..."`	Universal resource number.
`TITLE="..."`	The link's title.
`METHODS="..."`	Supported public methods of the object.

Allowed Inside: `<HEAD>`

`<META>`

Used to simulate HTTP response header messages in an HTML document.

Attributes:

`HTTP-EQUIV="..."`	HTTP response header name.
`CONTENT="..."`	Value assigned to the response header.
`NAME="..."`	Meta information name.

Allowed Inside: `<HEAD>`

`<NEXTID>`

Indicates the next document after this one (as might be defined by a tool to manage HTML documents in series).

Attribute: `N="..."`

Allowed Inside: `<HEAD>`

Headings

All heading tags have the following characteristics:

Attributes:

`ALIGN="CENTER"`	(HTML 3.0) Centers the heading.
`ALIGN="LEFT"`	(HTML 3.0) Left justifies the heading.
`ALIGN="RIGHT"`	(HTML 3.0) Right justifies the heading.
`ALIGN="JUSTIFY"`	(HTML 3.0 only) Block justifies the heading where possible.

Can Include: `<A>` `<IMG>` `<BR>` `<BIG>` `<B>` `<BLINK>` `<I>` `<SMALL>` `<SUB>` `<SUP>` `<TT>` `<CITE>` `<CODE>` `<DFN>` `<EM>` `<KBD>` `<SAMP>` `<STRONG>` `<VAR>`

Allowed Inside: `<BLOCKQUOTE>` `<BODY>` `<FORM>`

`<H1>...</H1>`

A first-level heading.

`<H2>...</H2>`

A second-level heading.

`<H3>...</H3>`

A third-level heading.

`<H4>...</H4>`

A fourth-level heading.

`<H5>...</H5>`

A fifth-level heading.

`<H6>...</H6>`

A sixth-level heading.

`<P>...</P>`

A plain paragraph. The closing tag (`</P>`) is optional.

B

Attributes:

ALIGN="CENTER"	(HTML 3.0) Centers the paragraph.
ALIGN="LEFT"	(HTML 3.0) Left justifies the paragraph.
ALIGN="RIGHT"	(HTML 3.0) Right justifies the paragraph.
ALIGN="JUSTIFY"	(HTML 3.0 only) Block justifies the paragraph where possible.

Can Include: <A> <IMG>
 <BIG> <B> <BLINK> <I> <SMALL> <SUB> <SUP> <TT> <CITE> <CODE> <DFN> <EM> <KBD> <SAMP> <STRONG> <VAR>

Allowed Inside: <BLOCKQUOTE> <BODY> <DD> <FORM> <LI> <TABLE>

<DIV>...</DIV>

Declares a block of text, but unlike the <P> tag, the <DIV> tag does not add a trailing double-line space.

Attributes:

ALIGN="CENTER"	(HTML 3.0) Centers the text defined by the division.
ALIGN="LEFT"	(HTML 3.0) Left justifies the text defined by the division.
ALIGN="RIGHT"	(HTML 3.0) Right justifies the text defined by the division.
ALIGN="JUSTIFY"	(HTML 3.0 only) Block justifies the text defined by the division where possible.

Can Include: <A> <IMG>
 <BIG> <B> <BLINK> <I> <SMALL> <SUB> <SUP> <TT> <CITE> <CODE> <DFN> <EM> <KBD> <SAMP> <STRONG> <VAR> <TABLE>

Allowed Inside: <BLOCKQUOTE> <BODY> <DD> <FORM> <LI> <TABLE>

Links

<A>...</A>

With the HREF attribute, creates a hyperlink to another document or anchor; with the NAME attribute, creates an anchor that can be linked to.

Attributes:

HREF="..."	The URL pointed to by a link.
TARGET="..."	The target window for the new document.
NAME="..."	The anchor name for a reference anchor.

Can Include: `<IMG>` `<BR>` `<BIG>` `<B>` `<BLINK>` `<I>` `<SMALL>` `<SUB>` `<SUP>` `<TT>` `<CITE>` `<CODE>` `<DFN>` `<EM>` `<KBD>` `<SAMP>` `<STRONG>` `<VAR>` `<TABLE>`

Allowed Inside: `<ADDRESS>` `<BIG>` `<B>` `<BLINK>` `<I>` `<SMALL>` `<SUB>` `<SUP>` `<TT>` `<CITE>` `<CODE>` `<DFN>` `<EM>` `<KBD>` `<SAMP>` `<STRONG>` `<VAR>` `<BLOCKQUOTE>` `<DD>` `<FORM>` `<LI>` `<TABLE>`

Lists

`<OL>...</OL>`

An ordered (numbered) list.

Attributes:

TYPE="..."	(NHTML) The type of numerals to label the list with. Possible values are A, a, I, i, and 1.
START="..."	(NHTML) The value to start this list with.

Can Include: `<LI>`

Allowed Inside: `<BLOCKQUOTE>` `<BODY>` `<DD>` `<FORM>` `<LI>` `<TABLE>`

`<UL>...</UL>`

An unordered (bulleted) list.

Attribute:

TYPE="..."	(NHTML) The bullet dingbat to use to mark list items. Possible values are DISC, CIRCLE, and SQUARE.

Can Include: `<LI>`

Allowed Inside: `<BLOCKQUOTE>` `<BODY>` `<DD>` `<FORM>` `<LI>` `<TABLE>`

`<MENU>...</MENU>`

A menu list of items. (Note: Removed from the HTML 3.0 specification.)

Can Include: `<LI>`

Allowed Inside: `<BLOCKQUOTE>` `<BODY>` `<DD>` `<FORM>` `<LI>` `<TABLE>`

B

`<DIR>...</DIR>`

A directory listing; items are generally smaller than 20 characters. (Note: No longer supported in the HTML 3.0 specification.)

Can Include: `<LI>`

Allowed Inside: `<BLOCKQUOTE>` `<BODY>` `<DD>` `<FORM>` `<LI>` `<TABLE>`

`<LI>`

A list item for use with `<OL>`, `<MENU>`, or `<DIR>`

Attributes:

> `TYPE="..."`   (NHTML) The type of bullet or number to label an item with. Possible values are `DISC`, `CIRCLE`, `SQUARE`, A, a, I, i, and 1.

> `VALUE="..."`   (NHTML) The numeric value this list item should have (affects this item and all below it in `<OL>` lists).

Can Include: `<A>` `<IMG>` `<BR>` `<BIG>` `<B>` `<BLINK>` `<I>` `<SMALL>` `<SUB>` `<SUP>` `<TT>` `<CITE>` `<CODE>` `<DFN>` `<EM>` `<KBD>` `<SAMP>` `<STRONG>` `<VAR>` `<P>` `<DIV>` `<OL>` `<DIR>` `<MENU>` `<DL>` `<PRE>` `<BLOCKQUOTE>`

Allowed Inside: `<DIR>` `<MENU>` `<OL>`

`<DL>...</DL>`

A definition or glossary list. The COMPACT attribute specifies a format that takes less whitespace to present.

Attribute: COMPACT

Can Include: `<DT>` `<DD>`

Allowed Inside: `<BLOCKQUOTE>` `<BODY>` `<DD>` `<FORM>` `<LI>` `<TABLE>`

`<DT>`

A definition term, as part of a definition list.

Can Include: `<A>` `<IMG>` `<BR>` `<BIG>` `<B>` `<BLINK>` `<I>` `<SMALL>` `<SUB>` `<SUP>` `<TT>` `<CITE>` `<CODE>` `<DFN>` `<EM>` `<KBD>` `<SAMP>` `<STRONG>` `<VAR>`

Allowed Inside: `<DL>`

`<DD>`

The corresponding definition to a definition term, as part of a definition list.

Can Include: <A> <IMG>
 <BIG> <B> <BLINK> <I> <SMALL> <SUB> <SUP> <TT> <CITE> <CODE> <DFN> <EM> <KBD> <SAMP> <STRONG> <VAR> <P> <OL> <DIR> <MENU> <DL> <PRE> <BLOCKQUOTE> <FORM> <ISINDEX> <TABLE>

Allowed Inside: <DL>

Character Formatting

All the character formatting tags have these features:

Can Include: <A> <IMG>
 <BIG> <B> <BLINK> <I> <SMALL> <SUB> <SUP> <TT> <CITE> <CODE> <DFN> <EM> <KBD> <SAMP> <STRONG> <VAR>

Allowed Inside: <A> <ADDRESS> <BIG> <B> <BLINK> <I> <SMALL> <SUB> <SUP> <TT> <CITE> <CODE> <DFN> <EM> <KBD> <SAMP> <STRONG> <VAR> <DD> <DT> <H1> <H2> <H3> <H4> <H5> <H6> <LI> <P> <PRE> <TABLE>

<BIG>...</BIG>

Big text; text uses larger font than standard text.

<B>...</B>

Bold; bold text.

<BLINK>...</BLINK>

Blinking; blinking text.

<I>...</I>

Italic; italic text.

<SMALL>...</SMALL>

Small text; text uses smaller font than standard text.

_{...}

Subscript; text is subscripted.

^{...}

Superscript; text is superscripted.

<TT>...</TT>

Typewriter; text uses monospaced typewriter font.

<CITE>...</CITE>

Citation; for quotes and references.

B

<CODE>...</CODE>

Program code; for computer program source code.

<DFN>...</DFN>

Defined; for word definitions.

<EM>...</EM>

Emphasis; when italic emphasis is required.

<KBD>...</KBD>

Keyboard; when showing text that users need to type in.

<SAMP>...</SAMP>

Sample; for examples.

<STRONG>...</STRONG>

Strong; when bold text is required.

<VAR>...</VAR>

Variable; for names of program variables.

Other Text Layout Elements

The following tags create standard page elements that resist categorization because they are not exactly text elements (although they may format text), but not exactly images or links, either. Call them *miscellaneous*.

<HR>

A horizontal rule line.

Attributes:

SIZE="..."	(NHTML) The thickness of the rule, in pixels.
WIDTH="..."	(NHTML) The width of the rule, in pixels.
ALIGN="..."	(NHTML) How the rule line will be aligned on the page. Possible values are LEFT, RIGHT, and CENTER.
NOSHADE="..."	(NHTML) Causes the rule line to be drawn as a solid color with no shading.

Allowed Inside: <BLOCKQUOTE> <BODY> <FORM> <PRE> <TABLE>

`<BR>`

A line break.

Attribute:

CLEAR="..."   (HTML 3.0) causes the text to stop flowing around any images. Possible values are RIGHT, LEFT, and ALL.

Allowed Inside: <A> <ADDRESS> <BIG> <B> <BLINK> <I> <SMALL> <SUB> <SUP> <TT> <CITE> <CODE> <DFN> <EM> <KBD> <SAMP> <STRONG> <VAR> <DD> <DT> <H1> <H2> <H3> <H4> <H5> <H6> <LI> <P> <PRE> <TABLE>

`<NOBR>...</NOBR>` (NHTML)

Causes the enclosed text not to wrap at the edge of the page.

Allowed Inside: <A> <ADDRESS> <BIG> <B> <BLINK> <I> <SMALL> <SUB> <SUP> <TT> <CITE> <CODE> <DFN> <EM> <KBD> <SAMP> <STRONG> <VAR> <DD> <DT> <H1> <H2> <H3> <H4> <H5> <H6> <LI> <P> <PRE> <TABLE>

`<WBR>` (NHTML)

Wraps the text at this point, only if necessary.

Allowed Inside: <A> <ADDRESS> <BIG> <B> <BLINK> <I> <SMALL> <SUB> <SUP> <TT> <CITE> <CODE> <DFN> <EM> <KBD> <SAMP> <STRONG> <VAR> <DD> <DT> <H1> <H2> <H3> <H4> <H5> <H6> <LI> <P> <PRE> <TABLE>

`<BLOCKQUOTE>...</BLOCKQUOTE>`

Used for long quotes or citations.

Can Include: <BLOCKQUOTE> <IMG> <H1> <H2> <H3> <H4> <H5> <H6> <P> <OL> <DIR> <MENU> <DL> <PRE> <FORM> <ISINDEX> <HR> <ADDRESS> <TABLE>

Allowed Inside: <BLOCKQUOTE> <BODY> <DD> <FORM> <LI> <TABLE>

`<CENTER>...</CENTER>`

All the content enclosed within these tags is centered. This tag is being phased out in favor of <P ALIGN=CENTER> and <DIV ALIGN=CENTER>.

Can Include: <A> <IMG> <ADDRESS> <BIG> <B> <BLINK> <I> <SMALL> <SUB> <SUP> <TT> <CITE> <CODE> <DFN> <EM> <KBD> <SAMP> <STRONG> <VAR> <DD> <DT> <H1> <H2> <H3> <H4> <H5> <H6> <LI> <P> <PRE> <TABLE>

Allowed Inside: <BLOCKQUOTE> <BODY> <DD> <FORM> <LI> <TABLE>

B

`<ADDRESS>...</ADDRESS>`

Used for signatures or general information about a document's author.

Can Include: `<A>` `<IMG>` `<BIG>` `<B>` `<BLINK>` `<I>` `<SMALL>` `<SUB>` `<SUP>` `<TT>` `<CITE>` `<CODE>` `<DFN>` `<EM>` `<KBD>` `<SAMP>` `<STRONG>` `<VAR>` `<DD>` `<DT>` `<H1>` `<H2>` `<H3>` `<H4>` `<H5>` `<H6>` `<LI>` `<P>` `<PRE>` `<TABLE>`

Allowed Inside: `<BLOCKQUOTE>` `<BODY>` `<FORM>`

Font Sizes (NHTML)

`<FONT>...</FONT>`

Changes the size or color of the font for the enclosed text.

Attributes:

`SIZE="..."`	The size of the font, from 1 to 7. The default is 3. Can also be specified as a value relative to the current size (for example, +2).
`COLOR="..."`	The color of the font. See the section titled "Colors by Name and HEX Value" later in this appendix.

Can Include: `<A>` `<IMG>` `<BIG>` `<B>` `<BLINK>` `<I>` `<SMALL>` `<SUB>` `<SUP>` `<TT>` `<CITE>` `<CODE>` `<DFN>` `<EM>` `<KBD>` `<SAMP>` `<STRONG>` `<VAR>` `<DD>` `<DT>` `<LI>` `<P>` `<PRE>` `<TABLE>`

Allowed Inside: `<A>` `<ADDRESS>` `<BIG>` `<B>` `<BLINK>` `<I>` `<SMALL>` `<SUB>` `<SUP>` `<TT>` `<CITE>` `<CODE>` `<DFN>` `<EM>` `<KBD>` `<SAMP>` `<STRONG>` `<VAR>` `<DD>` `<DT>` `<H1>` `<H2>` `<H3>` `<H4>` `<H5>` `<H6>` `<LI>` `<P>` `<PRE>` `<TABLE>`

`<BASEFONT>`

Sets the default size of the font for the current page.

Attribute:

`SIZE="..."`	The default size of the font, from 1 to 7. The default is 3.

Allowed Inside: `<A>` `<ADDRESS>` `<BIG>` `<B>` `<BLINK>` `<I>` `<SMALL>` `<SUB>` `<SUP>` `<TT>` `<CITE>` `<CODE>` `<DFN>` `<EM>` `<KBD>` `<SAMP>` `<STRONG>` `<VAR>` `<DD>` `<DT>` `<LI>` `<P>` `<PRE>` `<TABLE>`

Images

<IMG>

Insert an inline image into the document.

Attributes:

ISMAP	This image is a clickable imagemap.
SRC="..."	The URL of the image.
ALT="..."	A text string that will be displayed in browsers that cannot support images.
ALIGN="..."	Determines the alignment of the given image. If LEFT or RIGHT (HTML 3.0, NHTML), the image is aligned to the left or right column and all following text flows beside that image. All other values, such as TOP, MIDDLE, BOTTOM, or (NHTML) TEXTTOP, ABSMIDDLE, BASELINE, and ABSBOTTOM, determine the vertical alignment of this image with other items in the same line.
VSPACE="..."	The space between the image and the text above or below it.
HSPACE="..."	The space between the image and the text to its left or right.
WIDTH="..."	(HTML 3.0) The width (in pixels) of the image. If WIDTH is not the actual width, the image is scaled to fit.
HEIGHT="..."	(HTML 3.0) The height (in pixels) of the image. If HEIGHT is not the actual height, the image is scaled to fit.
BORDER="..."	(NHTML) Draws a border of the specified value in pixels to be drawn around the image. In the case of images that are also links, BORDER changes the size of the default link border.
LOWSRC="..."	(NHTML) The path or URL of an image that will be loaded first, before the image specified in SRC. The value of LOWSRC is usually a smaller or lower-resolution version of the actual image.
USEMAP="..."	(NHTML) Used to associate an image with a client-side imagemap specified by <MAP NAME=mapname>.

B

Allowed Inside: `<A>` `<ADDRESS>` `<BIG>` `<B>` `<BLINK>` `<I>` `<SMALL>` `<SUB>` `<SUP>` `<TT>` `<CITE>` `<CODE>` `<DFN>` `<EM>` `<KBD>` `<SAMP>` `<STRONG>` `<VAR>` `<DD>` `<DT>` `<H1>` `<H2>` `<H3>` `<H4>` `<H5>` `<H6>` `<LI>` `<P>` `<PRE>` `<TABLE>`

`<MAP>...</MAP>`

Defines a map for a client-side imagemap.

Attribute:

`NAME="..."`	Used to define the map's name.

Can Include: `<AREA>`

Allowed Inside: `<BODY>`

`<AREA>...</AREA>`

Define a clickable region for a client-side imagemap.

Attributes:

`TYPE="..."`	Used to indicate the type of region bound by the `<AREA>` tag. Possible values are `RECT`, `POLY`, and `CIRCLE`.
`COORDS="..."`	This attribute describes the points binding the region described by the `<AREA>` tag.
`HREF="..."`	The URL to load when the region bound by the `<AREA>` tag is clicked.

Allowed Inside: `<MAP>`

Forms

`<FORM>...</FORM>`

Indicates a form.

Attributes:

`ACTION="..."`	The URL of the script to process the form input.
`METHOD="..."`	How the form input will be sent to the gateway on the server side. Possible values are `GET` and `POST`.
`ENCTYPE="..."`	Only values currently supported are `application/x-www-form-urlencoded` and `multipart/form-data` (NHTML).
`TARGET="..."`	(NHTML) Target window for response following form submission.

Can Include: <H1> <H2> <H3> <H4> <H5> <H6> <P> <OL> <DIR> <MENU> <DL> <PRE> <BLOCKQUOTE> <ISINDEX> <HR> <ADDRESS> <INPUT> <SELECT> <TEXTAREA> <TABLE>

Allowed Inside: <BLOCKQUOTE> <BODY> <DD> <LI>

<INPUT>

An input widget for a form.

Attributes:

TYPE="..."	The type for this input widget. Possible values are CHECKBOX, FILE (NHTML), HIDDEN, PASSWORD, RADIO, RESET, SUBMIT, TEXT, or IMAGE (HTML 3.0 only).
NAME="..."	The name of this item to be passed to the gateway script as part of a name/value pair.
VALUE="..."	For a text or hidden widget, the default value; for a check box or radio button, the value to be submitted with the form; for Reset or Submit buttons, the label for the button itself.
SRC="..."	The source file for an image.
CHECKED	For check boxes and radio buttons, indicates that the widget is checked.
SIZE="..."	The size, in characters, of a text widget.
MAXLENGTH="..."	The maximum number of characters that can be entered into a text widget.
ALIGN="..."	For images in forms, determines how the text and image will align (same as with the <IMG> tag).

Allowed Inside: <FORM>

<TEXTAREA>...</TEXTAREA>

Indicates a multiline text entry widget.

Attributes:

NAME="..."	The name to be passed to the gateway script as part of the name/value pair.
ROWS="..."	The number of rows this text area displays.

B

COLS="..."	The number of columns (characters) this text area displays.
WRAP="OFF"	Wrapping doesn't happen. Lines are sent exactly as typed.
WRAP="VIRTUAL"	The display word wraps, but long lines are sent as one line without new lines.
WRAP="PHYSICAL"	The display word wraps, and the text is transmitted at all wrap points.

Allowed Inside: <FORM>

<SELECT>...</SELECT>

Creates a menu or scrolling list of possible items.

Attributes:

NAME="..."	The name that is passed to the gateway script as part of the name/value pair.
SIZE="..."	The number of elements to display. If SIZE is indicated, the selection becomes a scrolling list. If no SIZE is given, the selection is a pop-up menu.
MULTIPLE	Allows multiple selections from the list.

Can Include: <OPTION>

Allowed Inside: <FORM>

<OPTION>

Indicates a possible item within a <SELECT> widget.

Attributes:

SELECTED	With this attribute included, the <OPTION> will be selected by default in the list.
VALUE="..."	The value to submit if this <OPTION> is selected when the form is submitted.

Allowed Inside: <SELECT>

Tables (HTML 3.0)

The following tags are used to create tables.

`<TABLE>...</TABLE>`

Creates a table, which can contain a caption (`<CAPTION>`) and any number of rows (`<TR>`).

Attributes:

`BORDER="..."`	Indicates whether the table should be drawn with or without a border. In Netscape, `BORDER` can also have a value indicating the width of the border.
`CELLSPACING="..."`	(NHTML) The amount of space between the cells in the table.
`CELLPADDING="..."`	(NHTML) The amount of space between the edges of the cell and its contents.
`WIDTH="..."`	(NHTML) The width of the table on the page, in either exact pixel values or as a percentage of the page width.
`ALIGN="..."`	Determines the alignment of the given table. If `LEFT` or `RIGHT` (HTML 3.0, NHTML), the image is aligned to the left or right column, and all following text flows beside that image. If `CENTER` appears as the value for `ALIGN=`, the table is aligned with the center of the page (HTML 3.0 only).
`BGCOLOR="..."`	(NHTML) The background color of the cells in the table (Navigator 3.0 only).

Can Include: `<CAPTION>` `<TR>`

Allowed Inside: `<BLOCKQUOTE>` `<BODY>` `<DD>` `<LI>` `<TABLE>`

`<CAPTION>...</CAPTION>`

The caption for the table.

Attributes:

`ALIGN="..."`	The position of the caption. Possible values are `TOP` and `BOTTOM`.

B

<TR>...</TR>

Defines a table row containing headings and data (<TR> and tags).

Attributes:

ALIGN="..."	The horizontal alignment of the contents of the cells within this row. Possible values are LEFT, RIGHT, and CENTER.
VALIGN="..."	The vertical alignment of the contents of the cells within this row. Possible values are TOP, MIDDLE, BOTTOM, and BASELINE (NHTML).
BGCOLOR="..."	(NHTML) The background color of the cells in the row (Navigator 3.0 only).

Can Include: <TD>

Allowed Inside: <TABLE>

<TH>...</TH>

Defines a table heading cell.

Attributes:

ALIGN="..."	The horizontal alignment of the contents of the cell. Possible values are LEFT, RIGHT, and CENTER.
VALIGN="..."	The vertical alignment of the contents of the cell. Possible values are TOP, MIDDLE, BOTTOM, and BASELINE (NHTML).
ROWSPAN="..."	The number of rows the cell will span.
COLSPAN="..."	The number of columns the cell will span.
NOWRAP	No automatic wrapping of the contents of the cell.
WIDTH="..."	(NHTML) The width of this column of cells, in exact pixel values or as a percentage of the table width.
BGCOLOR="..."	(NHTML) The background color of the heading cell (Navigator 3.0 only).

Can Include: <H1> <H2> <H3> <H4> <H5> <H6> <P> <OL> <DIR> <MENU> <DL> <PRE> <BLOCKQUOTE> <FORM> <ISINDEX> <HR> <ADDRESS> <TABLE>

Allowed Inside: <TR>

`<TD>...</TD>`

Defines a table data cell.

Attributes:

ALIGN="..."	The horizontal alignment of the contents of the cell. Possible values are LEFT, RIGHT, and CENTER.
VALIGN="..."	The vertical alignment of the contents of the cell. Possible values are TOP, MIDDLE, BOTTOM, and BASELINE (NHTML).
ROWSPAN="..."	The number of rows the cell will span.
COLSPAN="..."	The number of columns the cell will span.
NOWRAP	No automatic wrapping of the contents of the cell.
WIDTH="..."	(NHTML) The width of this column of cells, in exact pixel values or as a percentage of the table width.
BGCOLOR="..."	(NHTML) The background color of the cell (Navigator 3.0 only).

Can Include: `<H1>` `<H2>` `<H3>` `<H4>` `<H5>` `<H6>` `<P>` `<OL>` `<DIR>` `<MENU>` `<DL>` `<PRE>` `<BLOCKQUOTE>` `<FORM>` `<ISINDEX>` `<HR>` `<ADDRESS>`

Allowed Inside: `<TR>`

Frame Tags

The following tags are used to create frame-based documents. To learn more about applying these tags, see Hour 18, "Dividing a Page into Frames."

`<FRAMESET>...</FRAMESET>` (NHTML)

Encloses a frameset definition in an HTML document.

Attributes:

COLS="..."	(NHTML) Defines the number of frame columns and their width in a frameset.
ROWS="..."	(NHTML) Defines the number of frame rows and their height in a frameset.

Can Include: `<FRAME>` `<NOFRAMES>`

Allowed Inside: `<HTML>`

<FRAME> (NHTML)

Used to define the contents of a frame within a frameset.

Attributes:

SRC="..."	The URL of the document to be displayed inside the frame.
MARGINWIDTH="..."	The size in pixels of the margin on each side of a frame.
MARGINHEIGHT="..."	The size in pixels of the margin above and below the contents of a frame.
SCROLLING="..."	Enables or disables the display of scroll bars for a frame. Values are YES, NO, and AUTO.
NORESIZE	The user is not allowed to resize frames.

Allowed Inside: <FRAMESET>

<NOFRAMES>...</NOFRAMES> (NHTML)

Used to define a block of text that will be displayed by Web browsers that don't support frames.

Can Include: <A> <IMG> <ADDRESS> <BIG> <B> <BLINK> <I> <SMALL> <SUB> <SUP> <TT> <CITE> <CODE> <DFN> <EM> <KBD> <SAMP> <STRONG> <VAR> <DD> <DT> <H1> <H2> <H3> <H4> <H5> <H6> <LI> <P> <PRE> <TABLE>

Allowed Inside: <FRAMESET>

Programming Tags

The following tags are used to embed program code in a document.

<SCRIPT>...</SCRIPT>

Encloses a JavaScript or LiveScript program definition and related functions.

Attributes:

LANGUAGE="..."	Either JavaScript or LiveScript.
SRC="..."	The URL of a JavaScript program stored in a separate file.

Allowed Inside: <HEAD> <BODY>

`<APPLET>...</APPLET>` (NHTML)

Used to incorporate a Java applet into a Web page.

Attributes:

`CODE="..."`	The name of the Java class to be included.
`CODEBASE="..."`	The URL of the directory where the Java class is stored if it is not located in the same directory as the HTML document.
`WIDTH="..."`	The width in pixels of the area taken up by the applet.
`HEIGHT="..."`	The height in pixels of the area taken up by the applet.

Can Include: `<PARAM>`

Allowed Inside: `<BODY>`

`<PARAM>` (NHTML)

Used to define values (or parameters) to be passed to the Java applet.

Attributes:

`NAME="..."`	The name of the parameter to be passed to the Java class.
`VALUE="..."`	The value of the parameter.

Allowed Inside: `<APPLET>`

`<EMBED>` (NHTML)

Use to embed files supported by plug-ins. Netscape calls such files *live objects*.

Attributes:

`SRC="..."`	A URL that describes the location and filename to be handled by a plug-in. The file extension specified in this attribute determines which plug-in module is loaded.
`WIDTH="..."`	The width in pixels of the area taken up by the live object.
`HEIGHT="..."`	The height in pixels of the area taken up by the live object.
Plug-in specific	Each individual plug-in defines its own list of attributes. Refer to the appropriate documentation for additional information.

B

Allowed Inside: \<BODY> \<TABLE>

\<NOEMBED>...\</NOEMBED> (NHTML)

Used to define a block of text that will be displayed by Web browsers that don't support plug-ins.

Can Include: \<A> \<IMG> \<ADDRESS> \<BIG> \<B> \<BLINK> \<I> \<SMALL> \<SUB> \<SUP> \<TT> \<CITE> \<CODE> \<DFN> \<EM> \<KBD> \<SAMP> \<STRONG> \<VAR> \<DD> \<DT> \<H1> \<H2> \<H3> \<H4> \<H5> \<H6> \<LI> \<P> \<PRE> \<TABLE>

Allowed Inside: \<BODY>

Colors by Name and HEX Value

Table B.1 contains a list of all the color names recognized by Navigator 2.0/3.0 and also includes their corresponding HEX Triplet values. These values are entered into the HTML code of a document automatically when you choose custom text and background colors (see Hour 7, "Formatting Text"), or table cell colors.

To see all these colors correctly, you need to have a 256-color or better video card and the appropriate video drivers installed. Also, depending on the operating system and computer platform you are running, some colors may not appear exactly as you expect them to.

TABLE B.1. COLOR VALUES AND HEX TRIPLET EQUIVALENTS.

Color Name	HEX Triplet
ALICEBLUE	#A0CE00
ANTIQUEWHITE	#FAEBD7
AQUA	#00FFFF
AQUAMARINE	#7FFFD4
AZURE	#F0FFFF
BEIGE	#F5F5DC
BISQUE	#FFE4C4
BLACK	#000000
BLANCHEDALMOND	#FFEBCD
BLUE	#0000FF
BLUEVIOLET	#8A2BE2
BROWN	#A52A2A

Color Name	HEX Triplet
BURLYWOOD	#DEB887
CADETBLUE	#5F9EA0
CHARTREUSE	#7FFF00
CHOCOLATE	#D2691E
CORAL	#FF7F50
CORNFLOWERBLUE	#6495ED
CORNSILK	#FFF8DC
CRIMSON	#DC143C
CYAN	#00FFFF
DARKBLUE	#00008B
DARKCYAN	#008B8B
DARKGOLDENROD	#B8860B
DARKGRAY	#A9A9A9
DARKGREEN	#006400
DARKKHAKI	#BDB76B
DARKMAGENTA	#8B008B
DARKOLIVEGREEN	#556B2F
DARKORANGE	#FF8C00
DARKORCHID	#9932CC
DARKRED	#8B0000
DARKSALMON	#E9967A
DARKSEAGREEN	#8FBC8F
DARKSLATEBLUE	#483D8B
DARKSLATEGRAY	#2F4F4F
DARKTURQUOISE	#00CED1
DARKVIOLET	#9400D3
DEEPPINK	#FF1493
DEEPSKYBLUE	#00BFFF
DIMGRAY	#696969
DODGERBLUE	#1E90FF
FIREBRICK	#B22222
FLORALWHITE	#FFFAF0
FORESTGREEN	#228B22

B

continues

TABLE B.1. CONTINUED

Color Name	HEX Triplet
FUCHSIA	#FF00FF
GAINSBORO	#DCDCDC
GHOSTWHITE	#F8F8FF
GOLD	#FFD700
GOLDENROD	#DAA520
GRAY	#808080
GREEN	#008000
GREENYELLOW	#ADFF2F
HONEYDEW	#F0FFF0
HOTPINK	#FF69B4
INDIANRED	#CD5C5C
INDIGO	#4B0082
IVORY	#FFFFF0
KHAKI	#F0E68C
LAVENDER	#E6E6FA
LAVENDERBLUSH	#FFF0F5
LEMONCHIFFON	#FFFACD
LIGHTBLUE	#ADD8E6
LIGHTCORAL	#F08080
LIGHTCYAN	#E0FFFF
LIGHTGOLDENRODYELLOW	#FAFAD2
LIGHTGREEN	#90EE90
LIGHTGREY	#D3D3D3
LIGHTPINK	#FFB6C1
LIGHTSALMON	#FFA07A
LIGHTSEAGREEN	#20B2AA
LIGHTSKYBLUE	#87CEFA
LIGHTSLATEGRAY	#778899
LIGHTSTEELBLUE	#B0C4DE
LIGHTYELLOW	#FFFFE0
LIME	#00FF00
LIMEGREEN	#32CD32

Color Name	HEX Triplet
LINEN	#FAF0E6
MAGENTA	#FF00FF
MAROON	#800000
MEDIUMAQUAMARINE	#66CDAA
MEDIUMBLUE	#0000CD
MEDIUMORCHID	#BA55D3
MEDIUMPURPLE	#9370DB
MEDIUMSEAGREEN	#3CB371
MEDIUMSLATEBLUE	#7B68EE
MEDIUMSPRINGGREEN	#00FA9A
MEDIUMTURQUOISE	#48D1CC
MEDIUMVIOLETRED	#C71585
MIDNIGHTBLUE	#191970
MINTCREAM	#F5FFFA
MISTYROSE	#FFE4E1
NAVAJOWHITE	#FFDEAD
NAVY	#000080
OLDLACE	#FDF5E6
OLIVE	#808000
OLIVEDRAB	#6B8E23
ORANGE	#FFA500
ORANGERED	#FF4500
ORCHID	#DA70D6
PALEGOLDENROD	#EEE8AA
PALEGREEN	#98FB98
PALETURQUOISE	#AFEEEE
PALEVIOLETRED	#DB7093
PAPAYAWHIP	#FFEFD5
PEACHPUFF	#FFDAB9
PERU	#CD853F
PINK	#FFC0CB
PLUM	#DDA0DD
POWDERBLUE	#B0E0E6

B

continues

TABLE B.1. CONTINUED

Color Name	HEX Triplet
PURPLE	#800080
RED	#FF0000
ROSYBROWN	#BC8F8F
ROYALBLUE	#4169E1
SADDLEBROWN	#8B4513
SALMON	#FA8072
SANDYBROWN	#F4A460
SEAGREEN	#2E8B57
SEASHELL	#FFF5EE
SIENNA	#A0522D
SILVER	#C0C0C0
SKYBLUE	#87CEEB
SLATEBLUE	#6A5ACD
SLATEGRAY	#708090
SNOW	#FFFAFA
SPRINGGREEN	#00FF7F
STEELBLUE	#4682B4
TAN	#D2B48C
TEAL	#008080
THISTLE	#D8BFD8
TOMATO	#FF6347
TURQUOISE	#40E0D0
VIOLET	#EE82EE
WHEAT	#F5DEB3
WHITE	#FFFFFF
WHITESMOKE	#F5F5F5
YELLOW	#FFFF00
YELLOWGREEN	#9ACD32

APPENDIX C

Online Resources for Web Authors

Browsers and Other Net-Surfing Programs

- Tucows Directory of Internet Clients

  www.tucows.com

- Cello

  www.law.cornell.edu/cello/cellofaq.html

- Client Software Directory

  www.w3.org/hypertext/WWW/Clients.html

- Lynx

  www.cc.ukans.edu/about_lynx/

- Microsoft Internet Explorer 4

  www.microsoft.com/ie4/

- NCSA Mosaic

  `www.ncsa.uiuc.edu/SDG/Software/Mosaic/`

- NetCruiser

  `www.netcom.com/netcom/cruiser.html`

- Netscape Communicator (Composer)

  `www.netscape.com or home.netscape.com`

- WinWeb

  `www.einet.net/EINet/WinWeb/WinWebHome.html`

Clip Art and Templates

- Free Graphics

  `www.jgpublish.com/free.htm`

- Internet Explorer Multimedia Gallery

  `www.microsoft.com/ie/author/mmgallry/`

- Netscape Gold Rush Tool Chest

  `home.netscape.com/assist/net_sites/starter/samples/index.html`

- Netscape Page Starter Site

  `home.netscape.com/assist/net_sites/starter/index.html`

- Netscape Templates

  `home.netscape.com/assist/net_sites/starter/samples/templates/index.html`

- WWW Homepage Starter Kit

  `www.isisnet.com/mlindsay/kitrex3.html`

- Cyberspace Portal

  `www.infomediacom.com/preview.htm`

- Clip Art Universe

  `www.nzwwa.com/mirror/clipart/`

- WebSpice

  `www.webspice.com`

- Yahoo's Clip Art Directory

  `www.yahoo.com/Computers_and_Internet/Multimedia/Pictures/Clip_Art/`

- Index to Multimedia Information Sources

  `viswiz.gmd.de/MultimediaInfo/`

- MPEG Archive

  `www.powerweb.de/mpeg`
- Multimedia/Clip Art Directory

  `www.clipart.com/`
- Animation Zone

  `www.teleport.com/~chrisdb/taz/`

General Web Authoring

- Netscape Developer's Edge

  `developer.netscape.com/library/documentation/jsframe.html`
- Off-the-Net Insider Newsletter

  `home.netscape.com/assist/net_sites/off_the_net.html`
- Yahoo's WWW Listings

  `www.yahoo.com/Computers/World_Wide_Web/`
- The Virtual Library

  `www.stars.com/`
- The Web Toolbox

  `www.rtis.com/nat/user/toolbox/`
- The Developer's JumpStation

  `oneworld.wa.com/htmldev/devpage/dev-page.html`
- All the HTML Commands

  `vzone.virgin.net/sizzling.jalfrezi/`
- The HTML Reference Guide

  `developer.netscape.com/library/documentation/htmlguid/index.htm`
- The HTTP Specification

  `www.w3.org/pub/WWW/Protocols/`

C

Plug-Ins, Helpers, and Other Browser Accessories

- Adobe Acrobat Reader

  `www.adobe.com/`

- Macromedia Shockwave

  www.macromedia.com
- Microsoft Free Downloads

  www.microsoft.com/msdownload
- Netscape Plug-Ins Directory

  home.netscape.com/comprod/products/navigator/version_2.0/plugins/
- Plug-In Plaza

  browserwatch.internet.com/plug-in.html
- Plug-In Gallery & Demo Links

  www2.gol.com/users/oyamada/
- RealAudio/RealVideo

  www.realaudio.com

JavaScript and Java

- Netscape Information about JavaScript

  home.netscape.com/comprod/products/navigator/version_2.0/script/
  index.html
- The Sun Microsystems Java Home Page

  java.sun.com/
- A Java Applet Directory

  www.gamelan.com/
- Yahoo Java Directory

  www.yahoo.com/Computers_and_Internet/Programming_Languages/Java/

General-Purpose Software Download Sites

- Association of Shareware Professionals

  www.asp-shareware.org
- Children's Shareware

  www.gamesdomain.com/tigger/sw-kids.html
- Download.com

  download.com
- Shareware.com

  shareware.com

- Shareware Junkies

  `www.sharewarejunkies.com`

- Softword Technology

  `users.aol.com/shareware/index.htm`

C

APPENDIX D

What's on the CD-ROM?

This appendix briefly describes the valuable shareware, freeware, and demo programs and files included on the CD-ROM bundled with this book.

To help you explore and install the CD-ROM, a directory to the CD-ROM is included in an HTML file. For more information, install the CD-ROM as described in its accompanying instructions; then open the directory in Communicator or another Web browser.

While viewing the HTML directory to the CD-ROM, you can selectively learn how to install any programs that interest you.

Netscape Communicator

The CD-ROM contains the complete standard version of Netscape Communicator for both Windows 95, 98, and NT and Macintosh. Communicator includes Composer (a Web page editing program used throughout this book), plus a Web browser (Navigator), email program (Messenger), and newsreader (Collabra).

To learn how to install and configure Netscape Communicator after installing the CD-ROM, see Appendix A, "Installing Netscape Communicator."

ACDSee

ACDSee is a fast, easy-to-use image viewer for JPEG, GIF, BMP, PCX, and TGA files. You can use ACDSee as a viewer with Netscape or to view and test images when adding them to your Web page. ACDSee features full-color image previews, panning, slide shows, drag-and-drop support, and more.

Adobe Acrobat Reader

This viewer enables you to view documents distributed on the Web in Adobe Acrobat (.pdf) format.

FrameGang

FrameGang, which is part of the SnagletPack from Sausage Software, is an easy-to-use program for generating HTML frame definition documents, the documents that break a Web page into multiple independent windows, each with its own URL. Using graphical tools, such as the ability to drag frame borders, you can easily customize frame documents while FrameGang automatically adjusts the HTML code for you. The SnagletPack includes all of the following programs: Egor 3, Image Wiz Plus, Swami, Background Builder, Clikette, Crosseye, FrameGang 32, Broadway, Flash 2, and AFKAL.

GIF Graphics

The CD-ROM contains a collection of GIF images for spicing up your Web page. Included are background textures, horizontal bars, bullets, and icons.

GoldWave

GoldWave is a utility for recording, playing, and converting sound files. You can use GoldWave to create or convert sound files to be linked to your page as external media, or you can test your sound files by using GoldWave as a helper application.

HTML Assistant

HTML Assistant is a full-featured, freeware HTML editor for composing pages that are to be published on the World Wide Web. It features a rich assortment of toolbar functions that simplify the application of HTML tags to create Web documents that include text formatting, graphics, links, and more.

JPEG Backgrounds

The CD-ROM contains a collection of JPEG images for use as backgrounds.

MapEdit

MapEdit automatically generates the code for imagemaps when you select an image file and then identify regions with your mouse. MapEdit can phrase its code for two popular Web server types or for client-based imagemaps.

Microsoft Internet Assistants for Word, Excel, PowerPoint, and Access

Microsoft Internet Assistants are add-ins to Microsoft's Office application suite: Word 95, Excel 95, PowerPoint 95, and Access 95. Each Internet Assistant transforms its application into a complete Web composition and HTML source editing tool. The add-ins enable you easily to convert Word, Excel, PowerPoint, or Access documents into HTML documents for display on the Web and to edit the HTML tags directly.

NetToob Stream: An MPEG Movie Player

NetToob Stream is a fast, easy-to-use Windows 95 MPEG movie player that you can use as a helper application in Netscape or to test your own MPEG files before featuring them in your Web document.

Paint Shop Pro

Paint Shop Pro is a sophisticated image drawing, painting, editing, and conversion tool. You can use it to create new images for inclusion in your Web document or to convert, edit, or prepare images you've acquired from other sources.

WinZip

WinZip is a Windows compression/decompression utility that allows you to conveniently decompress ZIP files and other compressed formats commonly downloaded from the Internet. When you install WinZip in a Windows environment, it automatically updates the File Types registry so that when you open any ZIP file, WinZip opens automatically to decompress the file and extract any separate files within the ZIP archive.

D

Glossary

applet   A small program or application, particularly one written in Java.

browse   To wander around a portion of the Internet, screen by screen, looking for items of interest. Also known as *surfing* or *cruising*.

browser   An Internet client that helps users browse.

CGI   (Common Gateway Interface) A facility for using scripts in Web pages.

client   A software tool for using a particular type of Internet resource. A client interacts with a server, on which the resource is located. Browsers are clients.

close tag   An HTML tag required at the end of a block of code beginning with certain tags. Close tags begin with </.

compression   The process of making a computer file smaller so that it can be copied more quickly between computers. Compressed files, sometimes called ZIP files, must be decompressed on the receiving computer before they can be used.

cyberspace   A broad expression used to describe the activity, communication, and culture happening on the Internet and other computer networks.

dial-up IP account   An Internet account, accessed through a modem and telephone line, that offers complete access to the Internet through TCP/IP communications. A dial-up IP account differs from a shell account in that a shell account does not employ TCP/IP on the user's PC, and it might not offer complete Internet access or offer the user the ability to use the client software of his or her choosing. Dial-up IP accounts come in two types: PPP and SLIP.

dial-up IP connection   A method that allows a computer lacking a direct connection to access the Internet through another computer that is directly connected to the Internet. Even though the connection is established with a modem, the dial-up user runs TCP/IP for a true Internet connection.

direct connection   A permanent, 24-hour link between a computer and the Internet. A computer with a direct connection can use the Internet at any time.

DNS   (Domain Name System) A method of translating IP addresses into word-based addresses that are easier to remember and work with.

domain   The address of a computer on the Internet. A user's Internet address is made up of a username and a domain name.

email   Short for *electronic mail*. A system that enables a person to compose a message on a computer and transmit that message through a computer network, such as the Internet, to another computer user.

email address   The word-based Internet address of a user, typically made up of a username, an @ sign, and a domain name (`user@domain`). Email addresses are translated from the numeric IP addresses by the domain name system (DNS).

Explorer   See *Internet Explorer*.

extension   See *Netscape extensions*.

FAQ file   Short for *Frequently Asked Questions file*. A computer file containing the answers to frequently asked questions about a particular Internet resource.

flame   Hostile messages, often sent through email or posted in newsgroups, from Internet users in reaction to breaches of netiquette.

form   A part of a Web page in which users can type entries or make selections that are passed on for processing by a script.

frame definition document   An HTML document whose purpose is to define the frames in a frame-based document as well as to identify the content files to go in each frame.

frames   Discrete sections of a Web page that have been divided into frames by a frame definition document.

freeware   Software available to anyone, free of charge (unlike shareware, which requires payment).

FTP   (File Transfer Protocol) The basic method for copying a file from one computer to another through the Internet.

GIF   A form of image file, using the file extension `.gif`, commonly used for inline images in Web pages.

Gopher   A system of menus layered on top of existing resources that makes locating information and using services easier.

Gopherspace   A metaphor for all the directories and other items accessible through Gopher menus. Taken together, these resources can be imagined as an online environment, or space, accessible through Gopher menus.

HTML   (Hypertext Markup Language) The document formatting language used to create pages on the World Wide Web.

HTTP   (Hypertext Transfer Protocol) The standard protocol used for communications between servers and clients on the World Wide Web.

hypermedia and hypertext   Methods for allowing users to jump spontaneously among onscreen documents and other resources by selecting highlighted keywords that appear on each screen. Hypermedia and hypertext appear most often on the World Wide Web.

imagemap   A block of code that assigns different URLs to different areas of an inline image.

inline image   An image that appears within the layout of a Web page.

Internet   A large, loosely organized internetwork connecting universities, research institutions, governments, businesses, and other organizations so that they can exchange messages and share information.

Internet Explorer   A browser for the World Wide Web created by Microsoft. Internet Explorer version 4 is built into Windows 98, and for other systems (Windows 3.1, 95, and NT; Macintosh; UNIX), it's available for free download from the Web and in a variety of software packages. It can be confused with Windows Explorer, which is the basic file/folder management system in Windows 95.

internetwork   A set of networks and individual computers connected so that they can communicate and share information. The Internet is a very large internetwork.

intranet   An internal corporate network, usually a local area network, that is based on Internet technologies such as TCP/IP and Web browsers.

Java   A general-purpose programming language sometimes used to add advanced capabilities to Web pages.

JavaScript   A programming language for creating scripts that add functions to Web pages.

JPEG   A form of image file, using the file extension .jpg, commonly used for inline images in Web pages.

menu   A list of choices on a computer screen. A user selects one choice to perform an action with a software program. Menus figure prominently in Windows and in the Internet resource Gopher.

MIME   (Multipurpose Internet Mail Extensions) A standard that allows graphics and multimedia information to be included in Internet documents such as email messages.

Mosaic   A browser for the World Wide Web.

multimedia   A description for systems capable of displaying or playing text, pictures, sound, video, and animation.

multitasking and multithreading   Two advanced techniques supplied by Windows 95/NT and 32-bit applications that allow multiple applications to run together more quickly, smoothly, and reliably.

netiquette   The code of proper conduct (etiquette) on the Internet (the Net).

Netscape   Short for *Netscape Communications*, a software company that developed and markets a popular World Wide Web browser called Navigator. Some people casually refer to Navigator and Communicator as "Netscape."

Netscape extensions   Nonstandard enhancements to HTML that can add features to Web pages. The features can be viewed only through browsers that support the extensions.

network   A set of computers interconnected so that they can communicate and share information. Connected networks together form an internetwork.

newsgroup   An Internet resource through which people post and read messages related to a specific topic.

password   A secret code, known only to the user, that allows the user to access a computer that is protected by a security system.

PPP   (Point-to-Point Protocol) A communications protocol that enables a dial-up IP connection.

provider   A general reference to an Internet access provider, a company that has its own dedicated access to the Internet and can therefore sell dial-up IP accounts to Internet users.

proxy server   In a network, a computer that uses its own Internet connection to provide Internet access to other computers on the network lacking their own Internet connections. These other computers connect to the Internet indirectly, by going through the proxy.

script   An external program opened by a link in a Web page to perform some special function.

scripting   The activity of writing a script.

search engine   A program that provides a way to search for specific information.

server   A networked computer that serves a particular type of information to users or performs a particular function. Users run client software to access servers controlling certain types of resources (email, newsgroups, and so on). Dial-up IP accounts are provided through Internet servers with direct connections to the Internet.

shareware   Software programs that users are permitted to acquire and evaluate for free. Shareware is different from freeware in that, if a person likes the shareware program and plans to use it on a regular basis, he or she is expected to send a fee to the programmer.

shortcut   A feature of Windows 95/98/NT that allows you to place an icon anywhere in Windows, even on the desktop, that you can click to open a file or program.

shorthand   A system of letter abbreviations used to efficiently express certain ideas in email messages, newsgroup postings, and Internet Relay Chat sessions. Examples are IMO (in my opinion) and BTW (by the way).

sign on   The act of accessing a computer system by typing a required username (or user ID) and password. Also described by other terms, including sign in, log on (or logon), and log in (or login).

SLIP   (Serial Line Internet Protocol) A communications protocol that enables a dial-up IP connection.

spider   A program that searches methodically through a portion of the Internet to build a database that can be searched by a search engine.

style sheets   A capability of Dynamic HTML that gives a Web author precise control over the appearance of a Web page when viewed through a compatible browser.

surfing   Another term for *browsing*.

tag   A code in HTML.

TCP/IP   (Transmission Control Protocol/Internet Protocol) The fundamental internet-working protocol that makes the Internet work.

Telnet   A facility for accessing other computers on the Internet and for using the resources that are there.

UNIX   A computer operating system widely used by Web servers.

URL   (Uniform Resource Locator) A method of standardizing the addresses of different types of Internet resources so that they can all be accessed easily from within a Web browser.

Usenet   A loose affiliation of sites that together controls the majority of Internet news-groups.

username   Used with a password to gain access to a computer. A dial-up IP user typically has a username and password for dialing the access provider's Internet server.

wizard   Automated routines, used throughout Windows 95, for conveniently performing a step-by-step procedure, such as setting up Windows 95 or configuring it for the Internet.

World Wide Web   (WWW or Web) A set of Internet computers and services that provides an easy-to-use system for finding information and moving among resources. WWW services feature hypertext, hypermedia, and multimedia information, which can be explored through browsers such as Netscape Navigator or Internet Explorer.

INDEX

X-Z

LICENSING AGREEMENT

By opening this package, you are agreeing to be bound by the following agreement:

Some of the software included with this product may be copyrighted, in which case all rights are reserved by the respective copyright holder. You are licensed to use software copyrighted by the publisher and its licensors on a single computer. You may copy and/or modify the software as needed to facilitate your use of it on a single computer. Making copies of the software for any other purpose is a violation of the United States copyright laws.

This software is sold as is without warranty of any kind, either expressed or implied, including but not limited to the implied warranties of merchantability and fitness for a particular purpose. Neither the publisher nor its dealers or distributors assumes any liability for any alleged or actual damages arising from the use of this program. (Some states do not allow for the exclusion of implied warranties, so the exclusion may not apply to you.)

Windows 95 and Windows NT: If you have AutoPlay enabled, insert the CD-ROM and choose installation options from the displayed splash screen.

NOTE: If you have AutoPlay disabled on your computer, the CD-ROM will *not* automatically display the installation splash screen. To browse the CD-ROM manually, double-click on My Computer on the desktop, and then right-click on your CD-ROM drive icon, and choose Explore from the shortcut menu. By doing this, you can immediately access the files for this CD.

Mac: Use the descriptions of the folder structure in the CD Guide to locate items.